Oracle CRM On Demand Administration Essentials

A one-stop implementation reference guide to Oracle CRM On Demand, the world's best-selling brand of CRM technology

Padmanabha Rao

Venkatesan Sundaram

BIRMINGHAM - MUMBAI

Oracle CRM On Demand Administration Essentials

First published: December 2012

Production Reference: 1121212

Published by Packt Publishing Ltd.
Livery Place
35 Livery Street
Birmingham B3 2PB, UK.

ISBN 978-1-84968-500-9

www.packtpub.com

Cover Image by Neha Rajappan (neha.rajappan1@gmail.com)

Credits

Authors
Padmanabha Rao
Venkatesan Sundaram

Reviewers
Hendrick Edwin
Tuhina Goel
Kelly Schultz
William Yu

Acquisition Editor
Rukshana Khambatta

Lead Technical Editor
Kedar Bhat

Technical Editors
Vrinda Amberkar
Dominic Pereira

Copy Editor
Alfida Paiva

Project Coordinator
Leena Purkait

Proofreader
Aaron Nash

Indexer
Rekha Nair

Graphics
Aditi Gajjar

Production Coordinator
Arvindkumar Gupta

Cover Work
Arvindkumar Gupta

About the Authors

Kadirenahalli Venkata Padmanabha Rao has been in the industry for 14 years. He started with India's National Resource Data Management System project in 1998, working on a decision support system for the Zilla Panchayat of the Raichur district in the state of Karnataka. He was a research assistant for the World Bank's Environmental Management Capacity Building project in India. Paddy was an educator and an information technologist in the non-profit sector before joining CRMIT in 2007. In CRMIT, he brings his familiarity with research, development policy, and education to the technology table.

He is a graduate of the National Institute of Technology at Hamirpur and lays equal store by atoms and bits with his training in engineering and economics. His academic interests include massive multiplayer mobile games and transportation problems. He is excited by the possibilities today to deliver a mind blowing experience on a large scale to customers.

This book was developed over an unfairly long period and across three time zones. It is bound to have some noise despite our — the authors — efforts to remove them all. We welcome your feedback, bouquets, and brickbats. You can write to us at crmondemandbook@gmail.com.

I would like to thank my customers for the opportunities to build and learn. We thank Oracle Corporation, whose excellent products prompted this book. Our publishers at Packt were friends on this journey and we are grateful for their generosity. Our reviewers came with humor and passion for their work, and we are thankful for their contributions. I would like to thank my co-author, Venky, for being the patience extraordinaire with my pace on this book. My schools and family provide the foundation upon which rests my work.

Venkatesan Sundaram is a co-founder of CRMIT and is positioned as the Senior Director of Project Delivery/Consulting.

Before CRMIT, he had worked in various consulting positions for Baan Info Systems, BroadVision, and Cognizant Technology Solutions.

He specializes in implementation of CRM solutions across multiple verticals and also architected many e-commerce solutions. One of the implementations (`www.irctc.co.in`) is the fastest-growing e-commerce site in India and the first mobile commerce application. At the time of its delivery, the project won PC Quest's "Maximum Social Impact for Indian people in 2004" and the "Best IT Implementation in India for 2005" awards.

He holds a Post Graduation degree in Software Enterprise Management from the Indian Institute of Management, Bangalore, Bachelor's degree in Electrical Engineering, is certified in Production and Inventory Management (CPIM) by the American Production and Inventory Control Society, and is a certified Project Management Professional (PMP) by the Project Management Institute (PMI).

I would like to thank MD and CEO of CRMIT, Mr. Vinod Reddy, co-workers Naga Chokkanathan, Tuhina Goel, and many of my colleagues in CRMIT, who contributed knowingly or unknowingly to the valuable contents in this book.

The reviewers provided valuable guidance and corrections and any errors still remaining are entirely mine. Finally, the team at Packt constantly nagged and cajoled to keep some sort of schedule, and without them this book would still be on the drawing board.

About the Reviewers

Hendrick Edwin currently holds the position of Senior Consultant CRM at Capgemini in The Netherlands. In his current position, he focuses on designing and delivering package-based Oracle and Salesforce CRM applications that have clear business benefits.

He has ample experience with Oracle products such as Oracle's Siebel, Oracle BI, and Oracle CRM On Demand. Among his areas of expertise are Enterprise Marketing and Business Intelligence. Recently, he was responsible for implementing CRM applications in an international setting. At the moment, he plays a leading role in developing the Oracle Fusion CRM capabilities at Capgemini.

He holds a BSc in Marketing and a MSc in Business Administration from Rotterdam School of Management, Erasmus University.

Tuhina Goel is a CRM consultant with more than 5 years of business consulting experience in enterprise as well as the cloud version of Oracle CRM. She is currently working with Amadeus Software Labs, India. Having worked with clients in diverse industries such as manufacturing, retail, banking, airline, and healthcare, she has developed a deep insight into the CRM domain. She is a person who takes on creative challenges and has a profound attention to detail. A self-confessed traveler and cook, she loves to explore new places and try out new recipes in her free time. Currently, she lives in Bangalore and can be contacted at her LinkedIn page.

Kelly Schultz is a geek against her will. She was coerced into a career in IT when she volunteered to liaise on some "little" marketing projects. After 12 years, having sampled all facets of the software development lifecycle as a PM and Business Analyst (including working for Oracle Consulting), she's still saying working with CRMOD is the best gig she ever had!

William Yu is an experienced SaaS CRM solution consultant. He is a solution consultant for Oracle's next generation CRM platform—Fusion CRM and Oracle Social Relationship Management offerings.

In the past, he has worked as a CRM sales consultant for a vendor, as a lead consultant for an implementation partner, and as a CRM go-to person for an enterprise client. This gives him a complete view of a CRM project/solution. He sold, designed, and implemented some of the most successful Oracle CRM On Demand projects in Victoria, Australia. He knows the CRMOD design, configuration, reporting, integration, and scripting inside out.

His experience was also adopted and published in the book *Oracle CRM On Demand Deployment Guide*.

I'd like to thank my wife, Ying Yan who supported me during the reviewing of this book as she takes good care of my two kids, Ella and Emily.

www.PacktPub.com

Support files, eBooks, discount offers and more

You might want to visit www.PacktPub.com for support files and downloads related to your book.

Did you know that Packt offers eBook versions of every book published, with PDF and ePub files available? You can upgrade to the eBook version at www.PacktPub.com and as a print book customer, you are entitled to a discount on the eBook copy. Get in touch with us at service@packtpub.com for more details.

At www.PacktPub.com, you can also read a collection of free technical articles, sign up for a range of free newsletters and receive exclusive discounts and offers on Packt books and eBooks.

http://PacktLib.PacktPub.com

Do you need instant solutions to your IT questions? PacktLib is Packt's online digital book library. Here, you can access, read and search across Packt's entire library of books.

Why Subscribe?

- Fully searchable across every book published by Packt
- Copy and paste, print and bookmark content
- On demand and accessible via web browser

Free Access for Packt account holders

If you have an account with Packt at www.PacktPub.com, you can use this to access PacktLib today and view nine entirely free books. Simply use your login credentials for immediate access.

Instant Updates on New Packt Books

Get notified! Find out when new books are published by following @PacktEnterprise on Twitter, or the *Packt Enterprise* Facebook page.

Table of Contents

Preface   1

Chapter 1: Overview of CRM On Demand   7

What is CRMOD?   8

The CRMOD service   9

Service infrastructure   10

The software   12

CRMOD administration   13

CRMOD out of the box   13

Custom administration   14

Summary   16

Chapter 2: Steps 1-2-3: Go Live Out of the Box   17

Step 1 – Knowing the prebuilt marketing, sales, and service organizations   19

CRM data   19

Function – Marketing   19

Function – Sales   21

Function – Service   24

CRM staff   26

Step 2 – Setting your company profile   29

The Company Administration data   30

The Company Profile   30

Company SignIn and Password Control   40

Activating languages   41

IP Address Restrictions   41

The Sign In Audit and Audit Trail sections   42

Currency definition   43

Creating the login IDs for users   44

Creating the product catalog   47

Enabling sales forecasts   48

Step 3 – Pass the word around   **50**
  Creating company-wide alerts and messaging   50
    Issuing the user IDs   51
    Ongoing support to users   52
Summary   **52**
Chapter 3: CRM On Demand Customization   **53**
  The application architecture   **54**
  Customizability   **55**
    The data model   56
      Data management   57
    The process model   57
      Object model   58
      Business rules   64
      Security model   65
    The interface model   67
      Online interface   68
      Web services interface   68
      Special interfaces   68
  Summary   **69**
Chapter 4: Application Customization   **71**
  Data model-level customization   **72**
    Adding, modifying, and deleting fields   73
    Cascading fields   78
  Layout management   **80**
    Page layout   80
    Dynamic layouts   86
    Search layouts   87
    Homepage and Action Bar layout   90
    List management   91
  Miscellaneous application customization   **92**
  Summary   **93**
Chapter 5: User Access Controls   **95**
  The user ID   **96**
    Manager hierarchy   99
    User group   99
  The accesses to data   **100**
    Team access   102
    Book access   103

The user role   **105**
Role name   107
Accesses to objects (record types)   107
The owner access profile and the default access profile   108
Accesses to objects' Homepages or tabs   108
The Homepage layouts   109
The Search page layouts   109
The Detail page layouts   110
    The default sales process for opportunity records   110
    The Lead Conversion layout   111
    The Action Bar layout   111
    The default Theme for UI   111
Privileges   112
    Accesses to customize the UI   112
    Accesses to data channels   112
    Accesses to user channels   113
Summary   **114**

Chapter 6: Business Process Automation and Management   **115**
Workflow configuration   **116**
Hold on!   116
About workflows   117
Adding and modifying the workflows   117
Record types   120
Trigger events   121
Workflow rule condition   122
Actions   125
    Ordering of actions   125
    Assign a Book   125
    Create Integration Event   126
    Create Task   127
    Send Email   128
    Update Field After Wait   130
    Update Values   131
    Wait   131
Actions available by events   133
Ordering the workflows   133
Deleting workflows   136
Active and inactive workflows   136
Workflow Monitor   137
Pending Instances   138

Error Instances 138
  Deleting instances from the Workflow Monitor 138
Assignment rules 139
About Assignment rules 139
Hold on! 139
Applicable objects 140
Defining a rule group 140
Lead Conversion Administration **144**
Hold on! 144
Converting a lead 144
Lead Conversion Mapping 144
Hold on! 144
  Mapping fields for converting leads 145
Creating a lead conversion layout 147
Sales methodology **149**
Sales process 149
Sales stage 150
Setting up a sales stage 151
  Mandatory fields 152
  Process coach 154
  Automated tasks 155
  Useful resources 156
Sales category 157
Setting up a sales stage category 158
Administering forecasts **158**
What type: Determining the types of forecasts 159
How to choose the right type of forecasting methodology 159
When: Determining the forecast duration 159
For whom: Designating forecasting roles 160
How often: Frequency of forecasting 160
  Setting up Forecast Definition 161
Updating and maintaining forecasts 162
Summary **163**
Chapter 7: Content Management **165**
Content **166**
The product catalog 168
  Product category 169
  Product 170
Assessment scripts 171
Reports/analytics folders 173
Attachment files 174
Summary **175**

Chapter 8: Web Services Integration   177

CRM On Demand integration abilities   178
Transferring data between systems   180
Surfacing data from other systems   181
Configuring Web links and custom applets   182
     Configuring a Web link   182
     Configuring a web applet   184
Configuring integration events   186
Enabling CRM On Demand web services   189
Listing the available CRM On Demand web services   192
Managing sessions in CRM On Demand web services   195
CRMOD web service best practices   196
CRMOD web service allotment and limiters   199
Monitoring web service allotment usage   199
Administrating service allotment   200
Setting alerts for service allotments   200
Service Allotment Usage History   201
Monitoring file and record utilization   202
Web Services Utilization   203
Summary   204

Chapter 9: Reports and Analytics   205

The Answers On Demand service   205
Prebuilt reports   206
     Interactivity   208
     Prebuilt dashboards   209
Writing a report   210
Report Folders   211
Manage Analyses   211
Open Existing Analyses   212
Subject Areas   213
     Building the report   216
     Define Criteria   217
     Create Layout   221
     Define Prompts   222
Summary   223

Chapter 10: Leveraging CRM On Demand Data and Integration Tools   225

Accessing CRM On Demand data and integration tools   226
Importing your contacts   226
Step 1 – choosing your data file   227
Step 2 – file validation   228
Step 3 – mapping your fields   229

Oracle Offline On Demand   **230**

Downloading data into Offline On Demand   232

Adding/updating data in Offline CRM On Demand   233

Uploading Offline On Demand data to CRM On Demand   234

Oracle PIM Sync On Demand   **234**

Oracle Outlook E-mail Integration On Demand   **237**

Oracle data loader   **239**

Oracle Migration Tool On Demand   **240**

CRM On Demand Connected Mobile Sales   **241**

Accessing CRMOD content outside the application using On Demand Widgets   **242**

Summary   **245**

Chapter 11: Help, Support Ecosystem, and Features in New Releases   **247**

Training and Support   **247**

Help—CRM On Demand usage manual   **249**

Support portal   251

Before creating the service request   252

Creating a service request   253

Support forums   255

Release notes   256

Product enhancements   257

Release upgrade activities   257

New features in recent releases of CRM On Demand   **258**

Summary   **261**

Chapter 12: Oracle Partner Offerings   **263**

Oracle's partner ecosystem   **263**

Oracle CRM On Demand implementation partners   **264**

Oracle CRM On Demand extensions   **267**

How to make a purchase decision for a CRM On Demand extension   **268**

Is the product certified?   268

Can I try it?   270

What level of support is available?   270

What about new feature requirements?   271

Is the source code available?   272

Is the solution built using an open or proprietary technology?   272

Most popular extensions   **272**

E-mail channel for CRM   272

Telephone channel for CRM   273

Mobile CRM   274
Quote and order management   274
Self-service portal   275
Social collaboration tools   275
Summary   **276**
Index   **277**

Preface

Is this book going to make you an expert with Oracle CRM On Demand? We think it can and we hope it does. How long can I expect to be the expert? Theoretically that would be till the cash cows come home but let's get real—you stop being one when you begin to think you are one. We debated long and hard whether this book should be the last word on Oracle CRM On Demand or a first word on Oracle Fusion CRM, the other product that is doing the rounds these days. Fusion is tall and sits on the shoulders of giants, one of them being CRM On Demand. Eventually, Fusion will consume these giants, but you will have gotten the lay of the land working with CRM On Demand. It is high time we got started.

What this book covers

Chapter 1, Overview of CRM On Demand, states the scope of this book and that of the Oracle CRM On Demand product. Starting with a brief history of the product, it explains the designed values of the system. The chapter is intended to leave you with a clear understanding of the technology and its objectives, which should help you assess its value to your organization.

Chapter 2, Steps 1-2-3: Go Live Out of the Box, is a description of how to go from purchasing the product licenses to creating login IDs for the users to generating analytics, all possibly within the course of a few days of a week. This chapter aims to explain the rich design and technology of Oracle CRM On Demand that is available out of the box. It critiques the need to customize the product. This chapter describes the administrator steps to implement the product in your organization without the assistance of technical specialists.

Chapter 3, CRM On Demand Customization, explains the extensive customizability of the product and the contexts in which to exploit them. Over time you will need to customize the product to meet your business requirements. This chapter covers the essentials for the administration of the product over the long term.

Chapter 4, Application Customization, describes the customization of the user interface (or screens as some might call them). The user interface is built from the ground up using a definition of business objects; objects are built from a definition of fields and rules, and defined by relationships to other objects. You will need to have read *Chapter 3, CRM On Demand Customization,* to gain from this chapter.

Chapter 5, User Access Controls, explains the product features available to build a system that reflects the real organization of people in your business. The product can be customized to provide for the most complex of organization charts. This chapter is essential to the administration of CRM On Demand in your evolving organization. You will need to have read the previous two chapters to appreciate this chapter better.

Chapter 6, Business Process Automation and Management, explains the construction of automatic validations and processes in your CRM On Demand. Workflows, assignment rules, conversion processes, and sales processes might need to be customized for your organization and this chapter explains their administration. The previous three chapters provide the context for the information in this chapter.

Chapter 7, Content Management, defines content and describes its administration. Content is corporate knowledge, and the system cannot afford to have outdated content.

Chapter 8, Web Services Integration, reviews the web services in CRM On Demand, with examples of requirements and solutions. Information systems are typically integrated to provide a consistent view of data and information across the length and breadth of the enterprise. Integration involves writing programs to transport data and contexts between systems. This chapter introduces the reader to the open world of web services and their use in CRM On Demand. A comprehensive description of web services and the art of writing programs would require a book in its own right.

Chapter 9, Reports and Analytics, is an introduction to the Answers On Demand product that comes integrated with CRM On Demand. While the preceding chapters help with customizing the system to generate better data, this chapter proceeds with the task of building the custom reports/analyses of all varieties (which are usually the originators of the customization in the first place). Answers On Demand is an extensive tool in the hands of users and administrators. A comprehensive lesson about it would occupy a book in itself. We recommend the books published by *Oracle Press* to get started on exploiting this powerful product that comes embedded with CRM On Demand.

Chapter 10, Leveraging CRM On Demand Data and Integration Tools, describes the product tools for data that is outside the online CRM On Demand system. Such data includes external data files and offline systems. This chapter describes the product tools that are available for importing data (transactional data and system data), synchronization with personal information management systems, and plugin software such as widgets and offline CRMOD.

Chapter 11, Help, Support Ecosystem, and Features in New Releases, informs you about the learning support provided by Oracle On Demand Customer Care, including the comprehensive **My Oracle Support** (**MOS**) portal. The current version of CRMOD is release 21 and the product management maintains a brisk pace of releases. It is imperative to be up-to-date with the latest release notes to be able to exploit the many enhancements to the product that come online in a release. This chapter includes a brief description of the enhancements in the last two releases. The enhancements are related to the core product function and as such the preceding chapters in this book are key to deriving value from the enhancements in each release.

Chapter 12, Oracle Partner Offerings, lists the custom products that are endorsed by Oracle for integration with CRM On Demand. These products use web services and provide surround functionalities. Oracle Partners are independent companies accredited by the Oracle product management. Partner offerings are reliable and high performance software, whose architecture and delivery is aligned with that of the core product.

What you need for this book

Information and technology are equally essential to business today, and they are increasingly becoming synonymous with each other; however, approaching IT as a single word would stop you getting the most out of this book. A passion for information and/or a passion for technology, at the altar of business, would help you digest this book rapidly.

Second, you will need to have access to Oracle CRM On Demand, the product that lives on the Internet. Oracle offers a 30-day trial license with administrative privileges, at no charge. CRM On Demand administration is largely driven by the users, who we hope are among the readers of this book. In having access to Oracle CRM On Demand, you are sufficiently equipped to understand its administration well enough, aided by this book, to raise service requests to your system's administrator.

For now, this book is composed entirely in English. With due apologies to the scores of users and administrators of CRM On Demand, who enjoy one or more of the 16 non-English versions of this product, you will need conversational English to engage with this book.

Who this book is for

This book will be useful to an architect, a product manager, a business analyst, an interface developer, and the professional administrator, who is working with or expects to be working with Oracle CRM On Demand. A long-time administrator of CRMOD whose technological socialization is largely with Oracle CRMOD customer care may find this book — written by independent analysts — a good read. The initial chapters of this book would be useful for project sponsors to get to know the product and its relevance. We do not think that this book will be of value to anyone who has been a full-time administrator of CRMOD continuously for the last five years or more.

Conventions

In this book, you will find a number of styles of text that distinguish between different kinds of information. Here are some examples of these styles, and an explanation of their meaning.

New terms and **important words** are shown in bold. Words that you see on the screen, in menus or dialog boxes for example, appear in the text like this: "Confirm that you want to delete the workflow by clicking on **Ok** in the **Confirm** dialog box".

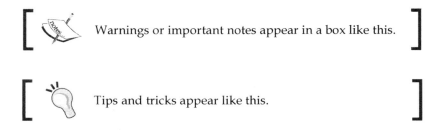

Warnings or important notes appear in a box like this.

Tips and tricks appear like this.

Reader feedback

Feedback from our readers is always welcome. Let us know what you think about this book—what you liked or may have disliked. Reader feedback is important for us to develop titles that you really get the most out of.

To send us general feedback, simply send an e-mail to `feedback@packtpub.com`, and mention the book title via the subject of your message.

If there is a topic that you have expertise in and you are interested in either writing or contributing to a book, see our author guide on `www.packtpub.com/authors`.

Customer support

Now that you are the proud owner of a Packt book, we have a number of things to help you to get the most from your purchase.

Downloading the color images of this book

We also provide you a PDF file that has color images of the screenshots/diagrams used in this book. The color images will help you better understand the changes in the output. You can download this file from `http://www.packtpub.com/sites/default/files/downloads/5009_images.pdf`.

Errata

Although we have taken every care to ensure the accuracy of our content, mistakes do happen. If you find a mistake in one of our books—maybe a mistake in the text or the code—we would be grateful if you would report this to us. By doing so, you can save other readers from frustration and help us improve subsequent versions of this book. If you find any errata, please report them by visiting `http://www.packtpub.com/support`, selecting your book, clicking on the **errata submission form** link, and entering the details of your errata. Once your errata are verified, your submission will be accepted and the errata will be uploaded on our website, or added to any list of existing errata, under the Errata section of that title. Any existing errata can be viewed by selecting your title from `http://www.packtpub.com/support`.

Piracy

Piracy of copyright material on the Internet is an ongoing problem across all media. At Packt, we take the protection of our copyright and licenses very seriously. If you come across any illegal copies of our works, in any form, on the Internet, please provide us with the location address or website name immediately so that we can pursue a remedy.

Please contact us at `copyright@packtpub.com` with a link to the suspected pirated material.

We appreciate your help in protecting our authors, and our ability to bring you valuable content.

Questions

You can contact us at `questions@packtpub.com` if you are having a problem with any aspect of the book, and we will do our best to address it.

1
Overview of CRM On Demand

If you think `https://sso.crmondemand.com/router/logon.jsp` is a practical and elegant URL, then we couldn't agree more. Oracle **CRM On Demand (CRMOD)** is designed better than any other service in its class. Effective change-management in the marketing, sales, or service practices of your enterprise cannot be accomplished with CRMOD alone. However, the state-of-the-art, on-demand software to support effective customer relationship management practices in an enterprise is best defined by CRMOD. This chapter is an introduction to the (software as a) service, contract, and party known as CRMOD. It gives an overview of CRMOD and of its administration. Legions of users and entire companies still refer to it as **SOD**, short for **Siebel On Demand** and have login passwords as "ilovesod". A rose is a rose by any other name!

By the end of this chapter, we will have understood the composition of:

- The CRMOD service — its history, technical, and commercial design
- The task of CRMOD administration

What is CRMOD?

It pays to know the history of CRMOD when learning its present and predicting its future.

The history of Siebel Systems Inc. as the provider of world-class software for customer relationship management in enterprises is well known and we shall not go into its rich history here. We will only recall that Siebel was synonymous with CRM systems in the 1990s. In 2003, Siebel Systems Inc. went live with Siebel On Demand (SOD), hosting at IBM's data centre in Texas, USA. The upshot of SOD was that it was "software as a service" (**SaaS**) and its delivery was helped by an amalgamation of Upshot and Siebel Enterprise. There were no global SaaSes at the time, for on-premise hardware and software could not be replaced as far as security, availability, and performance were concerned. Siebel OD was hosted on Windows, Siebel Enterprise 7.5 with DB2 and ran on Microsoft Internet Explorer, offering a subset of functionality of the on-premise version, that is, Siebel CRM Enterprise. It focused on rapid deployment for a reasonably homogenized marketing and sales department and after-sales service department. The user's interface to SOD was better than that offered by other websites, web portals, and web applications on the Internet at the time.

The year 2006 saw the acquisition of Siebel Systems by Oracle Corporation, renaming the service as Oracle CRM On Demand, and migration of the hosting to Oracle's data centre in Austin, Texas. A product versioning scheme conveyed the long term commitment for maintaining the CRMOD service. Just as with Siebel On Demand Release 13, you would continue to have no choice to stay on an outdated version; newer versions would be either bug fixes or new functionality, "free" of cost, so dare we ask why you would not want to be on the latest version? Oracle CRMOD has had regular enhancements to the application including releases of editions that are specific to some industries such as life sciences, automotives, financial services, and high-technology. A high quality, on-demand service is sustainable at a large scale so it goes without saying that Oracle CRMOD aimed to increase its clientele by orders of magnitude.

In 2012, it is now CRMOD release 21, which is available from data centers located in Australia, Ireland, and the USA. This release contains about 40 defined business objects, a robust analytic system including prebuilt analyses, usage analytics, a bulk data loader, a configuration migration tool, administration APIs, external file hosting, several prebuilt integrations with other Oracle enterprise products, and the option to host CRMOD on-premise in your data centre. It is delivered from Oracle Enterprise Linux and Siebel Enterprise 7.8 with Oracle 11g. This release runs on Microsoft IE, Mozilla Firefox, Apple Safari, and on the Apple iPad. Adjunct to this are the Desktop CRM and the Mobile CRM products that can be administered as your main form of CRMOD. The Oracle data centre provides you with three systems for every subscription: the **production** and the **stage** environments, and a **customer test environment** on request.

The CRMOD service

You do not implement CRMOD so much as release CRMOD to a suspecting workforce.

CRMOD is a web application, that is, you talk with it on HTTPS and in XML; your communications can be from web browsers such as Internet Explorer, Firefox, or Safari, or a web server such as Apache or IIS.

The commercial and technical currency of CRMOD is the user licenses, that is, you need to buy as many licenses as the number of users (both human and machines). The number of data records that you can store is a multiple of your user licenses, and the rate of use of the application resources (such as analytics queries and web service calls) is a multiple of your user licenses. The limits on the rate of the use of the application resources were introduced in release 19 and the limits are currently at a level high enough to meet the demands of a "normal outlier" as well.

CRMOD is built on a model of a customer relationship management software. It is not a mere database or just a collection of forms for data entries. It is a why-what-where-when-how-to structure for the application and performance of customer-centric data and information. Employees, customers, products, prices, and processes are some of the standard elements of its structure.

Service infrastructure

The hardware and software system that hosts the CRMOD application is called a **pod**. When you subscribe to CRMOD you can opt, at different prices, to be a single tenant or one of the many tenants of the host. The multi-tenant subscription is suitable if you are a small to medium-sized organization with fewer than 1000 users and/or 500,000 "accounts". A single tenant subscription should be your selection if you are a medium to large organization with a user base exceeding 1000 and/or 1 million "accounts". You can also opt to provision the pod in your private data center; this is the @Customer deployment of CRMOD. The comparative economics of hosting **CRMOD@Oracle** and hosting **CRMOD@Customer** varies depending on the number of users, growth, and regulatory costs. In the case of **CRMOD@Customer**, Oracle Corporation gives you the list of hardware and middleware to buy and provision in your data centre, and installs the CRMOD application on it. **@Customer**, Oracle maintains the application regularly on slightly negotiated schedules albeit as any other pod **@Oracle**.

The multi-tenant pod is one where multiple instances of a CRMOD application operate on the same physical infrastructure, for the many tenant companies. All companies' data is present in the same database; however, a company has no access to the data of another company. Every customer instance would have its own copy of the customer-specific application's configuration details such as its own fields, layouts, roles, reports, and so on.

In the single tenant pod, every company has a dedicated physical infrastructure providing better performance and independence from the fluctuating utilization of server resources of other companies as may happen in a multi-tenant pod.

The @Customer deployment is usually bought by companies that have legal restrictions on the storage of data in the countries where the Oracle data centers are located (USA, Ireland, and Australia) or in external locations. Examples of such companies are banks and government agencies.

In addition to the production instance of CRMOD, every company has a staging of CRMOD. About 3 months after you have purchased your licenses, the stage would have the copy of your production instance — the data as well as the application's configuration. The stage is refreshed periodically (quarterly as per current schedule) with a copy of the production instance.

The stage is officially meant for use by Oracle, to troubleshoot your production issues and test the patch releases before applying them to production. Technically, you are free to use the stage for your development activities as well, subject to some conditions; these are as follows:

- The availability of the stage is not assured on any given day or time. The stage may go offline for maintenance activity at any time without prior notice. The duration of downtime is not assured either. In the long history of CRMOD, the stages have rarely gone offline for more than once a month or for longer than 12 hours.

- The stage gets refreshed with a copy of the production on schedule. In this process you may lose any data between your stage and production as of the date of snapshot plus any difference between the date of snapshot and date of actual refresh. Typically there is a difference of a week between the snapshot and the actual refresh.

- You will need to identify and manage the risks of your production data residing on the stage. Access to the stage should be treated with the same amount of care that you would bring to the accesses to your production. It is your responsibility to ensure that your development team and the production data's copy on stage has appropriate access controls according to your company's requirements.

The advantage of using the staging environment is that you can rely on getting a full copy of your production system every quarter, at no manual cost.

The stage may not prove to be the complete environment for your development and testing activity. In such an eventuality, you can take recourse to the **CTE**, the **Customer Test Environment**. The CTE is a production quality environment and is designed for more reliability than the stage. You are not allowed to put large loads of data on the CTE. The CTE gets only the application updates and is not refreshed by Oracle with the copy of your production instance. The stage and the CTE are designed to complement each other as part of your agile CRM technology's release plan. The configuration migration tool combined with the schedules of the CTE and the stage can be used very effectively for your Production enhancement plans.

 What is the name of your pod? In the CRMOD URL `https://secure-ausomxPOD.crmondemand.com`, the letters in place of "POD" carry the three-letter name of the given pod. Your production pod, stage pod, and the CTE pod each have different names. Every pod in the CRMOD world, whether @Oracle or @Customer, is given a unique name.

The software

CRMOD out of the box has built-in sales, service, and marketing processes modeled after industry-leading best practices. A process consists of a set of activities in a sequence to achieve a specific objective. For example, a marketing process might have the following steps:

1. Segmenting your customers as campaign recipients.
2. Setting up a campaign.
3. Executing the campaign.
4. Collecting the response from the recipients.
5. Generating the leads from the campaign response.
6. Qualifying the leads.
7. Identifying opportunities.
8. Reporting and analyzing the effectiveness of the campaign.

To perform each of the steps in a process, CRMOD offers the following features:

*   A prebuilt data model with relevant fields
*   Facilities to associate related information to support the process
*   Embedded business rules
*   Embedded data visibility and access controls
*   A comprehensive set of 50 prebuilt reports and analytics
*   A collection of dashboards

All these features make a compelling case to go live out of the box.

Reports can be generated in real time, meaning that the information can be queried and presented from CRM transactional tables, or the reports can be historical (a day older) where data would be queried from de-normalized, high performance analytical tables. CRMOD maintains the transactional tables and the analytical cubes in a single database in the pod. Obviously, it is wiser to use analytic reports to ensure better reporting performances as well as to avoid load on the transactional database, thus slowing down your online CRM applications. Reports can be simple, presenting the data in a table format or can be interactive with filters, charts, pivots, tickers, facilities to drill-down, and scripted actions.

Industry editions

Customer management is a horizontal function, that is, it is existent in every enterprise. However, the practice of that management in, say, an insurance business, is distinct compared to that in an automotive business or in a pharmaceutical business. CRMOD provides industry editions of the software to support the industry-specific needs.

For retailing businesses, there is the partner relationship management module to facilitate partner management activities, such as partner recruitment, partner training, marketing development funds, fund requests, ROI tracking of marketing programs, and deal-management features to effectively leverage your partners. The wealth management edition defines a host of objects to support household relationships and financial accounts management. The insurance edition defines all the objects through the life cycle of a policy sale and service. The life sciences edition offers objects and reporting to manage samples, call planning, call tracking, and education events. The automotive edition has the objects, workflow, and reports for dealer management through post-sales vehicle revenue tracking.

The S.M.A.R.Test way to maximize returns and reduce your costs of deploying CRMOD is to merge Oracle's research with the industry's best practices and release it without customizing the software.

CRMOD administration

The CRMOD administrator is the business analyst and the information technologist, combined.

As an administrator you should avoid reinventing the wheels of your CRMOD as much as possible. So let us take a very quick look at the default definitions and processes in CRMOD that come right out of the box.

CRMOD out of the box

Contact, campaign, lead, opportunity, account, service request, and activity management are the standard functions that are available out of the box.

The lead management process comes up with a set of screens to create a lead, capture activities that are specific to the lead, run qualification scripts to qualify the lead, reject and archive the lead, convert the qualified lead to an opportunity, associate the opportunity to an new/existing contact, and associate the opportunity to a new/existing account.

The account management process provides a facility to create/edit your accounts' key information, associate the accounts to the contacts, opportunities, leads, activities, service requests, assets, and so on to build a comprehensive view of the account, define an account team with differential access rights to the account data, and establish a hierarchy of accounts if need be.

The contact management process provides a facility to record key information of your B2C customers or your B2B contacts, and associate the contacts to accounts, opportunities, leads, activities, service requests, and a contact team.

An **opportunity** is when you have a product/revenue identified and a date by when you expect to have a win/lose decision on it. The opportunity management process in CRMOD has a sales process that defines six stages, product revenue fields for recurring, and one-time sales and forecasting. Combined with the opportunity assignment manager, the opportunity assessment scripts, and the prebuilt lists and analytics on the opportunity home page, the default opportunity module is powerful.

The service request management process captures the product and a standard set of service definition fields to help route the requests to the relevant staff. Combined with the assignment manager, the service request call scripts, the solution object, and the prebuilt lists and analytics on the service request's home page, the default service request module can be released as a self-sufficient application for your service department.

In *Chapter 2, Steps 1-2-3: Go Live Out of the Box*, we will walk through the details of going live out of the box.

Releasing CRMOD out of the box makes for a stable growth and medium-to-high share of the adopter market. The next step in the business of change is making a "star" and eventually a "cash cow" out of it. This typically requires generating large scale demand and/or high value niches, and of course expanding your production to meet that demand. This customization activity usually involves configuration of the various features of the CRMOD and/or writing integration software for increased automation.

Custom administration

CRMOD has a full-fledged administration module that you can use to customize the object, accesses, and process definitions to suit the trademark marketing, sales, and service practices of your company.

The fields in the prebuilt data model can be customized. You can add new fields of many datatypes, namely `ShortText`, `LongText`, `Numeric`, `Integer`, `Picklist`, `Date`, `DateTime`, `MultiSelectPicklist`, `Currency`, and `Weblink`. A `LongText` datatype can hold 255 English characters, a `Numeric` field stores decimals, and `Weblink` is a hyperlink with intelligence. The `MultiSelectPicklist` datatype is a powerful construct and especially so when you find it neatly available in the report palette; to find an equally powerful use for it in the business process is the hallmark, we believe, of an administrator with a sound mind. Do note that once created a field cannot be destroyed. You can mask it by using the invisible character (*Alt* + 255) but you cannot delete it.

You can rename the custom objects to hold your company-specific information. For example, to capture the hobby details of your customers, you simply rename one of the custom objects as "hobby" and associate the "hobby" object to the standard contact object to capture one or more hobbies of the contact, and run workflows, processes, and reports upon that.

You can modify the page layouts to have the fields of your choice. The layouts can be associated to a specific role such that a sales manager may be able to see the gross profit information in an opportunity but a service officer may not be able to see if he views the opportunity details.

Tools such as the assignment manager, the assessment scripts, and the workflows are some of the other key facilities that are meant to be customized by nature.

You can opt to create new user roles or modify the prebuilt ones if you are certain you will not need the prebuilt definitions in the future.

CRMOD is built for practices in marketing, sales, and service in all their varied forms, and that means that across companies that use CRMOD, one would find it deployed for intermediate processes such as originations, approval workflows, self-service portals, presentation layer for a host of backend systems, product design portals, market research service, and so on. Many of these deployments, which we have been lucky to observe, advise, or deliver, are carefree exploitations of the rich feature set of CRMOD, namely its functional object model, simple user interface, web services, and analytics.

To customize CRMOD is to know it inside out. To that end, all the chapters after the next chapter will walk you through the particulars of customizing your CRMOD to suit your business process.

Summary

The CRMOD service is a fairly complex one wherein value is realized in the collaboration between Oracle and you. In this chapter, we looked at the deliveries by Oracle when you buy CRMOD, and the concomitant responsibilities on your part to exploit them for your business. We understood the design and objectives of the CRMOD application that should help compose the job description for the CRMOD administrator. We had an overview of the standard capabilities of the software that are available out of the box as well as the capabilities that can be customized. In the subsequent chapters we will look at the particulars of the CRMOD application in detail.

2
Steps 1-2-3: Go Live Out of the Box

In the previous chapter, we had an overview of the CRM On Demand product as an information system for customer relationship management. In this chapter, our focus is to explore more on how, with minimum customization, we can put the CRM On Demand system into production to save a lot of time and effort. Customizations incur new costs (of development, training, maintenance, and change management) and are typically sponsored to support the company's unique capabilities in both people and processes—capabilities that sustain its differentiation from competitors in the market. When the company is beginning or transitioning an information system for its CRM, it gets enormous value in simply adopting the information system that is already available in the CRM On Demand product, built on industry standard business process models of CRM. To go live out of the box, that is, without any customization, is effective for new companies and new organizations. When an enterprise has established its place in the market with custom-tailored CRM processes that may not map exactly to industry standards but at the same time work well for them as an organization, a customized CRM On Demand should be the order of the day.

Standard enterprise technology management, such as listing the business drivers, defining the business objectives, mapping the business processes, capturing master data, identifying the transactional data to be captured, and the overarching change management towards user adoption of the new system, is independent of whether you go live with a customized CRM On Demand or go live straight out of the box. Therefore, neither this chapter nor the book delves into the project management activity of the implementation.

The objective of this chapter is to provide you with the complete list of activities to be performed to go live with CRM On Demand without any customization of the product. For example, assume your company is a global logistics business with sales, marketing, and support teams operating in many countries, bought as many CRM On Demand user licenses as there are staff in the sales, marketing, and service teams, and intends to standardize its customer relationship management system across the board. The company management has opted to go live with CRM On Demand without any customization. With an additional user license for you to administer the new system, you have the responsibility of deploying the system to the users. Here, we will explore in detail the activities that a CRM On Demand administrator would perform to deploy CRM On Demand out of the box to the intended users across the countries.

We have grouped the activities in three steps. The steps are sequential and each step represents a reliable status of the deployment of the system. These steps are as follows:

1. The first step is to familiarize with the prebuilt content in the CRM On Demand for the marketing, sales, and service organizations.
2. The second step is setting your company-level parameters, which includes creating the login IDs, territories, and company content, such as the products catalog and the sales forecast reports.
3. The third and last step is issuing the login IDs to the users and sustaining their adoption of the new system.

By the end of this chapter, you will be able to do the following:

- Understand the business functionalities of the Vanilla CRM On Demand application
- Establish the primary settings in the CRM On Demand application to implement it in your company
- Create login IDs for the users of the application in your company.

The preceding information and skills will help you deploy CRM On Demand out of the box in a structured way.

Step 1 – Knowing the prebuilt marketing, sales, and service organizations

The CRM On Demand product comes prebuilt with a template to meet the common CRM needs of most organizations. Understanding that template in detail will enable you to map it to your company's CRM organization. Thus, as the CRM On Demand administrator, your business analytical skill and documentation of the mapping of the prebuilt organization to the real organization are key to a profitable adoption of the new information system.

As we saw in the previous chapter, there is more than one edition of the standard CRM On Demand. Apart from the generic edition, there are distinct editions for the different industries of financial services, life sciences, insurance, wealth management, and automotive, each of which has additional prebuilt content that is specific to the CRM organization practices in its industry. The industry-specific content, however, requires customization of the system before they can be deployed, and as such we will elaborate it in the next chapter.

A CRM system is essentially data (its generation and maintenance) and the usage of that data (by the staff that use the data to generate new values). In the following section, we will discuss in detail the preconfigured data structures that are available in CRM On Demand, steps involved in configuring the company level information to suit your organization needs, setting up the users in the system, and going live with the newly implemented CRM application.

CRM data

For the marketing suborganization, the data includes campaign, recipient, and lead. For the sales suborganization, the data are account, asset, contact, opportunity, sales process, revenue, and sales forecasts, and the service suborganization data are service requests and solutions. One could argue that the asset is a data of the service organization and the standard CRM model therefore defines asset as a common object. Activity is a data generated by all organizations.

The following section is the translation of the organization and its data in terms of the information system elements, namely function and business objects. It gives the definitions of these objects and their features in CRM On Demand.

Function – Marketing

The various marketing functions will be explored in the upcoming sections.

Campaign

The campaign module helps to create, update, and track campaigns. A campaign is a mechanism via which you convey a marketing message to your existing and potential customers. Typically, campaigns deliver a promotional offer or informational content on your organization's new products or services via different channels of communication, to cross-sell or upsell to you current customers or to acquire new customers. The goal is to generate additional interest in the company's products and services.

When you use campaigns, it enables you to do the following tasks:

- Store all campaign-related information, such as budgeted costs compared with actual costs, targeted leads, and marketing material (for example, brochures and artwork) in one place
- Share the campaign details to your sales and marketing team
- Analyze the campaign results in terms of generated leads, contacts, accounts, and opportunities
- Build reports and dashboards to analyze the return on investment of your campaign activities in real time
- Perform a trend analysis between the past and current campaigns
- Import leads and link them to an existing campaign

The list of preconfigured fields in the campaign object can be found in the CRM On Demand help text reference at `http://docs.oracle.com/cd/E27437_01/books/OnDemOLH/index.htm?toc.htm?CampaignEditHelp.html`.

Recipient

Recipients are the ones who receive the campaign information and store them as contacts in your CRM On Demand system. A recipient receives your marketing communications and you hope to receive his/her response. The same contact can be a recipient of one or more campaigns.

Lead

A lead is any addressable person who is in a potentially opportunistic position with a prospective or existing customer (account or contact) of yours, and with whom you can interact to develop an opportunity for the prospective/existing customer. The sales process might originate with lead generation. Leads move progressively through qualification to conversion. You can convert leads to contacts, accounts, deal registrations, and opportunities. After a lead has been converted to an opportunity, it enters the sales process. Certain fields in opportunity obtain their values from the lead record. These values are based on mapping the leads that have been converted during the sales process. The list of preconfigured fields in the lead object can be found in the CRM On Demand help text reference at `http://docs.oracle.com/cd/ E27437_01/books/OnDemOLH/index.htm?toc.htm?LeadEditHelp.html`.

Function – Sales

The various sales functions will be explored in the upcoming sections.

Account

Use the **Account Edit** page to create, update, and track accounts. Accounts are generally organizations that you do business with, but you can also track partners, competitors, affiliates, and so on as accounts.

If account records are central to how your company manages its business, as is the case in many companies, enter as much information about accounts as you can. Some of that information, such as the **Region** or the **Industry** field, can be used in reports as a way to categorize information. Similarly, if you link a record, such as an opportunity, to an account record with the **Region** or **Industry** field filled in, those opportunities can be grouped by the region. A list of preconfigured fields in the account object can be found in the CRM On Demand help text reference at `http://docs.oracle.com/cd/E27437_01/books/OnDemOLH/index.htm?toc. htm?AccountEditHelp.html`.

The **Account Name** and **Location** fields help us to uniquely identify an account record in the system, meaning there can't be two accounts in the system with the same **Account Name** and **Location** fields.

Contact

Use the **Contact Edit** page to create, update, and track contacts. **Contacts** are individuals that your company currently conducts business with or expects to conduct business with in the future. These individuals can be employees of other companies, independent consultants, vendors, or personal acquaintances. A contact is generally associated with an account, and often, an account record includes links to information about several different contacts at that company. A list of preconfigured fields in the contact object can be found in the CRM On Demand help text reference at `http://docs.oracle.com/cd/E27437_01/books/OnDemOLH/index.htm?toc.htm?ContactEditHelp.html`.

Opportunities

Use the **Opportunity Edit** page to create, update, and track opportunities. **Opportunities** are potential sales deals that, at some point, might be included in revenue forecasting.

You can create an opportunity by converting a qualified lead to an opportunity, or you can create a new opportunity from an existing account or contact.

Opportunity records help you to manage your sales pipeline as you work to close deals. All of your opportunity information is visible in one place and is linked to the related lead, contact, and account information. This information gives a complete picture of your opportunity and your customer.

To ensure that an opportunity record captures all the selling activity, the changes to the records can be tracked through an audit trail.

A list of preconfigured fields in the opportunity object can be found in the CRM On Demand help text reference at `http://docs.oracle.com/cd/E27437_01/books/OnDemOLH/index.htm?toc.htm?OpptyEditHelp.html`.

Sales process

The sales organization has time-bound goals. In the normal course of business, its pipeline of opportunities faces market competition and a variety of risks at the customers' end. The sales process is the discipline by which the sales organization generates reliable forecasts of revenues.

The sales process is the standardized workflow of selling. It has stages defined by the actions taken by the sales person and reactions received from the customer. The final stage of a sales process is either the **Closed/Won** or the **Closed/Lost** stage. Intermediate stages leading to the final stage are described, sequenced, and quantified in terms of the probability of reaching from that stage to that of the **Closed/Won** stage.

Thus, an opportunity at the sales stage X that puts a probability of 60 percent implies the opportunity with that customer having a 60 percent probability of reaching **Closed/Won** by the expected closing date for the given revenue.

Different sales processes may be defined for different types of opportunities. Multiple sales processes can be normalized using sales categories, to enable forecasting at a global level.

An opportunity can be associated with only a single sales process.

Revenues

You can link products or services (drawn from your product catalog) to opportunities in order to do the following tasks:

- Track which products belong to the opportunity
- Calculate revenue-based opportunity on product revenue
- Base your company's forecasts on product revenue or product quantities

If the product represents recurring revenue, you can input the **Frequency** and **# of Periods** information.

For usability, you can link a product to an opportunity when you create the opportunity in an unbroken sequential step, or alternatively at a later time.

To calculate the opportunity revenue based on the linked product revenue, follows these steps:

1. On the **Opportunity Detail** page, click the **Update Opportunity Totals** button available in the **Opportunity Product Revenue** section. This totals the product revenue for each linked product and displays it in the **Revenue** and **Expected Revenue** fields for the opportunity. The calculation behind this functionality differs depending on whether the **Product Probability Averaging Enabled** option is enabled on the company profile.

2. The company forecasting method determines which fields you must select when linking products to your opportunities.

3. If your company forecasts the revenue, based on opportunities, rather than products, do not select the **Forecast** checkbox on the **Opportunity Product Revenue** record.

4. If your company forecasts revenue based on product revenue, and you want to include this product revenue record as part of your forecasted revenue totals, or your forecasted quantities, or both, select the **Forecast** checkbox.

5. Make sure that the date in the **Start/Close Date** field falls within the forecast period, and that the record is owned by a forecast participant.

6. If a product is not sold, you can update the associated **Start/Close Date** and clear the **Forecast** checkbox on the **Product Revenue** page for that product to prevent the revenue for the product from being added to your company's forecasts. Alternatively, if one of the several products linked to the opportunity is on hold, you can remove the product from the opportunity, and create another opportunity for that product to prevent its revenue from being included in the forecast.

A list of preconfigured fields in the opportunity revenue line object can be found in the CRM On Demand help text reference at `http://docs.oracle.com/cd/ E27437_01/books/OnDemOLH/index.htm?toc.htm?opptyproducthelp.html`.

Assets

When you want to track a product that you have sold to a customer or company, link the product record to the account as an asset.

If you enter the **Notify Date** field's value on the asset record, a task is created when you save this asset record. The task appears as **Asset Name requires follow-up** on **My Homepage**, **Account Homepage**, and **Calendar**. A list of preconfigured fields in the asset object can be found in the CRM On Demand help text reference at `http://docs.oracle.com/cd/E27437_01/books/OnDemOLH/index.htm?toc. htm?acctassethelp.html`.

Sales forecasts

Use the **Forecast** page to review, adjust, and submit forecasts. A **forecast** is a saved snapshot of expected revenues over time. CRM On Demand calculates forecasts for each quarter and breaks down that information by fiscal month.

Forecasts in CRM On Demand automate a process that is often manual and sometimes inaccurate. Forecasts help companies to develop sales strategies. They also help companies to identify future business needs by giving managers accurate and up-to-date information about expected sales and quarterly progress toward sales targets. Individual sales representatives do not have to compile statistics. Instead, they decide when to include a record in their forecasts. The remainder of the process is automatic.

Function – Service

The various service functions will be explored in the upcoming sections.

Service requests

Use the **Service Request Edit** page to record, track, and address customer requests for information or assistance. A service request holds all the relevant and detailed information about a particular service activity. You can also use the service request to capture additional information, such as solutions or activities required to resolve the service request. Service representatives can access all the relevant information about service requests in one location. To ensure that a service request record captures all the service activity, the changes to records can be tracked through an audit trail. A list of preconfigured fields in the service request object can be found in the CRM On Demand help text reference at `http://docs.oracle.com/cd/E27437_01/books/ OnDemOLH/index.htm?toc.htm?SerReqEditHelp.html`.

Solutions

Use the **Solution Edit** page to create, update, and track solutions. Solutions contain information about how to resolve a customer query. By maintaining a knowledge base of solutions, your service representatives have access to a centralized knowledge base to help them resolve customer problems. In addition, the knowledge base expands as users interact with customers and create new solutions.

CRM On Demand tracks the usage of solutions and enables users to rate solutions. This information helps organizations to improve the solutions that they provide to customers and to identify problems in products or services. Frequently-used solutions give indicators to the organization on areas where product quality or supporting documents have to be improved. Poor solution ratings might indicate the need to improve solutions. A list of preconfigured fields in the solution object can be found in the CRM On Demand help text reference at `http://docs.oracle.com/cd/ E27437_01/books/OnDemOLH/index.htm?toc.htm?SolutionEditHelp.html`.

Activity

Use the **Calendar** page to review, create, and update your activities.

An activity consists of tasks that you need to accomplish before a certain date and appointments that you want to schedule for a specific time. Tasks and appointments can be meetings, calls, demonstrations, or events. The difference between tasks and appointments is that tasks appear in a task list and have a due date and status, whereas appointments are scheduled on your calendar with a specific date and time.

Activities can be associated to most of the standard and custom objects in the CRM On Demand application. A list of preconfigured fields can be found in the CRM On Demand help text reference at `http://docs.oracle.com/cd/E27437_01/books/ OnDemOLH/index.htm?toc.htm?AppointEditHelp.html`.

CRM staff

A user of your company's CRM On Demand gets access to the CRM data based on the accesses assigned to his user ID. Every user ID is associated to a user role, which defines all the access rights. A user ID can be associated to only one user role. There is no limit on the number of user roles that you can define on the system. The user role access levels are broadly captured in the following two types:

*   Feature access: Features (more commonly known as privileges) refer to the type of managerial/administrative workflows and actions that a user can perform in the CRM system. These actions include accessing all the data in the analytics tables, accessing prebuilt dashboards, accessing prebuilt reports, creating personal reports, creating custom reports, publishing list templates, creating campaigns, leads qualification and conversion, publishing solutions, sharing calendar with others, recovering deleted data, creating the assignment rules for automatic assignment of records, accessing CRM On Demand offline version, integrating the CRM On Demand with their e-mail client and PIM, exporting their data, importing personal data, and personalizing their homepages and detail pages.

*   Record access: These are the permissions to create/read-all/edit/delete the records in the system, and in reference to the user's ownership or absence of ownership on the record. For example, can the user create campaign records, can the user read all the leads available in the system, can the user delete his activity records, and so on.

The following table describes the prebuilt user roles. You will need to map this to the staff roles in your company's CRM organization:

User role	Privileges	Record access
Executive	Has access to all the features, other than administration and customization features	Has access and **Read all** records privilege to the most common horizontal record types such as accounts, contacts, activities, assets, campaigns, leads, opportunities, service requests, and solutions and sales forecasts. They can create records of these record types except solutions.

User role	Privileges	Record access
Advanced User	Has access to create custom reports, create assignment rules, publish lists templates, and leads evaluation (qualification, archiving, rejection, and conversion). Has access to all "non-admin" features, such as **Access All Data in Analytics**.	Has access and can create a privilege for the most common horizontal record types, such as accounts, contacts, activities, assets, campaigns, leads, opportunities, service requests, solutions, and sales forecasts. But advanced users can only read her/his own records.
Sales and Marketing Manager	Has access to sales and marketing related privileges such as create assignment rules, publish lists templates, and so on.	Has access to the most common horizontal type of records and can read all the records in the system. The sales and marketing manager has no access to generate sales forecasts (this means that the manager cannot force an automatic submit of the sales forecasts of his sales representative but has to wait for the sales representative to submit their forecasts).
Field Sales Rep	Has access to leads evaluation (qualification, archiving, rejection, and conversion).	Has access to the most common horizontal types of records and can read only those records owned by him.
Inside Sales Rep	Has access to leads qualification and archiving.	Has access to the most common horizontal types of records and reads all the records in the system.
Regional Manager	Has access to leads evaluation, Campaigns management and to create assignment rules.	Has access to the most common horizontal types of records and can read only those records owned by him.
Service Manager	Has access to publish Solutions, publish lists templates and recover deleted data.	Has access to the most common horizontal types of records (except Sales Forecasts) and can read only those records owned by him. The Service Manager can however read all the Accounts and Contacts records in the system.
Service Rep	-	Has access to the most common horizontal types of records and can read only those records owned by himself / herself. The service representative can however read all the accounts and contacts records in the system.

User role	Privileges	Record access
Administrator	Has access to all features in the system, and the access to modify the accesses of other user roles.	Has access to create/read/delete all types of records.

The previous table lists the permissions of each prebuilt role to access a record type, to create a record of a specific record type, and whether the user has access to view all the records created in the system. The permissions on each record (read-only/edit/delete) are defined by the **Owner Access Profile** and the **Default Access Profile** settings for each role as shown in the next screenshot; these profiles are explained as follows:

- **Owner Access Profile**: Defines permission on a record when the user is the direct owner and/or a derived owner through the manager hierarchy

- **Default Access Profile**: Defines the permission on a record to a user who is not directly or indirectly the owner of that record but is visible to the user because the **Can Read All Records** option is selected for the relevant record type in the **record-type access** settings on the user's role

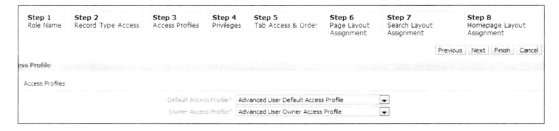

To understand the details of the access profiles of a particular user role you will need to know two things. First, that the name of the access profile follows the convention **[user role name] Default Access Profile** and **[user role name] Owner Access Profile**. Secondly, the path to the access profiles, which is **Admin | User Management and Access Controls | Access Profiles**. A screenshot of **Access Profile** is shown as follows:

This completes the first step. If you are a novice to the CRM On Demand service, we hope the preceding pages have given you the confidence and the "view" for step 2.

Step 2 – Setting your company profile

The second step of deploying out of the box involves giving the system the details about your company. The activities that comprise this step are as follows:

1. The **Company Administration** data.
2. Creating the login IDs for users.
3. Creating the product catalog.
4. Enabling the sales forecasts.

Each of these activities are explored in detail in the following sections.

The Company Administration data

The **Company Administration** page is the place where you define the company profile and some other global settings. The following screenshot details some of the important parameters that can be defined as part of the company administration. You can access this section by going to **Admin | Company Administration**:

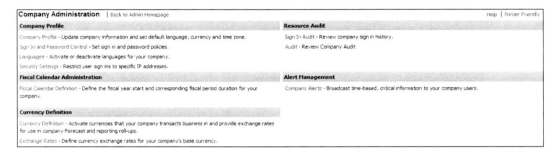

The Company Profile

The **Company Profile** page carries the key parameters. The screenshot is as follows:

Under **Company Key Information**, ensure that you set the CRM On Demand administrator user as **Primary Contact** along with his phone number. Don't make the mistake of setting the CEO of the company as **Primary Contact**. If you do so, Oracle support may end up calling your CEO on any support-related matters.

Under **Company Settings**, most of the default options such as **Language**, **Currency**, and **Time Zone** are set by Oracle, based on the inputs provided by you at the time of taking the trial run and/or the purchase order. As these are long-term and fairly static settings, you will need to select them thoughtfully at the start. You can change these settings with a service request to customer support. As a global company with staff distributed across various time zones, you would do well to set up the parameters in a manner that would be applicable for most of the users of the system at the company level. Note that CRM On Demand is designed for global deployments and therefore, these company-level defaults can be overridden at the user level using user-level settings.

The **In-Line Edit**, **Message Centre**, and **Heads-Up Display** options are meant to enhance user productivity when using the system.

In-Line Edit provides a facility to edit the details of the record in the list view or a detailed view without going to the edit mode. **In-Line Edit** reduces the amount of data sent from the client browser to the CRM On Demand server. In the following screenshot, the **Location** field under **Company Profile** can be edited without getting into the edit mode by clicking the **Edit** button:

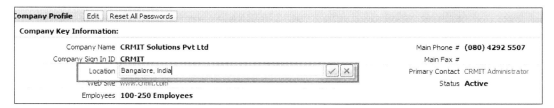

Similarly in the list view too, **In-Line Edit** facilitates a quick edit of the listed records without getting to the detailed record page.

Message Center is a mini collaboration tool available to the users to share general information with other users of the system-specific or record-specific information. As you can see in the following screenshot, on clicking the notes icon on the right-hand corner of the **Opportunity Detail** page, the notes pop-up appears displaying the notes written by users on this opportunity record. If you opt to subscribe for the notes, any message posted by any user of the system on this opportunity record will be displayed in the **Message Centre** section in the left-hand side navigation bar, giving an easy access to view all the messages posted by the users.

Heads-up Display provides quick links to go to a specific related information section of a record without scrolling the browser. On clicking the **Contacts** link, as shown in the following screenshot, the user is directly taken to the account's **Contacts** list applet that appears at the bottom of the **Account Detail** page. Clicking on the **Top** link will take you to the **Opportunity Detail** section.

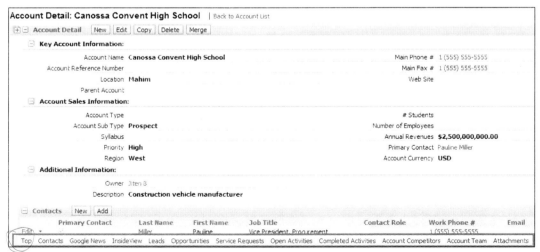

The **Record Preview** mode opens the preview window when a user points to a hyperlink or clicks the preview icon depending on the settings selected (click on the preview icon on the link). For example, if an opportunity is associated to an account, the account name is displayed as a hyperlink to navigate easily to the related **Account Detail** page. Enabling preview would help you to view the details of the account from the **Opportunity Detail** page without navigating to the **Account Detail** page. As shown in the following screenshot, on clicking the preview icon in the **Opportunity Detail** page, the details of **Account Action Rentals** are displayed in an overlay pop up:

Global Search Method provides a facility to specify the search option you would like to enable in the system. If you choose the **Targeted Search** option, the system provides a facility to search by one or more of the configured fields in the object to search the records stored in the object. As you can see in the following screenshot, I have set the **Targeted Search** option at the company level and as a result, on the left-hand side navigation search applet, I have a facility to search **Contacts** in the system by **Last Name**, **First Name**, and **Email**. If you key in more than one field, it performs an AND search. If you like to search by a different set of fields, you can either use the **Advanced** search facility or customize the **Search** panel for all users.

On the other hand if you have selected **Keyword Search**, the search applet in the left-hand side navigation appears as shown in the following screenshot, providing you with a single blank field where you can key in any text to do a wildcard search against a set of preconfigured fields. Unlike **Targeted Search**, here, the system uses the OR condition if there are more than one preconfigured field.

In the previous screenshot, when you key in **armexplc** as an input to the search field, it gets you all contacts with the e-mail domain ending with **armexplc-od.com**. The prebuilt **Search** panel has the relevant set of fields for each object. A complete list of the preconfigured keyword search fields, sorted by objects, is available in the online help file of CRM On Demand at `http://docs.oracle.com/cd/E27437_01/books/OnDemOLH/index.htm?toc.htm?defaultsearchfieldshelp.html`. The **Keyword Search** option can hinder the performance of the system as it runs on all the objects during every search.

Fiscal Year Start Date, Fiscal Year Start Month, and **Calendar Type** can vary by country or industry and can be changed on request to customer care.

Enabling **Product Probability Averaging** would compute the opportunity probability as a weighted average probability of opportunity revenues. In the following example, on clicking **Opportunity Totals** button, the probability at the opportunity level is calculated as (60% * 1000 + 40% * 2000) / (1000 + 2000) = **46.67**%:

Enabling **Opportunity Revenue Split** would provide an option to split the revenue of opportunity between more than one team member working in the same opportunity. In the screenshot, 20 percent of revenue is accounted to **Jiten** and the remaining 80 percent to **Donna**. The split gets reflected in the sales forecast and in reports that are used to measure the sales team member performance:

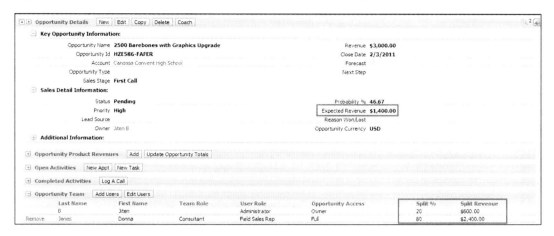

The field **Record Type Auditable Fields** sets the cap on maximum number of fields that can be audited across objects of different types. When a field is audited, for every change to the field value an audit log is created capturing the information changed. As you can see in the following screenshot, changes to the opportunity fields such as **Probability** and **Revenue** are tracked for reference in the **Audit Trail** applet in the **Opportunity Detail** page:

The **Audit Expiry (Days)** field specifies the age in days by which the audit records are purged. The value can be between 1 and 90 days. A value of 0 indicates the records are never purged and a 0 value can only be set by the Oracle customer care.

Themes provide a facility to customize the look and feel of CRM On Demand as per your corporate standards or your branding needs. You can choose one of the predefined themes available or you can create a custom theme. Custom themes can be defined under the **Admin | Application Customization | Themes** section. You should have the privilege **Manage Themes** set in your roles privilege to access the **Themes** section and create your own themes or to modify the existing ones. The following screenshot shows one of the available themes (**Technology**) under the **Themes** section. You can either modify it or you can copy the existing theme and customize the same. It is best to copy and modify an existing theme rather than changing the existing ones.

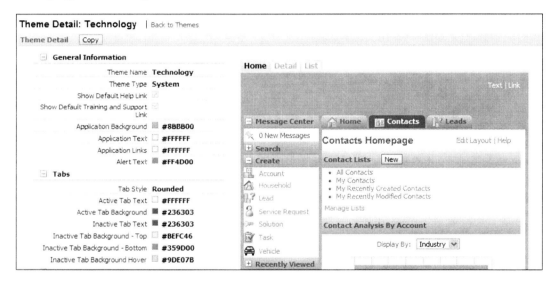

The **Company Data Visibility Settings** provides an option to turn on/off some of the security-related features of the data. *Chapter 7, Content Management*, discusses in detail the various mechanisms to secure the application data. These settings are shown in the following screenshot:

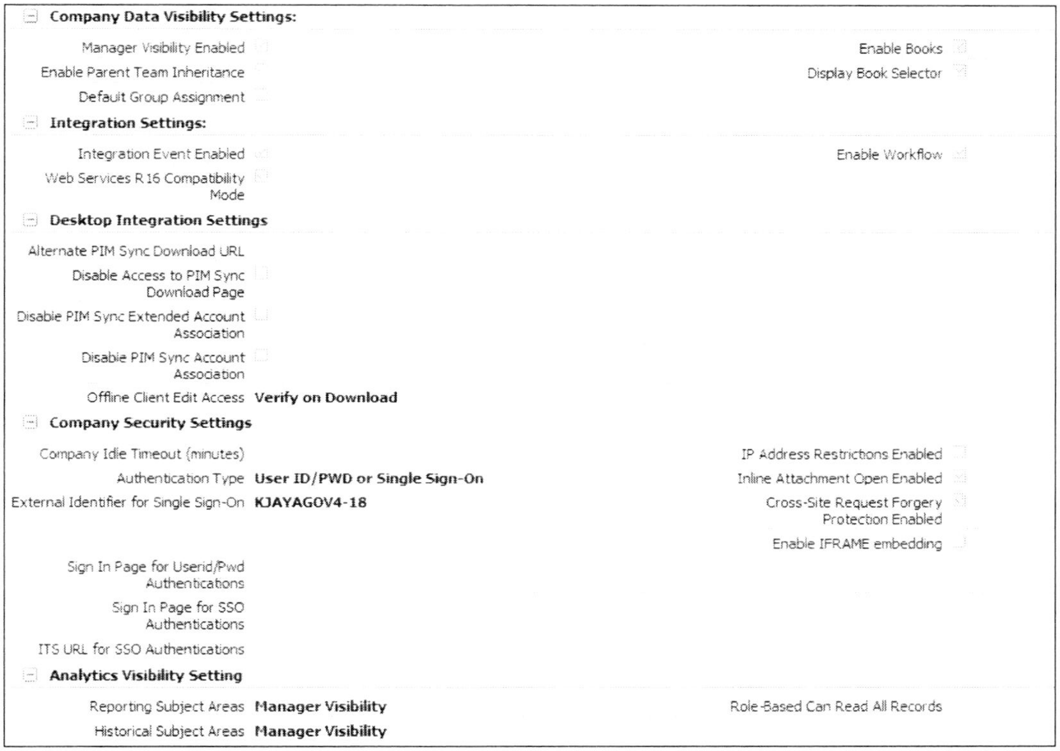

The **Manager Visibility Enabled** checkbox turns on/off the mechanism by which the reporting manager can view records of users who report to him.

Enable Parent Team Inheritance provides a way to automatically default the account team members as members of opportunity and contact teams, thereby providing an easy way for account team members to access opportunities and contacts related to the account.

Default group Assignment provides a facility for a group of users to have shared ownership of accounts, contacts, households, opportunities, and portfolio records created by any of the group members.

Enable Books enables the business feature book whereby a set of records associated to a given book can be accessed by a group of users associated to that book.

Display Book Selector enables a mechanism to filter the records by books applicable to the users.

The **Integration Settings** section is a place where you can turn on/off some of the web service integration features. We will discuss this in detail in *Chapter 8, Web Services Integration.*

The **Desktop Integration Settings** section provides facilities to customize some of the desktop productivity tools provided by CRM On Demand, such as **Personal Information Manager** (**PIM**) sync, offline tools, and Outlook e-mail integration plugin. We will cover this in more detail in *Chapter 9, Data and Integration Tools.*

Many of the fields under **Company Security Settings** are related to **Single sign-on** (**SSO**). Single sign-on is a mechanism by which the users of an organization can use a common username and password to access any of the company's application including CRM On Demand. For example, if there is an intranet portal for the company and the company authenticates the users by their intranet portal user ID and password, then after getting authenticated by the intranet portal, from the intranet portal page, users can seamlessly log in to CRM On Demand or any other internal application without logging in again.

Company Idle Time Out specifies the timeout value for an On Demand session in minutes. You can also request customer care to set the timeout value for an On Demand session. It can be set to a maximum of 60 minutes and a minimum of 10 minutes.

Authentication Type can be either by the CRM On Demand username and password combination or by Single sign-on or by both, depending on your company's policy settings. If you haven't enabled SSO, it is set as **User ID/PWD**.

If you wish to replace the standard CRM On Demand login page with a custom login page branded as per your corporate standards, you can specify the URL of the custom page in **Sign In Page for Userid/PwdAuthentications**; thus, after session timeout On Demand automatically takes the user to the custom page for relogin rather than the standard On Demand login page. Typically, this page is hosted by customers in their web server. The **Userid** and **Pwd** options are the same as the On Demand username and password.

SignIn Page for SSO Authentications is exactly similar to **Sign In Page for Userid/Pwd Authentications**, but applicable only when you enable Single sign-on where you use a common company's username and password to log into any of your corporate applications.

ITS URL for SSO Authentications is an intermediate page that transfers the user to the CRM On Demand's home page from the company's intranet portal, passing the authenticated token from the company's SSO server. After verifying the authentication token, On Demand logs the user automatically to CRM On Demand.

The **IP Address Restrictions Enabled** checkbox provides a facility to restrict access to CRM On Demand from a set of defined IPs. It restricts the user from logging in from anywhere in the world, but provides a security feature to limit the access, for example, strictly from the company's internal network.

The **Inline Attachment Open Enabled** checkbox provides a facility to open attachments inline in the On Demand window.

The **Cross-Site Request Forgery Protections Enabled** checkbox restricts external pages to directly make an HTTP post on a CRM On Demand page. If you enable this checkbox, the system forces the external pages to include a security token that can be authenticated by CRM On Demand before executing the action.

The **Enable IFRAME Embedding** checkbox provides an option to embed CRM On Demand in an `iframe` tag in an external application whereby on clicking on any of the internal links in CRM On Demand, the page opens within the embedded `iframe`. This provides a mechanism to embed CRM On Demand as a **portlet** in your corporate intranet.

The **Analytics Visibility Settings** section is related to reporting and analytics. We would cover the details in *Chapter 10, Introduction to Reports*. At a higher level, settings such as **Reporting Subject Areas**, **Historical Subject Areas**, and **Role-Based Can Read All Records** provide you with a facility to restrict the data displayed to users via reports.

The **Additional Information** section, which is located below the **Analytics Visibility Settings** section provides information on the number of active users, inactive users, and the total number of licenses purchased by your company. The number of active users can be at the most equal to the number of licenses.

Company SignIn and Password Control

The company's **SignIn and Password Policies** section is a place where you can define the **Sign In Policy Information** settings, standards you would like to impose on passwords set by users, authentication information to reset the password, and turn-on/off facilities that allow the user to change the login user ID and e-mail. The following screenshot shows this section with all its settings:

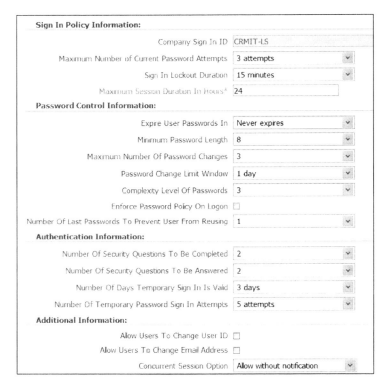

As most of the parameters are self-explanatory, let me explain only the tricky ones here. When you activate a user in CRM On Demand, the user receives two e-mails sent to his configured e-mail ID. One contains a temporary password generated by the system and the other contains a temporary link where a user can go and reset the temporary password by authenticating himself with the temporary password he received. The **Number of Days Temporary Sign In Is Valid** field is used to invalidate the temporary URL beyond certain days for security reasons. If you activate hundreds of users together and some of them are out of office and unable to reset the temporary password within the validity period, he may not be able to reset the temporary password when he is back in office. You may have to reset the password again to reissue a new temporary password and a temporary URL to facilitate his access to CRM On Demand.

The **Password Change Limit Window** and **Maximum Number of Password Changes** fields specify the maximum number of times you can change the password in a given period. If you set **Maximum Number of Password Changes** as **3** and **Password Change Limit Window** as **1 day**, you cannot change the password more than three times in a day.

It is optional to provide flexibility for the end users to change their user ID and e-mail. Typically, companies set the user ID and e-mail ID as the company's desktop sign-in ID and e-mail address without a facility for users to modify the same for simplicity and consistency purposes.

Activating languages

CRM on Demand is available in many languages. All default text fields supplied with the product, such as short text fields and picklist values, along with online help and tutorials, are shown in the available languages depending on the language settings in the user profile.

However, when you customize fields or picklist values, you must manually enter the equivalents in other languages if you want those to appear in their translated versions. Otherwise, they appear in the original language in blue text with brackets around them, regardless of the language you selected. Initially, the only active language is the one that was selected as the company's default language when your company signed up for Oracle CRM on Demand. To make the language choices available to your users, you must activate them in this section.

IP Address Restrictions

If you have checked the **IP Address Restrictions Enabled** checkbox at the company profile level with the help of customer support, then here you can specify the list of IPs from where access to CRM On Demand is allowed. For example, if you would like to restrict the access to CRM On Demand only from your office network, you can configure the Internet gateway's IP address over here to avoid access to the system from anywhere outside your office. Ensure you add the right IP address so that the administrator can still access the application. Otherwise, customer support has to grant access again.

The Sign In Audit and Audit Trail sections

This section provides a facility for the administrator to monitor the sign-in status and operations performed by the users of the system. The **Sign In Audit** section is shown in the following screenshot:

The different types of operations can be **Interactive** or **Web Services**, and the **Operation** tab's values can be **Reset Password, Forget Password, Answer Security Questions, Change SSO Identifier, Change to User ID, Change to Email Address, Set Password, Initial Password, PIM Sync, Offline**, and so on. The **Audit Trail** section is shown in the following screenshot:

Fiscal calendar definitions are generated by the system on the basis of the **Fiscal Calendar Type, Fiscal Year Start Month**, and the **Fiscal Year Start Date** fields set in the company profile. If it is set as **Calendar Quarters**, each of the four quarters will have three months with the first month of the first quarter as the starting date as per your **Fiscal Year Start Month** and **Fiscal Year Start Date** settings. If you have opted for week-based quarters such as 4-4-5 or 5-4-4, each quarter will have 13 weeks with either the first or the last month alone having 5 weeks. The fiscal definitions in the company profile can only be modified by raising a support request to customer care. Typically, business plans, reports, forecasts, and so on are created on the basis of the fiscal period rather than by calendar quarters or months, so setting this in accordance with your business needs is important. The **Fiscal Calendar Detail** section is shown in the following screenshot:

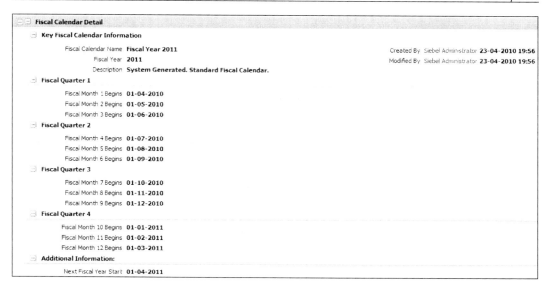

Currency definition

This is the place to activate all the currencies that are applicable to the company. Only on activating the currencies, will users be able to select the currency in defining, for example, the currency of the opportunity revenue.

The **Exchange Rate Edit** page is the place where you define exchange rates between a country's currency and your company's **Default Currency** defined in the **Company Profile** settings. For example, as shown in the next screenshot, if you set up the currency rates between **USD** and **EUR** and between **USD** and **AUD**, then CRM On Demand calculates the conversion between **EUR** and **AUD** by first converting **EUR** to **USD** and then from **USD** to **AUD**. You can specify the **Exchange Date** setting along with the **Exchange Rate** setting. You can click the **Exchange History** link to look into all the past exchange rates set in the system. The system picks up the appropriate exchange rate depending on the data of transaction for forecasting rollup. In case of opportunity, the opportunity revenue date is used to pickup the closest possible exchange rate available in the system. For example, if exchange rates are entered for only 05-15-2011 and 08-15-2011, then for forecasting rollup, the system follows this logic:

- For transactions prior to 05-15-2011, the 05-15-2011 rate is used
- For transactions between 05-15-2011 and 08-14-2011, the 05-15-2011 rate is used
- For transactions on or after 08-15-2011, the 08-15-2011 rate is used

In the case of reports, a single exchange rate for the month is picked up and for all the transactions that fall under the same month, that exchange rate is used for conversion to a single currency. For example, if exchange rates are defined for 05-10-2011, 05-20-2011 and 08-14-2011, then:

- The May 2011 rate will be the value set for 05-20-2011 (the latest rate set for May)

- The August 2011 rate will be the value set for 08/14/2011 (the only rate set for August)

- April 2011 and prior months will be assigned the rate for May 10, 2011 (there are 2 dates for the month of May)

- June 2011 and July 2011 will be assigned the August 2004 rate (closest future month)

- September 2011 and future months will be assigned the August 2011 rate (no future month, so first previous month is used)

Creating the login IDs for users

Users can be set up in the system by creating users one by one by using either of the following ways:

- Use the **New User** action under **Administration | User Management and Access Control | User Management**

- Use the **Quick Add** action under **User Management** or by importing users from a CSV file using the **Import Assistant** tool

As can you see in the following screenshot, when you use the **Quick Add** feature, the system prompts you only for the key-specific information that are required for setting up users, such as **Last Name**, **First Name**, **User ID**, **Email**, and **Role**.

User ID is the sign-in ID that the user uses to log in to the system. The full sign-in ID to log in to CRM On Demand is prefixed with the company identifier defined under the **Company Administration** section. If your company identifier is ABC and user ID is XYZ, the sign-in ID of the user would be ABC/XYZ.

The **Active** status determines whether the user can access the system or not. The number of active users at any point of time is limited by the number of licenses purchased by your company. Users once created in the system cannot be deleted; they can only be set as **Inactive**. If you intend to activate the user as soon as you create the user in the system, set the **Status** value as **Active** and check the **Email Password** checkbox. On saving the user status, the system automatically sends the sign-in information to the user by an e-mail, in two parts; one contains a temporary URL and the other contains a temporary password and details of the user's sign-in ID. A user has to click on the temporary URL, reset the temporary password with his own password, and can then start using CRM On Demand. If you don't intend to activate the user on creation, you can uncheck **Email Password** and later send the sign-in information using the **Reset Password** link in the **User Detail** page. Some of the other important fields required while defining a user are explained in the following table:

User property	Description
Reports To	The manager for the user. The definition of the manager of the user is required if you intend to use the **Manager Visibility** feature. Unless this reporting hierarchy is set up properly, managers may not have access to records created by their subordinates, they can't see the subordinates' records in reports and cannot review and approve the forecast submitted by the subordinates. Currently, CRM On Demand doesn't support reporting to more than one manager.

User property	Description
Reporting Subject Areas and **Historical Subject Areas**	These settings determine the data visibility for the users in reports developed from real-time subject areas and historical subject areas. The possible values are as follows: <ul><li>**Manager Visibility**: Allows the user to see the data that is owned by the user and the data owned by the user's subordinates.</li><li>**Team Visibility**: Allows the user to see the data that is owned by the user and the data shared with the user through teams.</li><li>**Full Visibility**: Allows the user to see the data that is owned by and shared with the user and data owned by and shared with the user's subordinates. The **Full Visibility** option is not available for real-time or reporting subject areas, meaning the user can't see together the records owned by subordinates as well as teams where he is part of it.</li></ul>
Role-Based Can Read All Records	If this flag is selected and if while defining the user's role, he/she has been assigned permission to read all the records, then the user would be able to access all the records in the **Reports** section too. Typically, this feature is used for administrators and managers.
External Unique ID	This is the unique ID of the user in the external system. If you have an organization-wide HRMS system, then this field would be the same as the identifier of the user in the external system. It helps to map the users of CRM On Demand with the external system users.
Integration ID	This can be considered as an equivalent of the **Row ID** field in CRM On Demand in an external system to uniquely identify the user in the other system for integration purposes.
External Identifier for Single Sign On	This is the sign-in ID for the user if the **Single Sign-On** option is checked under the **Company Administration** section. The value of this field is used by CRM On Demand to map the Single sign-on user ID to an On Demand user ID.
Authentication Type, **Records Preview Mode**, **Head-Up Display**, **Theme Name**, **Language**, **Local Currency**, and **Time Zone**	They are similar to the ones defined in the **Company Administration** section and defaulted automatically. You can override them at the user level if you wish to.

User property	Description
Never Call, **Never Email**, and **Never Mail**	These are the fields used by CRM On Demand marketing to avoid calling, e-mailing, and mailing users of the system.
Always Send Critical Updates	If this checkbox is selected, the user receives e-mails containing important information from Oracle CRM On Demand, such as product updates, service updates, and so on of CRM On Demand and the related products.

After you have created the login IDs and set them to **Active** status, you would proceed to set up the product catalog. Although the product catalog is normally assumed to be available as a standardized list, the reality in many companies (be they large or small enterprises) is that the lists tend to be standardized by multiple departments and teams. The sales and service teams may have slightly different definitions of the product category, which is not a problem in itself as long as they remained in their silos. However, CRM On Demand requires a single product catalog of the company. The set of login IDs that you have created will be handy in getting a quick consensus on the product catalog, right from your chief executive officer through the service and sales representatives.

Creating the product catalog

There are merely four things you need to know about the product catalog:

- First, you may not need the product catalog facility if your company sells custom services. The catalog is typically relevant for discrete goods businesses, or standardized service offerings.

- Second, product names have to be unique.

- Third, a product record cannot be deleted after it has once been created.

- Fourth, the path to the product catalog, which is **Admin | Content Management | Products**.

The product category records and product records can both be imported using the **Import UI Assistant** tool. We can edit the product name of an existing record but we should avoid that at all costs. The CRM On Demand product catalog is designed for a fair bit of product management practice. The **Orderable** field when unchecked, removes the product from the active catalog. We should use this feature to manage requirements to change the names of an existing product or to delete products from the catalog, and to schedule the release of new products to the sales force as well. The **Type** and the **Status** fields are useful too. Categories make a catalog and therefore we should prefer a generous use of the product category over creating a simple, long list of all the products. CRM On Demand updates all the analytics tables to reflect the latest catalog. So, product category names can be edited anytime, and product records can be edited to move them to a different category. Editing the product name however would lead to bad reports as the revenue or asset data do not get refreshed in the analytics tables.

Enabling sales forecasts

There are three things that you need to know about sales forecasts:

- First, the forecast engine has to be activated the first time, and updated every time there is any change in the forecast participants. Both the actions are simply called **Update**.

- Second, a forecast participant is any user who can submit his forecasts to the forecast computer. This translates to every user whose user role gives him the access to create a **Forecast** type of record.

- Third, changes in the forecast participants could be that of new (forecast creator) users being added to the system and existing (forecast creator) users leaving the system.

The path to update the forecast engine is **Admin | Data Rules and Assignment | Forecast Definition | Update**.

On clicking the **Update** button, you will see the definition settings displayed in three parts. Let us walk through these parts.

The next screen shot is of the first part. **Opportunity Revenue Forecast** refers to forecasting from the revenue field on the opportunity record. **Opportunity Product Forecast** refers to forecasting from the revenue field on the product revenue records under the opportunity. You can select both if your organization requires them, but in most cases there is usually an organization standard of what to use for the forecast. You can check the appropriate tick boxes as required in your sales organization, and then click on the **Next** button.

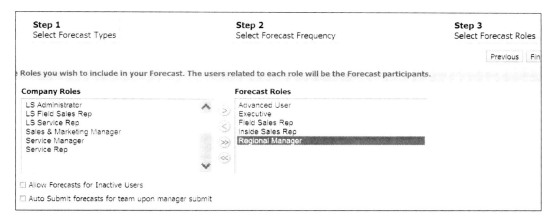

The second step of **Forecast Definition** is **Forecast Frequency**. This contains the preset frequency of the forecasting for one quarter and takes the submitted sales forecasts of the first day of every month. Keeping this frequency setting as it is, you can click on the **Next** button to get to the final step.

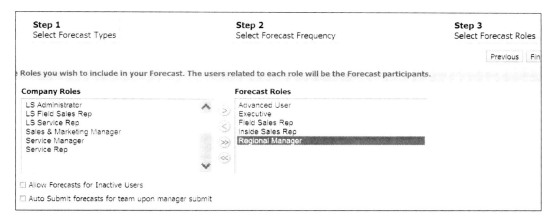

The previous screenshot is of the final step. Here, you need to define/add the forecast participants. The column labeled **Forecast Roles** should contain all the user roles that have users who are forecast creators. The **Field Sales Rep**, **Inside Sales Rep**, **Executive**, **Advanced User**, and the **Regional Manager** user roles have access to create forecasts and can engage in sales work that will produce forecasts. Therefore, assuming all of these user roles are assigned among your login IDs, you would use the chevron buttons to move the user roles from the column labeled **Company Roles** to the column labeled **Forecast Roles**. The **Sales & Marketing Manager** role does not have access to create forecasts so there is no point in adding this user role to the list of participants. The **Sales & Marketing Manager** role has access to read all forecasts and will view them at the **Forecast** tab when the forecasts have been generated on the first day of the month.

There are two other optional settings in this part of the definition. These are related to a customization of the organizational structure. We will revisit them later in this book.

You would thus complete the **Update** task by clicking on the **Finish** button.

This completes the second step of the deployment. It is a milestone that usually leads to a round of internal testing and final checks before the big bang of **Step 3**. A simple and clean approach to sanity testing is to have one of the advanced users on board. You could issue his login ID to him and then round-robin the user roles on his login ID. Needless to say, the administrator's login ID should never be switched to another user role, as that is a one-way ticket out of the system.

Step 3 – Pass the word around

Now that you have readied the system, the next step is to have the users login to the system and thereafter support their adoption and the use of this new system. The list of activities in this step are as follows:

* Creating company-wide alerts and messaging on CRM On Demand
* Issuing the user IDs
* Provide ongoing support to users on CRM On Demand

Creating company-wide alerts and messaging

You would likely prepare for the launch of the new system by e-mail and have departmental meetings announcing the new system and its launch process. These communications do help in preparing users to transition to the new system. Meanwhile, you could consider ways to welcome the users from within the new system when they log in for the first time, and through the initial few weeks after the launch.

The **Company Alerts** facility and the **Message Centre** section can be put to good use at this task.

You can broadcast alerts to all users of your company, and the alerts will appear on the main **Homepage** when the user logs into CRM On Demand. You would want to create welcome messages, support information alerts, and any other collateral suitable to your audience. An alert message can have attachment files and URLs. Perhaps an audio-video presentation of the new system and a "how-to" could be hosted on an internal HTTP server and the URL posted as part of the welcome message. The use of the alert facility is limited only by your imagination. The path to the alert administration is **Admin | Company Administration | Company Alerts**.

The **Message Centre** section at the upper-left corner of the CRM On Demand page can be used to engage with the users of your new system, at a personal level. If you are going live with a small number of users, you could actually consider leaving a personal message to each of the users. The **Message Centre** section's placement and its animations do invite attention, and certainly of the first-time users. To leave a message to a user, search for the user record using the search panel. A wildcard search would output all the user records. Hovering the mouse on the **Last Name** field invokes the **Message Centre** icon, clicking on which, would allow you to send a message to that specific user. The message would be available in the user's **Message Centre** when he logs in.

Issuing the user IDs

It is a rare administrator who recognizes that the end users could hardly care about the permanent URL of the new system or about the small lifespan of the temporary password, and yet these are fairly common problems—of users looking helpless on the second day because they either forgot to bookmark it on the first day or simply did not bother to note the easy URL of the CRM On Demand (`https://sso.crmondemand.com/router/logon.jsp`), of users logging in for the first time two weeks after you reset their passwords, and of course by then the temporary password has expired. It is the administrator's problem if a user is unable to log in to the system. A launch failure is never a good thing so we accept that it pays to take precautionary steps at the user level.

CRM On Demand issues the temporary URL and temporary password almost instantaneously, and it helps to trigger those password resets on launch day to exactly those users who can reliably be expected to login within the next couple of days. It would help you more to send a personal e-mail to all those users, stating the permanent URL of the application and their login ID format.

Related to user friendliness is the CRM On Demand **Help** window that can popup when the user logs in. The technical page doesn't add any value to the end users and therefore you should consider disabling it in the user record at the time you are resetting the password. The **Show Welcome Page on Sign In** field, if set to **N** will not display the CRM On Demand welcome page to your users when they login.

Ongoing support to users

Having gone live out of the box, it will not be long before users begin to raise requests and alarms about and around the CRM On Demand. As the data accumulates in your system and reports take a while longer to generate, users and you would likely see the need for a service request management system. To eat your own dog food is the hallmark of the professional, and to that end, we recommend that you use the service request functionality available in the system for you to receive and process service requests of your customers.

In the next chapter, we focus on the art of customizing the CRM On Demand application to meet our business needs.

Summary

In this chapter, we learned about the default sales, marketing, and service functions that come embedded as part of an out of the box CRM On Demand instance, went through some of the key objects that are available in the system to capture the CRM data, learned about turning on/off company-wide features, setting up users in the system, utilizing some of the predefined user roles available, and a list of activities to be performed to activate the users and go live with an out of the box CRM On Demand system. In the subsequent chapters, we will discuss in detail customizing the CRM On Demand system to meet any of your organization-specific needs if the standard out of the box features we learned in this chapter are not good enough to meet your requirements.

3
CRM On Demand Customization

After your business has conceptualized a customer relationship as a profitable object of management, it expects the **Customer Relationship Management** system, that is, the CRM application software, to be fit for the business. The reason you have bought CRM On Demand instead of building a CRM application in-house is because, as we learned in the preceding chapter, the out of the box CRM On Demand application delivers the software and functionalities that will meet the needs of your CRM organization. The CRM On Demand application is built to a world-class industry reference model of customer relationship management practice, and therefore, going live out of the box is quite common among its buyers as it meets most, if not all, of the business requirements for the introductory stage. In such a case, one will of course need to follow through on the newly introduced system to fit it with the custom nuts and bolts required by the business. In some cases the business may require that the new CRM application be introduced with all the custom nuts and bolts in place before deploying it to the users. This exercise of configuring the out of the box application (either after the introduction or as part of the introduction itself) and/or writing new external software that integrates with the application is called **customization**. CRM On Demand is designed to be extensively customized to the specific needs of your CRM organization. CRM On Demand is unlike its peers in the industry in terms of both the features it delivers out of the box and the easy facilities it provides for modifying the application. As such, the terms configuration and customization are fairly synonymous when you are implementing CRM On Demand.

The objective of this chapter is to introduce the customizability available in the CRM On Demand application. To efficiently and effectively customize any given thing, one needs to know the art, design, and technology, in other words, the architecture of that thing. You are already aware of the architecture of your business and now you need to understand the architecture of the CRM On Demand application to be able to integrate it neatly to the requirements of your business. This process of integrating the two systems — that of the business system with its line and staff of "CRM" thinkers and doers with that of the electronic system, that is, the CRM application capable of high velocity collection, storage, processing, and publication of "CRM" data to and from both individual business people and other electronic software systems — usually involves customizing the business as well to adopt some of the CRM practices implicit in the CRM On Demand application.

It is the role of a good analyst to understand the business process as it stands today — and at the same time also retain the concept of flexibility — to determine a cost/benefit of which business processes can be adjusted to accommodate the application's best practices sans customization, as well as to determine which parts of the application specifically must change to meet the business need. Documented business processes are the foundation of good CRM project management. A description of the process of such an integration system is out of the scope of this book, but it suffices to note here that the overarching decision of the enterprise to buy the CRM On Demand application "off-the-shelf" instead of building an application in-house should guide every question you ask and every decision you make on the customization of the CRM On Demand application.

By the end of this chapter, you will know the following:

* The architecture of the CRM On Demand application
* The customizable components of the CRM On Demand application

The application architecture

CRM On Demand is an application software, used to consume and produce CRM-related data, by business users who are operating by processes that are defined by the enterprise. The following diagram is a representation of the logic of the CRM On Demand application. In this diagram, **Data** refers to the data model. **Business Processes** refers to the process model including the business objects, the user organization (of responsibilities and authorities), business rules, and workflow integrations with other systems. **User** refers to the interface model in the application, including the online and web services available to the user of the application.

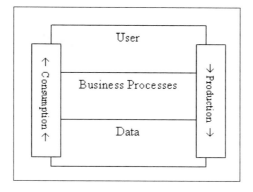

If you are familiar with the Siebel Enterprise application software and its construction, the terminologies used in this chapter about the CRM On Demand application are not meant to be read in relation to those of the Siebel Enterprise application. The CRM On Demand application is a deployment of the Siebel Enterprise application with significant simplifications and enhancements of functionalities of the Siebel Enterprise application, to deliver it as SaaS. Specifically, the separations between the data, business, and UI layers that are visible and accessible in the Siebel Enterprise application are invisible in the CRM On Demand application. As such, the data layer that is distinct from the business layer is not a practical concept for administration of CRM On Demand.

Customizability

The three parts: namely the data model, business model, and the interface model that make the software are separable and are individual parts of the software. This means that, technically, each of them can be subject to customization.

The application software is a single piece of the CRM On Demand service; the hardware on which the software runs is the other piece. The hardware and the software together provide the quality of service, that is, the application's performance, reliability, and scalability. The CRM On Demand service does not have an automated hardware provisioning and therefore each of the three parts of the software has specific limits to its customization. In the following sections, we will look at the customization limits of the three parts of the CRM On Demand software.

The data model

The data model of CRM On Demand is not available for customization. However, it helps to understand the data management tools available to the administrator. The relevant sections in the **Admin Homepage** page of the application, are depicted in the following screenshot:

CRM On Demand defines the following two types of data:

- Transactional data
- Files

Files are stored in a separate file system. Files are represented as attachments in CRM On Demand.

The database, data tables, columns, and rows that constitute the physical and logical storage and management of transactional data is out of the scope of the CRM On Demand application customization. Service allotments define the amount of transactional records storage that is available to your organization.

Except executable files, a file can have any type of extension. A single file cannot exceed 20 MB in size. Service allotments define the amount of file storage available to your organization. A central **Attachments Management** console is provided in the **Content Management** section of the administration page, to enable the administrator to manage the consumption of file storage space.

Data management

A record that is deleted by a user is marked for actual purging from the database 30 days from the date of deletion. The **Deleted Items** list has prebuilt display columns and these cannot be customized. The schedule of purging cannot be customized. The records in the **Deleted Items** column can be recovered. The ability to recover deleted items is a customizable feature.

The application provides prebuilt tools for the batch export, import, and deletion of data. The tools cannot be customized. The tools provide industry-standard facilities and options for the task of batch exports, imports, and deletions.

The process model

The process model comprises the object model, business rules, and the security model. The vast bulk of the process model is available for customization.

The following screenshot highlights the sections in the **Admin Homepage** page that are related to the process model of the application:

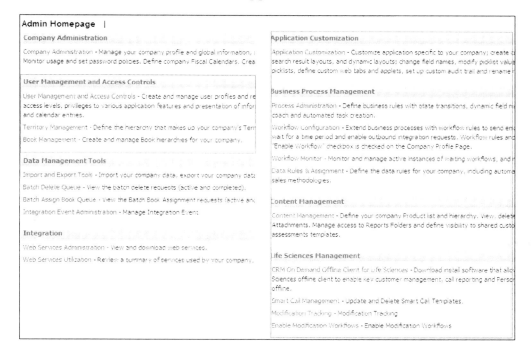

Object model

The business objects and their inter-relationships constitute the object model. The object is also known as a **record type**. An object is one of two types; namely, the **standard object** and the **custom object**. While the standard objects are predefined, the custom objects, as their name implies, get their definitions when you customize them. The names and display icons of all the objects can be customized, in all the activated languages.

An object comprises the main/parent object and its relationship with other/child objects. It would be useful to think of the business object as a collection of business components, with a main component, and its relationships with the other/child components. For example, the account object is a collection of the account component; it has an M:M relationship with the contact component, a 1:M relationship with the service request component, an M:M cardinality with the `CustomObject1` component, a 1:M cardinality with the activity component, and so on. Similarly, the service request object is a collection of the service request component and its relations are 1:M activity, 1:1 product, M:M `CustomObject1`, 1:1 account, 1:1 contact, and so on.

A business component is manifest by its fields. A component comprises key fields, other input fields, record auditing fields, and audit fields.

The standard objects include lead, activity, campaign, account, contact, opportunity, service request, business plan, objective, price list, insurance policy, insured party, financial account, opportunity competitor, contact role, contact interests, service request team, vehicle, dealer, product samples, medical event, among many others totaling about 50 objects covering the various industries. The modeling of the standard objects cannot be customized.

The custom objects are devoid of any functional definition and you give them business names and definitions when you have configured them as part of your application. The custom objects are available in specified quantities depending on the type of CRM On Demand service that you buy; a single-tenant pod of CRM On Demand can be set to provide any required number of custom objects, while a multi-tenant pod provides up to 30 custom objects. The custom objects have two subtypes among them. The ones numbered 1 to 3 are prebuilt with an M:M cardinality with all the standard objects and themselves, and a 1:M cardinality with the custom objects numbered 4 and above. The custom objects numbered 4 and above are prebuilt with a 1:M cardinality with all the standard objects and custom objects in the application.

In other words, the custom objects numbering from 1 to 3, have prebuilt intermediate tables, while the later custom objects are simpler in builds and are expected to be used as intermediate tables themselves if you need to construct an M:M cardinal relationship with custom objects. By the same token, for reports/analytics, the custom objects numbering from 1 to 3 have many prebuilt subject areas while the later custom objects have a single, comprehensive subject area that brings all the objects together. Understanding the business processes and business object needs before starting your project can ensure that the right processes, which require an M:M cardinality, are assigned to the right custom objects.

A business object is manifest by the **Record Detail** page, **Record Edit** page, **Targeted Search** page, and the home page; these pages are customizable.

A **Record Detail** page consists of the main/parent component record page, followed by sections of related information. Except the key fields, all the other input fields on the record page can be set to be a **Required** field and/or a **Read-Only** field on that page.

The parent component record page form is a layout of two columns and six sections in which the fields are positioned. The form layout of 2 X 6 cannot be customized. Unused sections do not display on the screen. Each of the six sections can be customized to have section headings in every active language. Every object is prebuilt with one field that can be inputted with 16,350 characters; the placement of this field is customizable in the custom objects and is not customizable in the standard objects where its default position is at the bottom of the parent record page. A sample **Customer Details** page is shown in the following screenshot:

Related information refers to views of records of the associated components and views of external/unlinked data (that is, web applets). The records are displayed in a list view. The list view displays five records on a random sort, and a link to view the full list. The list view cannot be customized; however, the list columns can be customized to a maximum of 9 columns. The vertical sequence of the related information sections can be customized on every **Record Detail** page. There is no standard facility to customize the pool of related information; such a customization calls for the use of web applets, which can programmatically fetch the data from the various sources and provide the custom views.

> In release 20, the related information sections can be opted to be displayed in a Tab view. The Tab view displays all the sections as tabs, in a line horizontally. The Tab view reduces the length of the **Record Detail** page and reduces the data that needs to be fetched when the **Record Detail** page is loaded. One downside of the Tab view is that as the number of sections exceed the horizontal space available, they automatically collapse into a drop-down icon at the right-hand side. See the last chapter in this book for details of the release 20 of CRM On Demand.

In general, related information refers to all those associated records that are non-mandatory to the business processing of the parent record. While components that have a 1:M and M:M relationship would have a section of their own as part of the related information, the components that have a 1:1 cardinality with the parent component can be either placed as a related information section or included in the parent record page. The placement of a 1:1 associated component in the **Record Detail** page would be dependent on the business rules and the security model that you plan to implement in your process model. To elaborate, if the associated 1:1 component is a mandatory record without which the parent record is deemed incomplete for business processing, the placement on the parent record page is necessary to enforce the rule of creating or supplying that associated record before creating the parent record. On the other hand, placing it as related information and manual verification by dedicated user/roles (as part of the security model) would well meet the requirements with its different efficiency.

Fields

A field has a unique name in each language, a data type, a default value (either pre-default or post-default), a validation rule, a validation error message, and web service integration tags. An object is provided with relevant predefined fields and a limited quantum of custom fields, including a fixed quantity of fields that are indexed.

The set of fields for indexing cannot be customized.

Every object has its key fields, that is, user keys, which may be a single field or a set of fields. The key fields are the defining fields of that object; the values of the key fields in a record provide a unique identity to that record. Duplicate records are identified at the time of input based on the values in the key fields. The de-duplication feature is available in the standard objects of account, opportunity, lead, and service request. The de-duplication feature cannot be customized to apply to the other objects. The fields that are defined as the key fields for the object cannot be swapped with another field.

The tabulation of the business objects and their key fields is given in the following table. This table does not list all the objects available in the CRM On Demand application. To illustrate, **Opportunity Name** and its **Account Name** constitute the key fields of an opportunity. The key fields of all objects are predefined and cannot be customized.

> Another easy way to know the key fields of an object is to launch the **Data Import** wizard. The key fields will be listed on top of the first wizard page!

The record auditing fields are a fixed set of fields that audit the user manipulation of the record. Examples of such fields are `CreatedBy`, `ModifiedTimestamp`, and `CreatedByEmailAddress`. These fields are updated by system workflows and can be displayed on the record page. The calculation logic of the record auditing fields cannot be customized.

The quantity of custom fields available is not the same across all objects. The tabulation of the quantity of custom fields by data type available in each object is given in the second table. **Name** and **Integration Tag** of a custom field can be changed any number of times; however, the data type of a field cannot changed after it is created.

Auditing fields of an object refer to the set of key fields and/or other input fields that you want audited. Every object can have a maximum of 35 fields marked for auditing. You can select, that is, customize, the set of fields for auditing. The columns of the **Audit Trail** section cannot be customized.

External objects

The business processes of your CRM may require the users to access external systems from within the CRM On Demand application window. The access may be mediated by security features such as **Single sign-on** (**SSO**) and common identities stored across the two separated systems. The CRM On Demand integration point for such customization is the **Custom Web Tabs** and **Global Web Applets** links. The set of user object fields available for URLs and/or HTML in the **Custom Web Tabs** and the **Global Web Applets** links cannot be customized.

The following table lists the business objects and their corresponding key fields:

Name of the business object	Key fields
Account	**Account Name and Location**
Contact	**First Name, Last Name, and Email**
Product Category	**Category Name**
Product	**Product Name**
Opportunity	**Opportunity Name and Account**
Opportunity contact role	**Opportunity Name and Contact Full Name**
Opportunity product revenue, asset	**Product**
Campaign	**Source Code**
Campaign recipient	**Campaign, Contact, and Source Code**
Lead	**First Name, Last Name, Company, and Email**
Service request	**SR Number**
Solution	**Title**
Task, appointment, and note	**Subject**
CustomObjects 01 and higher	**Name**
Partner	**Partner Name and Location**
Price list	**Price List Name**
Business plan	**Plan Name**

The following table lists the quantity of custom fields available, by business object:

Record type/ Business object	Check Box	Currency	Date	Date/ Time	Integer	Multi-select Picklist	Number	Percent	Phone	Picklist	Text (Long)	Text (Short)	Web Link
Account	35	80	25	25	35	10	33	30	10	100	30	45	100
Contact, opportunity	35	25	25	25	35	10	33	30	10	100	30	70	100
Lead, activity	35	25	25	25	35	10	33	30	10	100	30	45	100
Campaign, MedEd, solution, household, funds, portfolio, fund request, MDF request, SP request	35	25	25	25	35	0	33	30	10	100	30	45	100
Vehicle	70	50	60	50	70	0	33	30	10	100	30	45	100
Service request	35	25	25	25	35	10	68	60	30	200	60	105	100
Customobject 1-3	35	25	35	25	35	10	35	30	20	100	30	60	100
Dealer	70	105	60	50	70	0	35	30	20	100	30	60	100
Product	35	25	25	25	35	0	35	30	20	100	30	60	100
Asset, revenue	35	25	25	25	35	0	68	60	30	200	60	105	100
User	35	25	35	25	35	0	35	30	20	100	30	60	100
Customobjects 4 and higher	35	25	25	35	35	0	35	30	20	100	30	90	100
Industry-specific record types other than those listed in this table	35	25	25	35	35	0	35	30	20	100	30	90	100

Business rules

Business rules refer to the policies and workflows to govern the user's production of business data. Examples of validations are: a lead must have a physical address, the opportunity owner's location must be less than 200 miles from the customer's address, the user cannot create a task record with a past due date, a contact must have either the date of birth or a valid phone number, the area and cause of a service request must not be changed after the service request is closed, **Company Name** must be minimally four characters long, and so on. Validations on fields, which have typed inputs, listing of values of a field, default values for fields, cross-fields validations for record-level integrity, insistence of the state model of the record (that is, particular paths of the status) are field-related rules that are meant to have custom content.

Workflow actions, be they instantaneous or time-based, are rules-based facilities that are meant to be deployed for your custom processes. Workflow actions include updating field values, e-mail notifications, tasks scheduling, assignment of records to specific users, and integration of the data with external systems.

The integration of the objects of the CRM On Demand application with the external objects/pages that are accessed via the **Custom Web Tabs** link can be tightly customized using the web link fields and web applets in the objects.

The list of values of the status fields of the activity and service request objects cannot be customized. The state model of the lead qualification cannot be customized. For sales processes, the final two stages of **Closed/Won** and **Closed/Lost** cannot be changed.

The hierarchy of territories, the hierarchy of the books of business, the opportunity product catalog, the assessment scripts for leads, opportunities, contact and service requests, the lead conversion rules, opportunity forecast rules, and the opportunity sales processes are the content that are meant to be customized to your organization. However, none of these rule engines can be customized.

Assignment rules for automated routing of the opportunity, lead, service request, and account records to specific users, teams, and territories are examples of customizable content for the workflows. However, the **Assignment Manager** tool itself cannot be customized; for example, **Assignment Manager** stops evaluating rules once a match is found and you cannot customize this process.

When you do want multiple rules to be evaluated before an assignment is made, you would use the workflows, with their sequences and ordered actions. In release 20, you can set a workflow to stop all subsequent workflows, and this at a simple level is nearly the same as how the **Assignment Manager** tool operates. For other details on release 20, see the *Chapter 11, Help, Support Ecosystem, and Features in New Releases*, in this book.

Security model

The security model refers to the accesses to the object, data, and application features, in what is called the user role, that is assigned to every user of the CRM On Demand application. User roles can be created and definitions of the prebuilt user roles can be customized.

Apart from the mandatory user role, a user can be given accesses through four other ways: namely, the manager hierarchy, the team, groups, and the books of business. The definition of each of these four access controls are predefined and cannot be customized.

Delegated user is another access control that is available in CRM On Demand. A user can delegate his/her access profiles to other users. The access to create data cannot be delegated.

The manager hierarchy refers to the linear organizational chart of the users, which is represented in the **Reports-To** field of the user's object. A user cannot report to more than one manager, and a manager cannot report to a subordinate (that is, circular hierarchies are not permitted). The manager hierarchy is organization-wide and therefore the access applies over all the data in the system, independent of the business objects.

A **team** is defined at each object and is therefore a record-level access control. Teams created by users for a particular record apply to that particular record. The access to create and modify the teams is customizable. Team members may have differential accesses to the particular record, in terms of reading/editing/deleting that record as well as on the team itself. The team accesses are available for all the objects in the CRM On Demand application.

A **group** is a simpler construct of the team, which applies across all the standard business objects. A group access is limited to the records that are owned by any one member of the group. It provides a common-owner access to the particular record to all the group members.

Groups were an early implementation of predetermined teams. By assigning an account or contact or opportunity to a group, the members of the group become automatically assigned to the team. Groups have generally been replaced by books of business and are not recommended for continued use as an access-control mechanism. Groups do offer an advantage in sharing calendars; however, groups allow you to provide several users with access to each other's calendar.

The books of business is a combination of a security object and a business object. A hierarchy of books can be set up, and a book can have only one parent book. A book has data and users of that book. The users can access that data with specific rights. The cardinality of the book and the user is M:M and that of the book to data is M:M. A book need not contain data in it and can instead be an organizing folder or a general record for any other purpose; a book that is tagged to contain data cannot later be reverted.

A book hierarchy has its cost and benefit. A hierarchy is easy for access and workflow maintenance but it takes longer for the system to go through the hierarchy when searching for a record. At the user profile, a book can be set as default for searching, for each record type and/or for the entire system, and these facilities should be exploited if you are designing complex book structures.

The books administration section appears on the **Admin Homepage** page as **Book Management**. The following screenshot shows the administrative work in this section, including creating a book, its sub-books, and associating users for a book:

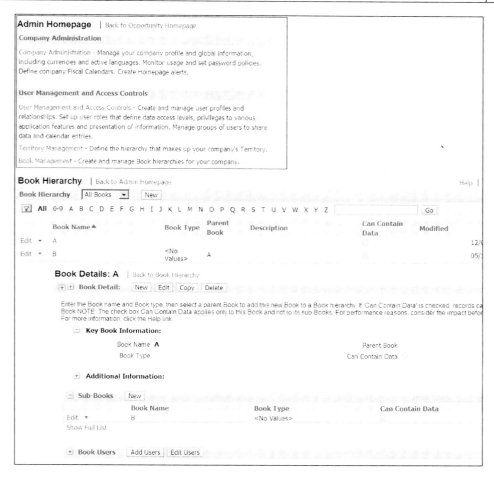

The interface model

The CRM On Demand application has multiple interfaces for the users. Every one of these interfaces is predefined and cannot be customized. The interfaces are as follows:

- The entire application, online via Internet Browsers IE7 and higher, Firefox 3 and higher, and Safari 5x on iOS

- The transactional data and application data, via web services using HTTPS SOAP XML

Online interface

The browser-based interface for the online application contains four elements in the window; namely the global header, the action bar, the tables (tabs), and the global footer. The content of each of the four elements can be customized for every user role. Thereafter, every individual user can customize/personalize the action bar and the tables, provided the user's role has access to personalization. The four elements in themselves cannot be customized.

Web services interface

The web services interface provides **Web Services Description Language (WSDL)** files and schema files by a business object. The WSDLs are available in two notations: namely WS 1.0 and WS 2.0, which differ in the kind of data operations they support. The WSDLs are available in two representations for each of the business object fields: namely the custom tags WSDL and the generic tags WSDL. The schema files are available in the WS 1.0 notation.

The CRM On Demand application WSDLs cannot be customized.

The access to the WSDL files is an independent, role-level privilege, that is, a user who has access to web services does not automatically get access to the WSDLs.

Special interfaces

The CRM On Demand application provides additional, specific interfaces that utilize the published web services and other non-published web services that are accessible to Oracle Corporation alone. Such interfaces include the following:

- The core CRM model application, offline, in an MS Excel-based utility, using web services for synchronization
- The core CRM model application, online, on designated Mobile device platforms
- The core CRM model application, online, as widgets
- The core CRM model application, integrated synchronization with MS Outlook, and Lotus Notes (personal information manager)

Summary

In this chapter, we learned the scope of customization that is available across the CRM On Demand application. We began with the application architecture to understand the structures in the application. The CRM On Demand application has three parts, that is, the data model, the process model, and the interface model. We then proceeded to understand the scope of customization available in each of the three individual parts.

Understanding the scope of customization is essential to efficient customization of the application to fit it to your business requirements.

In the subsequent chapters we will learn the details of the customizable elements, including how to customize them.

Application Customization

As you saw in the previous chapter, the CRM On Demand application logic consists of data, business process, and user layers. The spotlight of this chapter is to detail out the level of customization possible at the data and user interface layer of CRM On Demand. The chapter focuses on customizations at the business process and user layer. By the end of this chapter, you will know the following:

- The level of customization possible at the data and user interface layers
- Steps to perform customization
- Best practices associated with it

For better clarity, this chapter is divided into three major sections, which are explained as follows:

- Addressing customizations at data model level: Here, we talk about customizing the CRM On Demand data model
- Layout-level customization: Here, we discuss surfacing the changes to the underlying data model to the end users
- Other assorted customizations: Here, the focus is on customizing any other configurable user interface section in CRM On Demand

Data model-level customization

We have seen in the earlier chapters that CRM On Demand provides, by default, a range of objects such as accounts, contacts, leads, and so on to store and retrieve your vital CRM data. Though these objects look independent, your CRM database is not complete without them being related to each other. For example, information about the companies that your organization deals with can be stored in the account object and the contacts in these companies can be stored in the contact object. Though these accounts and contacts, as standalone, are valuable sources of information in your CRM database, typically, your needs doesn't stop here. You might be interested to know the list of contacts with whom you deal with in each of the companies. This apparently requires a third object "account-contact" to capture the relationship between accounts and contacts. The third object "account-contact" can be a simple one, which just stores the accounts and contacts to establish the relationship or it can enrich it with additional information at the relationship level such as the role a particular contact plays in relation to an account. The same contact can play the role of decision-maker for a company but an influencer for another company which makes the relationship between accounts and contacts as M to M.

As a company administrator, you should be able to access the entity-relationship diagram of the CRM On Demand application from support.oracle.com. In the support portal under the **Knowledge** section, search for **CRM On Demand: Entity Relationship Diagram (ERD) for CRM On Demand Industry Editions** to get access to it.

It is an important point to note that you don't have flexibility to customize the default relationship between the CRM On Demand objects but you do have flexibility to add fields to some of the relationship objects such as the one that relates accounts and contacts.

In addition to this, CRM On Demand also provides you a set of custom objects (1 to 15) to capture some of your business entities that are not available out of the box. For example, a standard CRM On Demand object model doesn't have a standard object called **orders** but you can rename one of the available custom objects to orders and use it to store order information in CRM On Demand.

The custom objects numbered 1 to 3 are prebuilt with an M:M cardinality with all the standard objects. They have an M:M cardinality among themselves, and 1:M cardinality with the custom objects numbered 4 and above. Similarly, the custom objects numbered 4 and above have 1:M cardinality with all the objects including among themselves. It is important that you understand the difference in the relationship between custom objects "1 to 3" and "4 and above".

You can smartly use the custom objects to alter the relationship between any two standard objects or between a standard object and a custom object or between two custom objects. For example, the standard data model defines the relationship between contact and service requests as one-to-many, which is the most common scenario where you have multiple service requests coming from a single contact. But let us say your business situation demands a many-to-many relationship as you may like to associate the same service request from many of your contacts possibly due to the reason that all of them have similar issue on your products/services. Though the prebuilt On Demand data model doesn't provide the flexibility to handle this, you can introduce a custom object (4 and above) as an intermediate object between account and service requests there by altering the relationship between service requests and contacts as M:M from 1:M.

Adding, modifying, and deleting fields

As you saw in the earlier chapters, standard On Demand objects come with a wide set of standard fields that are ready to use. In addition to these, there are precreated custom fields that can be used for any of your customization needs. Though the custom fields are precreated at the On Demand database level, you have to explicitly add the field to make it available for your customization needs.

Deleting the field (standard as well as custom) is not possible in CRM On Demand, so think twice before adding a new custom field to avoid cluttering your system with too many unused custom fields. Field names are sorted by alphabetical order in the administrative screens of CRM On Demand, so if there are unused custom (or standard) fields, they can be renamed to a convention (typically prefixed with ZZ) that pushes the field to the end of the list and thereby keep your field list concise. Fields can be "recycled"; but as in any DB model, be wary of historical data residing in fields planned for re-use. Renamed standard fields may show in default reports.

To add a field, say `Region`, to a standard account object, go to to **Admin | Application Customization | Account | Account Field Setup** and click on the **New** action. This opens the screen that is shown in the following screenshot to capture the properties of the field to be created. Note that before you start creating new fields, you should check whether the fields are available in the list of preconfigured CRM On Demand fields. Start creating new fields only if you don't find them. Also, if the field is going to be used heavily in lists, search, or in real-time reporting, ensure you use an indexed field for optimal system performance. Indexed custom fields are preconfigured and available in the system with prefix "indexed". As the number of indexed fields is limited, use them judiciously.

The **Display Name** textbox of the field obviously takes the value `Region`. The checkbox **Mark for Translation** assists you to overwrite the **Display Name** value as well as field validation error messages in other languages if you intend to configure the system in multiple languages.

If you like to make the field as mandatory in the CRM On Demand data entry form, mark it as **Required**. Note that designating a field as mandatory here makes the field mandatory in all the standard/custom layouts that you create. If you want to selectively make it mandatory only for a designated layout of one or more roles, don't make it mandatory here but make it mandatory in the appropriate layout.

If the field is only for displaying information and assuming there is a way to determine the region on the basis of the selected account's country using field default, you can set it as **Read-Only**.

By selecting **Copy Enabled**, we determine whether the field value has to be copied when we perform a record-copy action at record level.

As you learned in the previous chapter, On Demand provides a wide variety of field types such as, Checkbox, Currency, Long Text, Short Text, and so on; and depending on your needs, you can chose the right one. Once a field type is selected, it cannot be modified later. In our example of adding a custom field named `Region`, the obvious choices are Short Text, Long Text, or Picklist. Selection between Short Text and Long Text is determined by your field length requirements, whereas choice of Picklist is determined by whether the field has the predetermined, limited set of values or not.

The **Default Value** textbox helps to default the field value with a default region. For example, let us assume that predominantly your customers are from America, you can then default region to America. If you select **Post Default**, America is defaulted after you hit the **Save** button in the account data entry form, whereas if you haven't checked it, it is prepopulated and surfaced in the new account data entry form. The user always has an option to overwrite. Irrespective of whether you have selected **Post Default** or not, if the user overwrites the information by keying in a value for the field in the form, the keyed-in value takes precedence over the default value that you set at the configuration level.

Field Validation helps to build some validations on the field. Assuming you decided to keep the field as Short Text instead of Picklist so that the user can key in any value, but at the same time you want to enforce that the user uses only capital letters, you can include a validation rule similar to the following:

```
(FindOneOf ([<Region>], "qwertyuiopasdfghjklzxcvbnm") = 0)
```

The **Field Validation** lookup window provides a clever editor to write your field validation rules. This window is shown in the following screenshot:

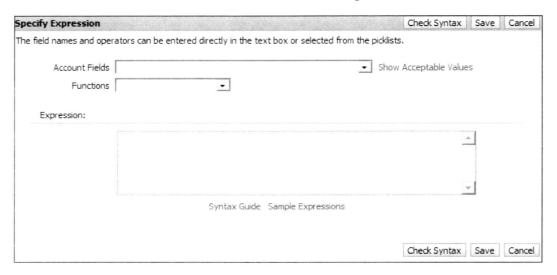

The steps to write the field validation rules are as follows:

1. Select the `findNoneOf()` function from the functions drop-down menu.
2. Select the `Region` field from the **Account Fields** drop-down menu.
3. Expand the validation as provided in the code snippet.
4. Check whether the syntax is valid using the **Check Syntax** action.
5. If you need any additional help on syntax or some sample expressions for reference, click the **Syntax Guide** and **Sample Expressions** links.

As you have observed in the previous validation syntax, if the validation expression evaluates to `true`, that is, if there are no lower-case letters found in the field, the system doesn't throw an error; but on the contrary, if the validation expression evaluates to `false`, the system throws an error to the end user.

These steps complete the process of writing the field validation rules for any of the custom or standard fields. Writing advanced/complex field validation in CRM On Demand is a knack by itself and it can only be built with practice and experience over a period of time.

If the field is of type Picklist, save the field, go back to the page that list all the fields, and click the **Edit Picklist** link to add the new Picklist values. The pop-up window that appears on clicking the **Edit Picklist** link is shown in the following screenshot:

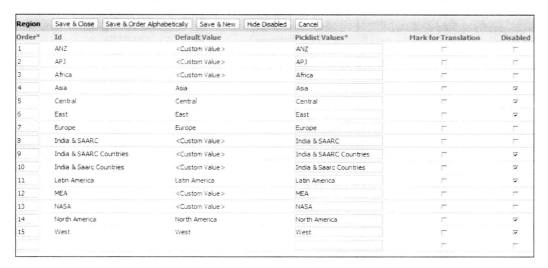

You can add new fields, order the sequence in which the fields in the drop-down should be listed, and mark the Picklist values for translation to overwrite the Picklist values for different languages. Although you cannot delete an existing Picklist value such as an existing field, you can disable them and suppress the disabled field using the **Hide Disabled** action.

The easiest way to manage translations is to use the **Rename Fields** action in the **Account Fields** page, where in a single window you can provide the translated label values for all the fields depending on the language that you have selected at the top. You still have to get to the **Edit Picklist** window to provide translated values for validation error messages and Picklist values; this is shown in the following screenshot:

Similar to the way you manage fields of account object, you can manage the fields specific to the relationship between two objects such as account and contact, account and account, account and team by going to **Admin | Application Customization | Account (Object) | Field Management**. Note that there are inconsistencies in the system in terms of the flexibilities to add custom fields in the relationship object. For example, you can add custom fields in **Account Contact** and **Account Relationship** whereas it doesn't provide an option to add a custom field in **Account Team** field setup. You can observe these inconsistencies across the objects. As an administrator, you have to be familiar with these limitations. Also, note that the custom fields that are added to the relationship objects doesn't appear in CRM On Demand reporting/analytics. Don't be surprised if it is made available in your current version of CRM On Demand as Oracle is making consistent progress in removing these limitations in every new release. If you are stuck with this limitation, you can consider building a custom relationship between these standard objects using one of the available custom objects.

Cascading fields

Cascading Picklists provide you with a facility to limit the related Picklist values on the basis of the selected parent Picklist value. For example, assume that depending on **Account Industry**, you want to limit the value of **Account Priority**, then you can define a cascading Picklist definition to enforce the same. The steps to implement cascading Picklist constraints are shown in the following screenshot and they can be accessed from **Admin | Application Customization | Account | Cascading Picklist**:

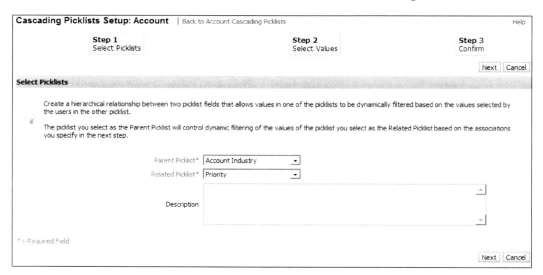

In **Step 1**, select **Parent Picklist** as **Account Industry** and **Related Picklist** as **Priority**. In **Step 2**, define the constraints. The constraints here are basically to set the applicable values for **Priority** depending on the selected industry. As you can see in the following screenshot, for the **Aerospace & Defence Industry**, we have constrained the applicable priorities as **Low** and **Medium**. You can do the same for each of the industry Picklist values in the same screen; these settings are shown in the following screenshot:

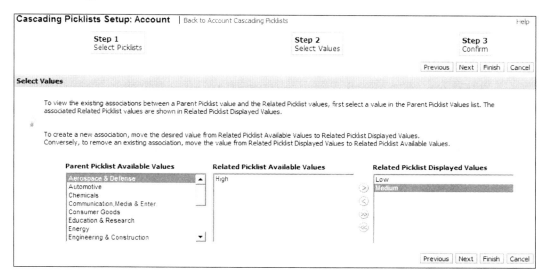

The last step is a confirmation page which lists the details of constraints that you have selected for your review and on hitting the **Finish** button, the definitions are saved in the system and the constraints are enforced to users in account's data entry forms; the final step is shown in the following screenshot:

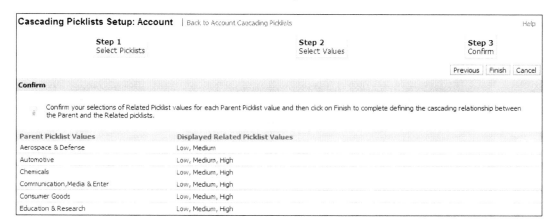

Note that for **Related Picklist Values**, you cannot have two **Parent Picklist Values**. Similar to the cascading Picklist definition for main objects, you can establish similar constraints between Picklists at related objects such as **Account Relationship**. Note that this cascading Picklist feature is not available for all related objects. For example, for account object, it is only available for **Account Relationship**. You are limited by what is exposed by CRM On Demand at this stage.

Layout management

Under layout management, we would cover customization of different types of layouts such as page layouts, search layouts, homepage layouts, lists layouts, and so on.

The standard CRM On Demand application comes with a set of layouts for each of the objects. You can create custom layouts by copying the available standard layout. Typically, additional layouts would be created for the following reasons:

- To expose your custom fields that is not present in standard layout.
- To create role-specific layouts. For example, the layout that you would like to present for a sales representative could be different from the layout for a sales manager. Sales manager may have visibility to additional fields, such as account level revenue figures, may have privileges to modify the account status field, and so on; whereas a sales representative should not be seeing the account level revenue information nor should they be able to modify the account status.

Page layout

Page layout determines the fields exposed in the **New/Edit** screen in standard/related/custom objects in CRM On Demand. As we discussed in the previous chapter, you have to be aware of the fact that page layouts are two-column layouts with a maximum six sections. You don't have the flexibility to add more columns or more sections but you can place your fields in the desired sections in the layout. Page layouts can be static or dynamic. Dynamic layouts are explained in detail in the next section.

Under **Admin | Application Customization | Account (Object) | Page Layout Management**, you can create/modify/delete the page layouts for the selected main object or any of the related information objects. The steps involved in creating/modifying the page layout for the main object are explored in the following sections.

In **Step 1**, give a brief name and a detailed description for the page layout. **Description** is used to capture the necessity of creating a custom layout instead of re-using the standard layouts or any of the already existing layouts. If you create layouts for different roles, then the recommended best practice is to prefix the layout name with the role name for easy manageability in the future; **Page Layout Wizard** is shown in the following screenshot:

In **Step 2**, determine whether you would like to make any of the fields in the object **Required** or **Read-Only** at the layout level. If the fields are made as **Required** or **Read-Only** at the field definition stage, you cannot modify those properties here. So unless you like to make the fields **Required** or **Read-Only** across all layouts, don't set these constraints at the object field while defining; **Step 2** is shown in the following screenshot:

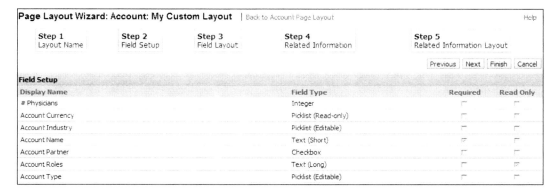

In **Step 3**, move the available fields to any of the available sections in the two-column layout. Note that you cannot increase or decrease the number of columns in the layout or use a custom style for page layouts. The mandatory fields defined in **Step 2** or in the Object field definition have to be added to one of the page layout sections. If not, then the system throws an error when you try to save the layout definition. Note that the **Description** field available in most of the objects to capture large text inputs from the user always appears at the bottom of the screen layout and its location is fixed. You don't have an option to customize it. **Step 3** is shown in the following screenshot:

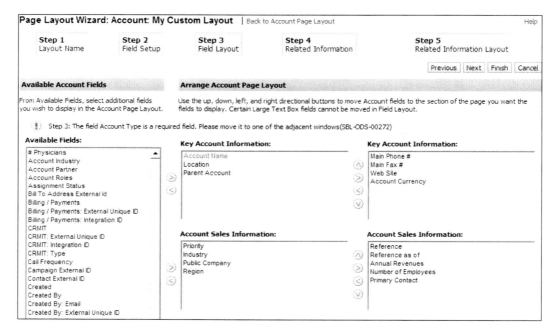

In **Step 4**, determine the list of related information sections that you like to display under the main object. All applicable and related objects are listed on the left-hand side and it is predetermined by the entity-relationship diagram that we had discussed in the beginning of the chapter. If you move them to the **Available Information** section, the section would be available for the user and users interested in the related information can add it to their screen using the **Edit Layout** button available in the record **Detail** page. If you move them to the **Displayed Information** section, the information is displayed by default to the users in the record **Detail** page and users can hide it using the **Edit Layout** button available in the record **Detail** page. **Step 4** is shown in the following screenshot:

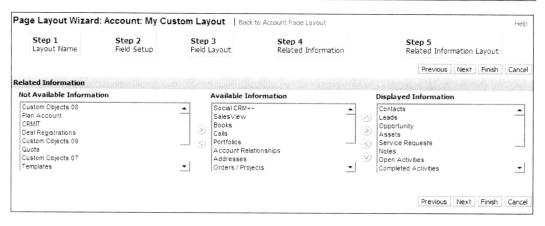

As you see in the following screenshot, the **Account Detail** section is the layout for the main object and the **Contacts** section is the layout for the related information section. When you drill down to one of the selected contacts, you would then be taken to the **Contact Detail** page where contact would be the main object and related accounts would be presented as child objects.

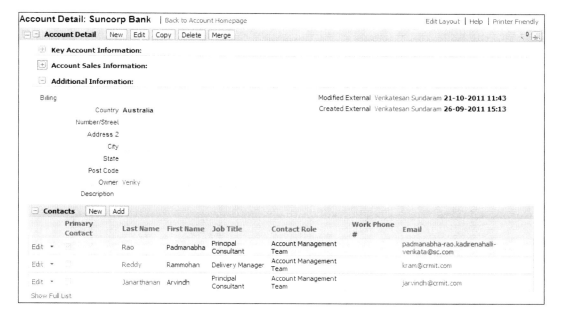

In **Step 5**, you can select the **Related Information Layout** option applicable for each of the selected **Related Information Section** names. This is to customize the fields that are listed in the related information section. The related information layout can be a standard one or any of the customized layouts that you have created. **Step 5** is shown in the following screenshot:

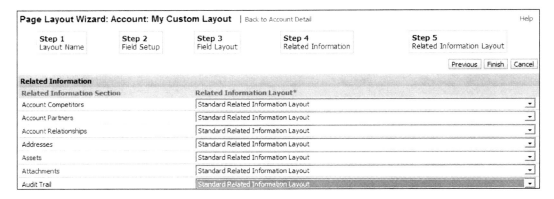

To create a customized related information layout, go to **Admin | Application Customization | Account | Page Layout Management**; you can find the list of related information sections available for customization under the **Account Related Information Layout** link. The next screenshot shows this link for an **Account** object. Note that not all the fields defined in the main object are available for display here. For example, under the **Contacts** section of the account object, you may not find all the contact fields available for display. Also, note that the number of fields that can be displayed in **Related Information Section** is limited to 9. Unlike the five-step process used to define the page layouts for the main object, defining the **Related Information Layout** page is a simple, two-step process where in **Step 1**, you provide a name for the customized layout and in **Step 2**, you select a list of relationship-specific fields that you would like to display under **Related Information Section**.

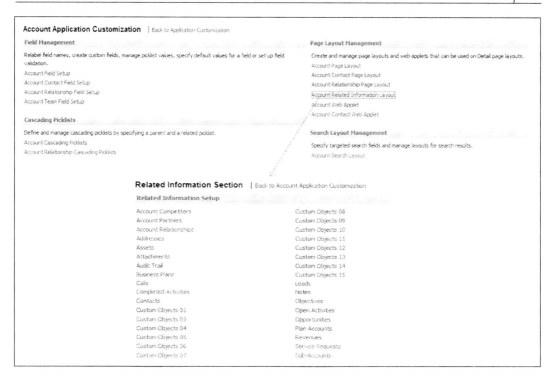

If the data displayed in **Related Information Section** stores any relation-specific information, you can define a detailed page layout for the same by going to **Admin | Application Customization | Account | Page Layout Management**. As you can see in the following screenshot, on clicking the **Edit** link, the application opens the related information page details, whereas if you click on the **Last Name** link, you would then be taken to **Contact Detail** page:

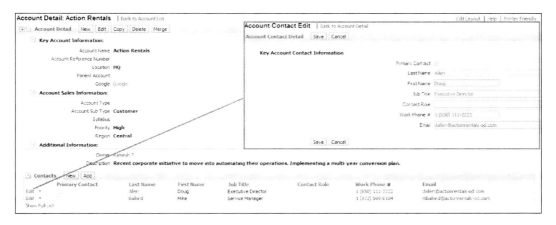

We will discuss a special type of applet called web applets in *Chapter 8, Web Services Integration*. Note that until you link these layouts to a use role, the user will not be able to see these layouts. The steps involved in linking the layout to the user role will be discussed extensively in *Chapter 5, Business Process Management*.

Dynamic layouts

Dynamic layouts are a special type of layout that change the layout of the screen on the fly depending on the selected Picklist value by the user. For example, the kind of information that you capture for a service request of a specific type of product, say credit cards, could be different from say mortgage. Presenting all the fields of a credit card and mortgage in the same form would make it cumbersome for the end users to fill in the relevant fields depending on the product selected.

Dynamic layouts addresses this problem by providing a facility to dynamically change the layouts depending on the value of the driving Picklist field the user selects. The driving Picklist values are predetermined by CRM On Demand for every object and cannot be changed. You can create dynamic layouts by going to **Admin | Application Customization | Account | Dynamic Layout Management**. Creating dynamic layout is a two-step process where in **Step 1**, you assign a name for the dynamic layout and in **Step 2**, you select the applicable page layout for each of the driving Picklist values. These steps are shown in the following screenshot:

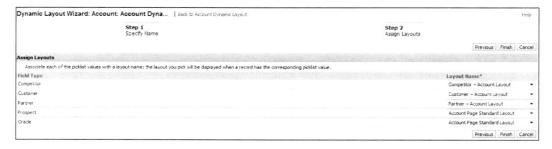

The predefined driving Picklists for the standard objects, industry-specific objects, and custom objects are available in the CRM On Demand help-text reference at `http://docs.oracle.com/cd/E27437_01/books/OnDemOLH/ dynamicpagelayoutshelp.html`.

Note that the combination of dynamic layouts along with the role-based layouts is very powerful and is useful to meet many of your data visibility needs. There is a wide spectrum of options available to you, such as the following:

- A single standard layout for all users
- Different layouts for people falling under different roles
- Different layouts for different type of records classified by the **Record Type** field
- Different layouts for every combination of role and records classified by the **Record Type** field

Depending on your needs, you should be able to choose the right option for your deployment.

Search layouts

The information stored in CRM On Demand should be easily accessible to the end users for their day-to-day needs. You can locate records in the CRM database by using the **Search** option in the left-hand side, navigation bar. Also, we can locate records by using the **Advanced** option that is available in the **Search** section, by creating predefined lists, or by using the lookup icon when you intend to search and associate records with other records.

The **Search** field layout management provides the facility to customize these aspects. The **Search** layout for every object can be configured by going to **Admin | Application Customization | Account | Account Search Layout**.

It is a three-step process, where you define the name and description of the
Search layout in **Step 1**, and the list of fields by which you would like to search
in the left-hand side navigation bar on the click of the **Search** lookup window
in **Step 2**. These steps are shown in the following screenshot:

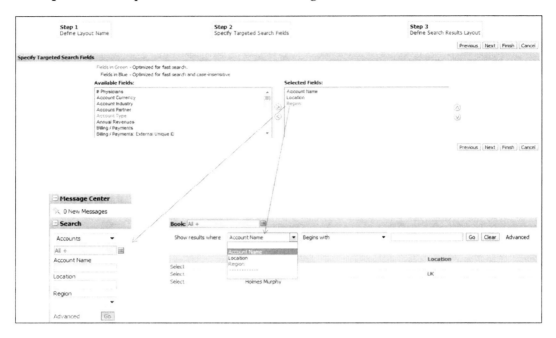

In **Step 3**, you can define the list of fields that you would like displayed when search
results are presented to the users. Note that in **Lookup Window**, the maximum
number of fields that can be displayed is restricted nine and in the **Search Results**
page, in addition to those nine fields, you can add 11 more fields limiting the total
number of fields to 20.

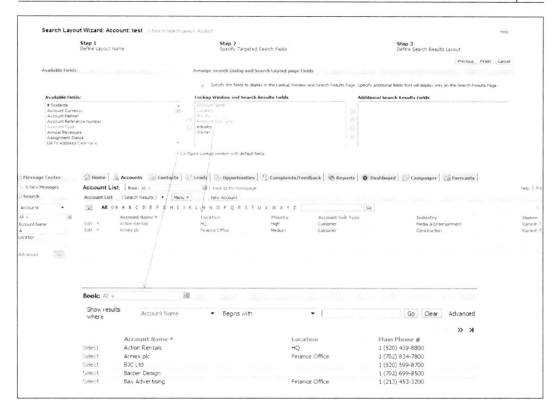

As you can see in the previous screenshot, in a standard **Search Results** page, the fields that you selected in the search layout, such as **Account Name**, **Location**, **Priority**, **Account Sub Type**, **Industry**, and **Owner** are displayed. But in the account lookup window, the standard fields **Account Name**, **Location**, and **Main Phone #** are displayed even though we have selected the same set of fields for **Lookup Window and Search Results Fields**. The difference is due to the fact that you have checked the **Configure Lookup window with default fields** checkbox. If you do not check this checkbox, the fields that are configured in the standard **Search Results** page would be displayed in the lookup window too.

Note that for optimal performance, use indexed fields when defining your targeted search fields. Indexed fields are displayed in green text. Indexed fields that are also case insensitive are displayed in blue text. It is important to use indexed fields for fields that are expected to be queried often. In implementations where the number of records runs in the thousands, you may end up with performance issues if you use default text fields for **Search** instead of indexed fields.

Homepage and Action Bar layout

When you click any of the object's tabs that is displayed in CRM On Demand, you will be taken to the homepage of the object. Similar to the **Record Detail** page layout, the homepage layout is again a two-column layout and the applets that you can surface in these columns are limited by a set of applets provided by CRM On Demand. The set of applets can vary depending on the object. Creation of a custom homepage is fairly straightforward; here, you would arrange the list of applets in either of the two columns available. These steps are shown in the following screenshot:

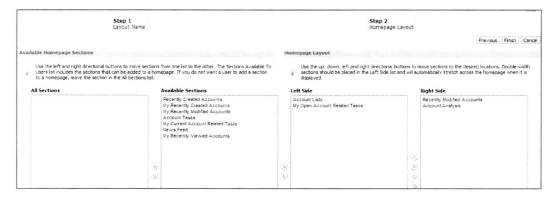

All Sections contains the list of all the available applets provisioned by CRM On Demand along with any other custom applet that you have created. We will discuss extensively about custom applets in *Chapter 8, Web Services Integration*. When you move these applets to **Available Sections**, these applets would be made available for the user and they can surface the desired applets by arranging them in their homepage using the **Edit Layout** button, provided the user has **Personalize Homepages** privilege to modify the homepage layouts in their role definition. In line with the previous customization settings, you can find **Account Homepage** displayed accordingly. Homepage layouts can be customized by going to **Admin | Application Customization | Account | Homepage Layout Management**. **Account Homepage** is displayed in the following screenshot:

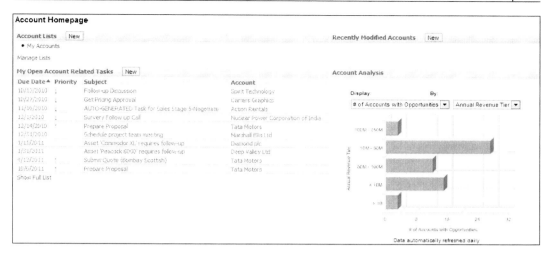

Similar to object homepage layout customization, the homepage that is displayed when logging into CRM On Demand under the **Home** tab can also be customized by going to **Admin | Application Customization | Application Setup | My Homepage Layout**. The steps involved in displaying it are exactly same as the object layout customization.

The list of applets displayed in the left-hand side navigation bar can also be customized by going to **Application Customization | Action Bar Layout**. The standard applets that you can pick and chose to display in the left-hand side navigation bar are limited to the predefined set of applets provisioned by CRM On Demand but you create custom applets wherever there is a need.

List management

Lists provide a simple way for the users to get a set of frequently accessed records on the basis of a predefined query criteria. You can create a list by clicking on **New** under the **Object Home Page | <Object> List** applet. The list that you create as an administrator can be made available for all users, for users belonging to a specific role, or only to yourself.

Under **Admin | Application Customization | Account | List Access & Order**, you can customize the availability of these lists in the **List** applet displayed in the object homepage. The list management is role-specific, where on selection of the role, all lists that are created for this role are listed under the **All Lists** section. You can make the desired lists available for the role. When you move them to the **Show in Short List** section, these lists would be available in the **List** applet in the object homepage.

As you see in the following example, all the available lists excluding one are made available to this role and a small subset is made available under **Show in Short List**, which is displayed under the homepage applet. You can access the rest of the defined lists using the **Manage Lists** link:

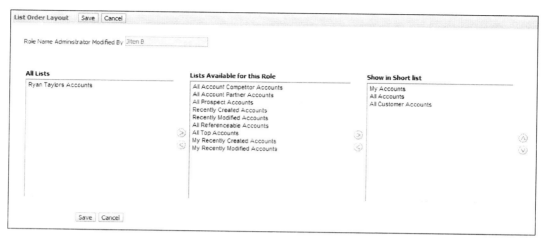

Miscellaneous application customization

There are a few other miscellaneous customizations that you can perform by going to **Admin | Application Customization**. The object names can be changed under **Admin | Application Customization | Application Setup | Customize Record Types**.

As you can see in the following screenshot, apart from specifying the **Singular**, **Plural**, and **Short** names (used in the tabs), you can also chose a custom icon for each of the objects. A list of the available icons are displayed on clicking magnifying glass:

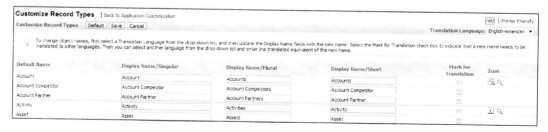

Similarly, translated values for the object can be provided by selecting the appropriate language in the translation drop-down box.

CRM On Demand provides a facility to audit changes in the field value of the records. You can customize the fields that you like to audit by going to **Admin | Application Customization | Account | Field Audit Setup**. Auditing is available only for certain record types. For some of the record types, by default, the system turns on auditing and for others you may have to explicitly turn on auditing. Maximum number of fields that can be audited is limited to 35, but you can request customer care to add more fields but note that it dampens the application performance. A list of objects and fields audited by default for each of the objects is available in the CRM On Demand help-text reference at `http://docs.oracle.com/cd/E27437_01/books/OnDemOLH/customizingaudittrailhelp.html`.

Summary

In this chapter, we learned the scope of application customization that is available across the CRM On Demand application. We began with the object-relationship customization, followed by customization of various types of layouts such as page layouts, search layouts, homepage layouts, and also touched upon how to customize miscellaneous user interfaces.

Understanding the scope of customization is essential to effectively customize the application and meet your business needs. We haven't touched some of the elements of application customization such as web applets, homepage custom reports, as it is more apt to go over them in the relevant chapters that follow.

5
User Access Controls

An organization is essentially a structure of people, each of whom has designated responsibilities and the requisite authority to maintain those responsibilities. The CRM organization in your business includes the swathe of people from the chief executive to the billing executive, with service technicians, marketing directors, sales managers, campaign executives, call centre agents, salespersons, external consultants, and many other line and staff people in between, each of whom expects to have access to the CRM information system in order to perform their work. The CRM organization might include people such as system auditors, report writers, and trainers. Automated integration between the CRM system and other information systems (be that such systems are internal to your business or external publicly available services) would introduce machines as users of the CRM system. The objective of this chapter is to learn to customize the CRM On Demand application to fit the structure of your CRM organization. The collection of users is the CRM organization entity, a.k.a. **organizational chart**. Among other things you would want to differentiate between what the various staff do and functions they need to perform, and therefore what their role is in the organization, what the staff need to see (or not see) and therefore their access to view the data within the CRM system. In *Chapter 3*, *CRM On Demand Customization*, we looked at the concept of CRM staff. This chapter will go into detail about how to build the system for the staff in terms of their business functions, data visibilities, and access rights.

The users of the system may include machines as well as humans. Some organizational charts may admit to having no machines in their CRM business process, stipulating that every conduct of the process be the responsibility and authority of a specific human. With the advent of industry and business-specific mark-up languages, and increased computing power leading to better quality of data, a host of web services and computing capabilities allow for reliable machines in the business processing. Some organizations may thus define a great number of machines in the CRM processes in conjunction with humans. The definition therefore is of user identities (**user ID**), and the CRM system/organization is simply the collection of user IDs.

In a large organization where a particular job may be divided among multiple user IDs for reasons of efficiency and scale, we see the need for a common Job Title to identify the different user IDs with the same quantum and quality of work. When the work is organized at a larger scale, the Job Titles and other demarcations such as Divisions and Regions of the many user IDs would coalesce into business **user roles**. For example, the CRM organization of a large multinational company may define a business role of the Regional Field Salesperson, which is applied commonly to its 300 salespersons that are each assigned separate regions of their own and who are field based (in contrast to being based at a telecom centre). In this case, the 300 user IDs would all have the same business user role, however their individual access to the data in the system would be mediated by other controls that represent the region, the field type, and the sales work. The controls become extensive if the regions overlap or if the field type responsibility overlaps with that of the telesales type of responsibility, or if the selling work overlaps with other responsibilities, and so on.

In this chapter we will learn about the following:

- The definition of the user ID
- The accesses to data for a user ID
- The definition of the user role

By the end of this chapter you will be able to define and build user IDs, user roles, **groups**, **books of business**, and **access profiles** to operate on individual or hierarchies of books of business, **teams**, and user IDs.

The user ID

In an ideal case the CRM organization is composed of user IDs each with a unique non-overlapping set of business responsibilities and authorities. At the other extreme of the organizational ideal is the communal one where all users have access to all data, with no distinct responsibilities and authorities amongst them. These two theoretical extremities illustrate the concept of the user ID. A user ID is either an **owner** or a non-owner of data. The non-owner is labeled as "default user" or "unrelated user". Thus a user ID has either owner access or the default access to any given data. A user ID does not have both owner access and default access to any given data. Where the user ID is the owner of the data, the owner access is applied, and where the user ID is not the owner of the data the default access is applied. The owner access and default access being two separate definitions for a user ID, it is conceivable to have the same access for both ownership and non-ownership, or for the owner access to be "less" than the default access. The user ID merely establishes the ownership on the data, while the access establishes what operations can be done in either case (of ownership and non-ownership).

A user ID is sustainable in the system only if it has its owner/default access definitions for the entire data set in the system. The collection of owner access definitions across all the objects is called an **owner access profile**. The collection of default access definitions across all the objects is called a **default access profile**.

 In the CRM On Demand object model, the Service Request does not mandate an owner. However, you can customize to make ownership mandatory for SR records.

The **Access Profile Management** section of the **User Management and Access Controls** section of the **Administration** page is shown in the following screenshot:

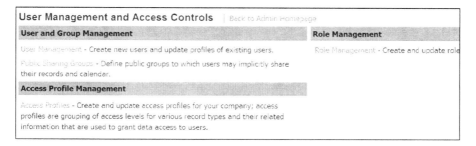

An example access profile creation, through the Access Profile Wizard, is shown in the following series of screenshots.

The Access Profile Wizard provides two main steps. Step 1 sets the basic properties of the access profile in terms of its name, whether the profile is to be active/available or disabled, whether it is to be available in the lists of access profiles for team access and for book access (see the *Team access* and *Book access* sections for more details).

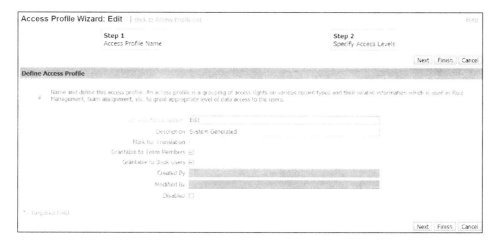

Step 2 of the Access Profile Wizard lists all the objects available in your CRM On Demand application:

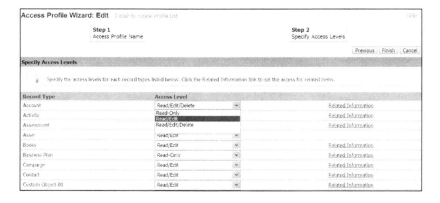

For each of the objects in step 2, you would also set the access levels for their child/related objects. Clicking on the **Related Information** link in each line item, will show you the page that lists the child objects for that parent object. Here you can set the accesses for the child objects.

 This is a critical piece that should be systematically documented in the design. Among the configuration templates that are available in the CRMOD Support portal, the template for the User Access Controls is comprehensive. It has the work sheets to capture all the details of an access profile.

The following screenshot shows the **Related Information** section for the Account parent object:

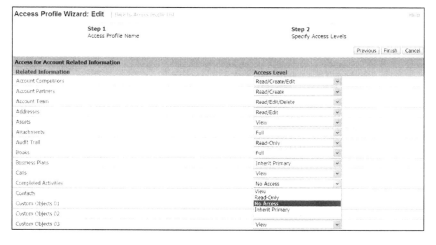

Manager hierarchy

A hierarchy of user IDs is a common form of organization. If you have enabled the **manager hierarchy** in your company profile then the manager access will apply to the data accesses of every user ID in your organization. The manager access operates on the basis of the **Reports-To** field in the profiles of all the user IDs of the organization. The manager access operates independently of whether a given manager user ID is active or inactive in the system. A manager gets access to all the data that is accessible to his/her subordinates. The manager's owner access profile will apply on all data that becomes accessible to the manager by virtue of the hierarchy.

 A manager user has the facility to filter the data by individual subordinate, in the targeted search, advanced search, and lists.

User group

A group of some user IDs sharing all their data may be found in some small organizations. If you have enabled the **group assignment** in your company profile then the group access will apply to the data accesses of the user IDs that are included in the user groups. A user ID can be a member of only one user group. There can be any number of user groups in the organization.

All member user IDs of a user group gain owner access to the records that are owned by any one of the member user ID. Each member user ID of a user group exercises their personal default access profile over the records that are not owned by the user group (not owned by any of the member's user IDs).

The group assignment access operates prospectively. When a user ID gets added to a user group the user ID does not gain owner access to the group's prior records but only gains owner access to the records that are produced from the time of joining the group.

The accesses to data

A user ID has the following accesses to any given record:

- Create/add association to another record
- Read/view/inherit primary
- Edit (or update)
- Delete/remove association with another record
- Add/remove association to other user IDs (team)
- Add/remove association to other data access controllers (books of business)

The create access is notionally part of the owner access as the user ID that creates a record becomes its first owner. For business and commerce, authoring new data (record) automatically implies additional responsibility and downstream authority for the owner, for a duration that is determined by the lifespan of that record. Therefore it is common to rationalize the authority to create such primary data as accounts, partners, plans and the like, in order to ensure a high quality of "master" data.

An organization may need to restrict reading access to data to the owner of that data, and/or leave the decision on publication of that data in the hands of the owner of that data. The trivial case is of the user ID having access to read all the records. Some organizations might restrict reading access to specific fields of the record. Such restrictions are normally designed over specific types of data and to specific types of staff. Such normalization of data accesses and users leads to the concept of user roles. In CRM On Demand, while the read access for any given record is captured in the owner and default access profile definitions, the extent of reading access, that is whether the user can read all the records and/or whether all the fields of a record (also known as **visibility**) are captured in the user role definition.

The View/Inherit Primary accesses are defined for the records that are related/ child to the reference parent record. Both "View" and "Inherit Primary" imply that on the record Detail page where the related/child records are listed, the user ID will have edit and/or read-only and/or delete access to those child records based on the access given for that particular object in its parent-level definition. For example, for the Opportunity records that are child/related to an account record, a "View/Inherit Primary" access to Opportunity child records under the account access definition implies that the user ID will be able to edit and/or read-only and/or delete those child Opportunity records based on the setting at the parent Opportunity Access definition.

View and Inherit Primary

The View and Inherit Primary accesses are different when the user role does not have access to read all the records of the object. Inherit Primary provides access to merely owned/related user records, in the form of child lists, if the user role does not have access to read all the records of the object, whereas the view provides access to all the records, in the form of child lists, even if the user role does not have access to Read All the records of the object. The view here is that the user ID can get a "glimpse", a view of the child records. However, a detailed reading of those child records would be available only if the user ID is an owner/related user of that child record. Thus the View is a lenient version of the Inherit Primary.

An authority to create data need not necessarily imply an authority to edit the data after it has been created. Some organizations may find it feasible to separate the authorities to create and to edit data, some others may need to restrict edit rights to the parent record while not restricting it to the related/child records, and some may need to restrict edit rights to the related/child record while allowing only reading of the parent records. These constitute the access profile definitions. Organizational needs such as to restrict editing to certain fields of a record while allowing reading of the rest of the fields, different sets of fields to be available for editing for different types of users and the like, lead to the composition of the user role, and appropriately in CRM On Demand these latter accesses are captured in the user role definitions while the record-level accesses are captured in the access profiles.

Data once created is not merely the property of its owner/related users but also the property of the legal organizational entity. It is normal therefore that the access to delete single records or relationships between the parent and associated child records is restricted to specific types of users (be they owner/related or unrelated), leading to the concept of the user role. Further, the authority to delete records may be organized in terms of whether it will be available at the level of individual records and/or for bulk operations as well. Expectedly, the authority to delete is captured in the access profile while the privilege of bulk deletion is maintained in the user role definition.

The access profiles definition captures the "when and what access" while the "where, which, and how access" is captured in the user role definition. A user ID is meaningless if it is lacking in either its set of owner and default access profiles or its user role definition. The organizational and business considerations that we have discussed above are underlined in the design of the CRM On Demand's **User Access Management** administration section. The relationship between access profiles and the user role is provided for by including the access profiles as one of the components of the user role definition, and keeping the user role as the lone access-related mandatory association for a user ID. The other mandatory fields of the user ID, namely the first name, last name, work phone, e-mail address, and the login ID serve for the unique identification of humans/machines that are members of the organization.

Team access

By adding or removing other user IDs to the record, the current owner of a record can potentially share and/or relinquish its ownership of that record with another user ID. Two or more user IDs that are associated to a record constitute the **team** for that record.

The team is a separate object and therefore super to the related record. The team could also be super to the user ID that has owner access on that record. Therefore the addition of another user ID to a record, that is, creating a team, requires defining the data accesses for the incoming user ID over that record and all its related/child records as well. This leads to definitions of the **team access profile**. The team access profile of a user ID defines the data accesses for that user ID on that specific record.

The user ID, the individual member of the organization, brings to the organizational table platform capabilities, or skills, to be exploited by and in the organization. Some examples of skills are contract writing, trading, product designing, administering, selling, buying, legal counseling, managing, researching, mass communication or marketing, and servicing. An efficient organization captures the skills in the user role definition, allowing for the user ID to play various operational roles on different teams. This is the concept of a team role. Thus, a user ID who is skilled at "selling" might play the role of a consultant in one team, the main seller in another team, a partner seller in yet another, an observer in another, and any other form of **collaboration** that is feasible in the organization.

Thus in the presence of a team the access control necessarily moves away from being based on individual user IDs to more normalized structures such as user roles and team roles.

The team access operates over the record in entirety. A corollary of defining teams in the organization is that you should not need to control a user ID's access at the level of the fields of a record, based on that user ID's team role. Any such organization would require increasingly complicated definitions of the user role and team role matrix, making the matrix eventually unsustainable. While user ID based accesses at the field level can still be applied in the presence of teams it becomes practically limited when the size of the organization is 5 or more, as the access validations become too complex to maintain reliably. The CRM On Demand application maintains a restriction on the length of validations precisely to prevent such constructions.

An organization is a discipline of competent, self-aware parallel-computing user IDs, an automaton as it were; therefore any organization that requires intensive computation and control of accesses at every operation by a user ID would ordinarily not have teams within it. The team is a super entity that subordinates the user ID in relation to the given record. The team is a record level access control and therefore requires eschewing large scale requirements of team role specific field level access controls in the organization. In most, if not all, cases if you find yourself trying to draw complex matrices of user roles and team roles to meet the business requirements, it is safe to assume that either the requirements have not been refined or the organization does not presently need a Customer Relationship Management system to operate its business.

Book access

The book of business (or book) is a tag that can be associated to a user ID and to a record. A user ID and a record become related by virtue of having the same tag. Thus books can bring a group of user IDs and a group of data together, by associating those given user IDs and those given data to the same tag, the book. The books provide a matrix on the physical organization. It provides for user IDs to participate, and be available across the entire business organization, overcoming divisional and departmental silos of data. The same book can be associated to different types of records, such as an account, opportunity, and service request.

The book is a type of record, and can be created by user IDs. Similar to other records, the access to books is defined in the access profiles and the user role.

By adding or removing books to the record the current owner of a record can potentially share and/or relinquish its ownership of that record with a group of user IDs each of whom may have differential accesses on the record. By adding new books to the system, a user ID can potentially share and/or gain ownership over records that get associated to those books.

The book is a separate object and therefore super to both the records in it and the user IDs in it. The book could also be super to user IDs that have owner accesses on the records in that book. The book is also super to the records in it, in that a book cannot be deleted until all the records are removed from it. Therefore the addition of a book to a user ID i.e. creating a book user, requires defining the data accesses for the incoming user ID over all the records that might ever get associated to that book. This leads to definitions of **book access profile**. The book access profile of a user ID defines the data accesses for that user ID on all the records in that book.

In comparing the book to the team, we can summarize as follows. A team associates multiple user IDs to a single record. A book associates multiple user IDs to multiple records. The team constitution is controlled by the first owner of the specific record. The book constitution is controlled by the management access that user IDs have to books plus the distributed usage of the book.

An efficient organization might capture the skills of its user IDs at a very high level in the form of user roles, and allow for the user ID to play various operational roles at different "spaces" and "times" in the organization through association with relevant books. This is the concept of a book role. Thus, a user ID who is competent about "Nordic culture" might play the role of a consultant in the Nordic Opportunities Book, Nordic Service Requests Book, Nordic Accounts Book or simply in the Nordic Book of the organization, and any other kinds of **isolation** that are feasible in the organization. As another example, if you are a Health Insurance business in the USA the governmental mandate on restricted data access would require you to create books to isolate user IDs who have not signed the HIPAA agreements from those who have signed them, to ensure your business is compliant with the HIPAA regulations.

Thus in the presence of a book the access control necessarily moves away from being based on individual user IDs to more normalized structures such as user roles and book roles.

The book access operates over the entire record and all the records in it. A corollary of defining books in the organization is that you should not need to control a user ID's access at the level of the fields of a record, or over specific records in the book, based on that user ID's book role. Any such organization would require increasingly complicated definitions of the user role and book role matrix, making the matrix eventually unsustainable. While user ID based accesses at the field level can still be applied in the presence of books it becomes practically limited when the size of the organization is 5 or more, as the access validations become too complex to maintain reliably. The CRM On Demand application maintains a restriction on the length of validations precisely to prevent such constructions.

An ideal organization is a discipline of competent self-aware parallel-computing user IDs. An organization that requires intensive computation and control of accesses at every operation by a user ID would ordinarily not have books within it. The book is a super entity that subordinates simultaneously both the individual user ID and individual record in relation to other records and user IDs in it. The book is a data access controller by itself. It requires the organization to eschew requirements of book role based field level access controls and/or book role based record level access controls. In most, if not all, cases if you find yourself trying to draw complex matrices of user roles and book roles to meet the business requirements, you should look to refine the requirements.

Books are an ideal, flexible mechanism for additional data visibility settings. A record can be added to a book manually or automated by workflows. A large number of books usually entail a large number of workflows to be added. When there are too many workflows and especially with frequent maintenance a web services program may be more efficient at the job of moving records amongst the books.

The user role

As you have probably realized by now, the variety of data and accesses, when operative in any organization made of more than 5-10 users, leads you to rationalize the data accesses in terms of business user roles. You begin to move away from the following equation:

user ID = user role

Instead you compose it as the following:

user role = {user IDs}

Or perhaps the following:

user ID = f (user Role)

It is important to bear in mind though that at its simplest the user role is the data access definitions for the user ID. In the CRM On Demand application all the transactions on the system are mediated by the user ID and the number of access definitions that are packed together in creating a user role definition is tagged to the user ID; it is not that the user ID is tagged to the user role definition. This is manifest in that the user role field is a mandatory field when you create a user ID.

The items in the user role definition are as follows. They are listed here in a particular order for conceptual clarity:

- Role name
- The accesses to objects (record types)
- The owner access profile and default access profile
- The accesses to objects' Homepages (tabs)
- The Homepage layouts for the accessible objects
- The Search page layouts for the accessible objects
- The Detail page layouts for the accessible objects
- The default sales process for opportunities
- The Lead Conversion page layout
- The Action Bar page layout
- The default Theme for the UI
- The accesses to customize the UI
- The accesses to data channels
- The accesses to user channels

In the Administration page of CRM On Demand, the role definition is done with the Role Management Wizard, which provides eight steps for completing the role definition, as shown in the following screenshot. The sequencing and organization of these eight steps are meant to help you rapidly set up a user role; hence it has the label "wizard".

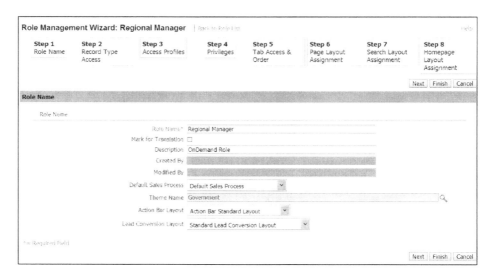

The Role Management Wizard is a configurator and therefore it begins at the Data layer followed by the Business layer and finally the UI layer. The wizard builds the internal code in real time as you progress from start to finish. Therefore, it expects information from the ground upwards. For instance, the user role will require a Search layout for leads (step 6) only if that role has access to the Lead record type (step 2). In contrast to the configurator as a system builder you would, of course, follow the top-down approach, starting with building the Homepage layouts, Search layouts, and Detail page layouts. The user role definition would logically be your final task in building the system, where you bring together the built custom layouts to combine with the relevant set of system privileges and the foundational data accesses.

In the conceptual descriptions of the following 14 items we give the mapping to the specific step in the eight-step wizard.

Role name

The role name (and its translations in the selected languages) is the first and mandatory value for the user role definition. The role name can be 50 alphanumeric characters in length, in each of the selected languages. This appears in step 1 of the wizard.

> The Action Bar layout, Lead Conversion layout, and the default sales process are multiobject and multisystems constructions. If your customization of CRMOD involves those multiple elements it is essential that they have been analyzed and designed as necessary for each user role, which is why they appear in step 1 of the Role Management Wizard.

Accesses to objects (record types)

This appears in step 2 of the Role Management Wizard. The access to each of the objects (objects that are enabled in your CRM On Demand application) is defined in three inter-independent controls, with Boolean values (yes or no). The three controls are as follows:

- Can (this role) access (this object)?
- Can (this role) create (new records of this object)?
- Can (this role) read all (the records of this object present in the system)?

The "can access" control determines the application of the other two controls. If the "can access" is set to "no", its values of "can create" and "can read all" are immaterial and irrelevant. When "can access" is "yes" and "can read all" is "no", the visibility of the records will be entirely controlled by the owner access profile, including the child records accesses therein. See the tip on "View and Inherit Primary" in the *The accesses to data* section earlier in this chapter.

The owner access profile and the default access profile

As described earlier in this chapter, you would have previously created the access profiles, and in the step 3 of the Role Management Wizard, you have associated the relevant owner access profile and the default access profile.

Accesses to objects' Homepages or tabs

Accesses to objects' Homepages is step 5 of the wizard. Every main object in the CRM On Demand object model has for the UI a **tab** (short for "table") for the visual representation of the object. The tab contains the space to display a Homepage of the object. A tab has a name and a pictorial icon to represent it. You can customize the name, and its translations in all the selected languages. You can change the pictorial icon to any one of the 50 icons that are available in the icon collection. The tab is also the space to display the Detail page of a record of that object, however it is not necessary for the object tab to be present on the UI to display the object record.

For the given user role you would select the tabs and their horizontal ordering based on the UI that suits the requirements of the user role. This is known as the **Tab layout** for that user role. It is worth noting that the tab is derived from the record type access; if the role is not given access to a record type, the tab related to that record type would not manifest on the UI even if you select it for the Tab layout. The Homepage layout that is assigned to the record type in step 8 of the wizard displays on the tab of that record type. That is, when a tab is absent from the Tab layout the object Homepage layout becomes unavailable to the user ID. A tab cannot exist without a Homepage layout and therefore CRMOD defaults to the seed Homepage layout of the record type. See the next section for descriptions of the Homepage layouts.

The CRM On Demand application automatically adjusts the number of tabs on the screen based on the user's display device. The wider the screen, the more all the assigned tabs are displayed horizontally, and where the screen is not as wide the tabs that are down the line are automatically put into the drop-down menu that appears after the last tab.

Custom Web Tabs are tabs that you create, to operate any interactive content be it a CRM On Demand page or an external page. We will study the utility of Custom Web Tabs later in *Chapter 8*, *Web Services Integration*.

The Homepage layouts

The Homepage layouts for each of the tabs are created priorly. The Homepage of an object can have **lists** and **applets**. Applets are used to operate interactive content from within the CRM On Demand application or external systems.

In step 8 of the wizard we tag the Homepage layouts created for each tab that will be displayed for the user role. Assigning a Homepage layout to an unselected tab does not have any impact as the tab access in step 5 is the container, and in its absence the Homepage has no container in which it is to be displayed. A user role can be assigned only one Homepage layout for an object/tab, and an object/tab can support any number of Homepage layouts each of which are destined for assignment to different user roles. In a small- to medium-size organization it would be effective to design a global Homepage layout that contains all the various lists and applets, and can train users to customize their Homepage layout. We learnt about building custom Homepage layouts in *Chapter 4*, *Application Customization*.

The Search page layouts

The Search page layouts for each of the accessible objects are created priorly. The Search page layouts for objects is relevant where the **default search method** of the company is the **targeted search**. If you select the keyword search as the search method for your company, the Search page layouts are irrelevant and have no impact. The Search page layout has the search input fields and the search output fields. In addition, it defines the output fields separately for searching from the panel on the Action Bar and for searching via the lookup on a record.

In step 7 of the wizard, we tag the Search page layouts created for each object that is accessible to the user role. Assigning a Search page layout to an inaccessible object does not have any impact as the object access in step 2 determines whether the object page constructors are enabled for the user ID. A user role can be assigned only one Search page layout for an object, and an object can support any number of Search page layouts, each of which are destined for assignment to different user roles. It is usually effective to design common Search page layouts for all or sets of user roles, utilizing fields optimized for fast search and output, and subsequently train users to run custom searches using the Advanced Search feature on a needs basis.

The Detail page layouts

The Detail page layouts for each of the accessible objects, for the user role, are created previously. The Detail page layout has the parent record fields and the related information applets sequenced below the parent record. The Detail page layout also sets each field as editable, mandatory, or read-only (for that layout). The Detail page layout can be static or dynamic for the user role.

In step 6 of the wizard we tag the Detail page layouts created for each object that is accessible to the user role. Assigning a Detail page layout to an inaccessible object does not have any impact as the object access in step 2 determines whether the object page constructors are enabled for the user ID. A user role can be assigned only one Detail page layout (whether static or dynamic) for an object, and an object can support any number of Detail page layouts (both static and dynamic), each of which is destined for assignment to a different user role. We learnt about building custom Detail page layouts in *Chapter 4, Application Customization*.

The default sales process for opportunity records

This appears in step 1 of the Role Management Wizard. Sales processes are created previously. *Chapter 6, Business Process Automation and Management*, provides the details on setting up custom sales processes. If your company has defined multiple sales processes (with or without normalized categorization of sales stages) there are various ways in which your company may have designed to employ those processes.

One approach would be to associate every process to every opportunity type that is handled by the organization. A second approach would be to associate processes to user roles, without regard to the opportunity types. A third approach would be a mix of the two approaches but where some opportunity types are left free of a process. In the latter case, the default sales process of the user role would become available on such undefined opportunity types as there may be. The default sales process is also used by the Revenue Forecast engine for such unlinked opportunity types, where the user role is a forecast participant.

As a sales process can define mandatory fields by sales stages for the Opportunity page, it is important to synchronize the Opportunity Detail page layouts assigned to the user role with the default sales process of that user role (if the default sales process is actually of relevance in your organization). Any gaps in the process validations and layout would cause errors during run time, preventing the user from editing/saving those opportunity records.

Assigning a default sales process to a user role which has no access to the opportunity object is still relevant, if the user role is a participant in the Revenue Forecast and submits forecasts.

The Lead Conversion layout

This appears in step 1 of the Role Management Wizard. Lead Conversion layouts are created previously. *Chapter 6, Business Process Automation and Management*, provides the details on setting up custom Lead Conversion layouts. Your company may have defined multiple Lead Conversion layouts to be used across various user roles.

As a Lead Conversion process defines field mapping across objects and involves creation of new records of multiple objects, it is important to synchronize the Lead Conversion layout that is assigned to the user role with the object accesses and access profiles assigned to that user role. Any gaps between the conversion process and object access profiles would cause errors during run time, preventing the user from completing the conversion.

Assigning a Lead Conversion layout to a user role which has no access to any of the related objects and/or to the Lead Qualification/Conversion process, does not impact the system.

The Action Bar layout

The Action Bar is available as a standard page for all users of the CRM On Demand application. The custom Action Bar layouts for user roles are created priorly before they can be assigned to user roles. *Chapter 4, Application Customization*, provides the details on setting up custom Action Bar layouts. The custom Action Bar layout can have the full or subset of the pre-built applets of CRM On Demand in addition to custom global applets that operate interactive content from within the CRM On Demand application or external systems.

In step 1 of the wizard we tag the custom Action Bar layout created for the user role. A user role can be assigned only one Action Bar layout, and the CRM On Demand application can support any number of Action Bar layouts. In a small- to medium-size organization it would be effective to design a common custom Action Bar layout containing all the various custom applets and train users to customize their Action Bar layout to surface the applets that are relevant to their needs.

The default Theme for UI

Custom Themes are created previously. Themes can contain corporate imagery, branding, and links to hosted corporate content. From the collection of Themes available in the system, in step 1 of the wizard we can tag the default Theme for the user role. The default Theme is relevant if the user role will have no access to select their choice of Theme or does not select their choice of Theme. A user can assign their choice of Theme via the **My Profile** page in the **My Setup** administration section. The Theme has to be an editable field on the User Owner page layout for the user to be able to edit and select their choice of Theme.

Privileges

In step 4 of the definition you would assign privileges at the system level. The privileges can be categorized as those relating to personalization of the UI and those relating to accesses.

Accesses to customize the UI

The UI consists of the Action Bar layout, the Homepage layout, the Detail page layout and the Tab layout. The user's personal password is part of the user's personalization with the CRM On Demand application. Step 4 of the wizard lists all the **privileges** that can be enabled for the user role. These are Boolean settings; checking the checkbox activates the line item. The privileges pertaining to the **My Setup** category define whether the user role can customize the layouts and reset their personal password.

Accesses to data channels

The data channels in CRM On Demand consist of the online UI channel, the data management channel of data exports and imports, the Integration channels of online Web Services and Widgets/Web applets, and the desktop/mobile channels of PIM Sync, Outlook/Notes e-mail integration, and the offline application.

The access controls that we have discussed in this chapter are relevant to the main channel of the online UI. The other data channels provide their specific prebuilt accesses to data and which cannot be customized by the CRM On Demand administrator. In step 4 of the wizard, which lists all the privileges that can be enabled to the user role, these specialized channels can be enabled to the user role as necessary. We will briefly discuss the characteristics of each of these specialized data channels. The common characteristic of these alternative channels of access is that they are useful when one needs to extract the CRM data to an external system be it a networked server or the local desktop.

The channel of data exports and imports provides unrestricted access to export all the fields of a record and/or import data to any fields of a record, without being subject to the visibility restrictions of the online UI.

The channel of online web services is a programmatic interface to query all fields of a record and insert into any field of a record however it is subject to the record type accesses that are defined for that user role (in step 2 of the wizard). The programmatic interface allows high velocities of data operations compared to the online UI channel.

The channel of online Widgets/Web applets provides a programmable interface to transmit all fields of a record to external systems, and/or receive data from external systems, after the user has logged into the online UI channel.

The desktop/mobile channels refer to supplementary applications that integrate with surrounding applications, such as the e-mail clients and desktop processors. In these integrations, the data is downloaded, stored, and maintained in the local clients. The data is synchronized on demand, based on the synchronization rules set by the user in their local application. The data access is subject to the visibilities and controls that are set for the online UI channel of the user role; however, custom fields, validations, and custom Page layouts are not supported.

Accesses to user channels

The user channels in CRM On Demand refer to channels by which data and/or accesses of one user can be channeled to another user. Calendar sharing and user delegation are the two user channels available in CRM On Demand for normal business users. User channels are initiated and controlled by the 'giver' at all times. The channels have prebuilt and fixed definitions which cannot be customized by the CRM On Demand Administrator.

In step 4 of the wizard, the Calendar Sharing and User Delegation privileges can be enabled to the user role as necessary. Enabling the Calendar Sharing privilege merely allows the user to share their calendar with others if they personally choose to. Calendar includes only the appointment records and those which are not marked "private". Enabling the User Delegation privilege allows the user to delegate access to their secured data to any number of other users. The delegates receive the same access to the data that is available to the user who is delegating to them, that is the delegator's owner and default access profiles apply. Delegation applies to all the data of the delegator and limited delegation cannot be made. However, the create accesses of the delegator are not conveyed to the delegates.

The other user channel is that of the Administrator. The CRM On Demand application Administrator is the primary user who channels accesses to all the other users of the system. In step 4 of the wizard, a host of privileges pertaining to the administration of the application are maintained for the user role. All the privileges are enabled by default to the prebuilt user role of "administrator" and newer definitions are enabled to the Administrator by the On Demand Customer Care service. Any of these privileges, in their logical combinations, can be enabled for other technical or business users as necessary.

Summary

In this chapter we learnt to customize the CRM On Demand application to the business organization of users. We learnt how to conceptualize the organization and the central idea of the user ID. We learnt the types of accesses on data that are available in the application. We learnt the various mechanisms available to control the data accesses to user IDs, and thus map the real organization of people to the user IDs in the CRM On Demand application. A keen understanding of the user management and access controls facilities in the CRM On Demand application goes a long way in the successful implementation and adoption of the information system, meeting the business objectives.

Business Process Automation and Management

6

Customer relationship management (CRM) is a combination of people, processes, and technology that seeks to understand a company's customers. In this chapter, we are going to focus on the "process" part of CRM.

On a day-to-day basis, any company runs on business processes. Just about everything that goes on—from general business operations, sales, customer services, to industry-specific activities—has well-defined processes. Thus, to improve the efficiency of any company, it is vital to identify, optimize, and automate the business processes to reduce the manual effort as well as operational inconsistencies. This is where the concept of business process management comes into the picture.

Business Process Management (BPM) in CRM's perspective means identifying, optimizing, and automating those processes which increase customer satisfaction. This helps to cut down the lead time involved in many of the customer-centric business processes from weeks to a few hours.

Consider a typical scenario where an existing bank customer calls up a bank and wants to inquire about the rate of a home loan. The bank should ideally have a set of business rules which can be applied to customer details such as salary, bank balance, occupation, and credit record for quoting the rate. The business process should be optimized and automated in such a way that the system retrieves these details automatically based on the customer ID/phone number and applies the applicable business rules, coming up with the quote straight away, without a customer representative carrying out these processes manually and holding the customer on the call. Automating such day-to-day business processes can attribute towards better personnel and organizational productivity, quick and improved decision making, and enhances operational excellence. Business process management can therefore prove to be a strong reason that businesses run smoothly.

In CRMOD, our allies for BPM are workflows and assignment rules. We will see in this chapter how they help us in aligning the operational procedures and practices of a company as per the business needs. The workflows and assignment rules help to automate process steps that are done manually, perform business rules validation to improve the quality of data keyed in the CRM system, and facilitate automatic assignment of records to cut down the processing lead time and so on.

Workflow configuration

Workflow configuration in CRMOD is used to automate business processes to increase efficiency and adherence to business policies. Simple examples of what can be achieved through workflows are:

- Sending e-mails
- Creating follow-up tasks
- Updating customer data in CRM On Demand
- Assigning a record to a book
- Creating integration events
- Deleting data from CRM On Demand
- Creating a wait action on a workflow to delay the execution of other (following) actions

Hold on!

Before you actually log in to the CRMOD application and start configuring the workflows, don't forget to complete the prerequisite steps for successfully structuring your workflows; these are as follows:

1. Ensure you have the **Manage Data Rules - Manage Workflow Rules** privilege assigned to your role.

2. Check the **Enable Workflow** option in the **Company Profile** page.

3. Work with business stakeholders to identify workflow and assignment requirements.

4. Follow best practices while creating new workflows or updating the existing ones in CRMOD. The most methodical way is to document workflow rules, corresponding actions, as well as the expected outcome before configuring them in the CRMOD application. Follow a relevant naming convention to name each workflow created in the system; for example, adding a prefix to each name can describe the job function or even geographic assignments. This will help you to group workflows visually on the screen and accelerate the process of troubleshooting for consultants.

5. A thorough test strategy with realistic sample data is required to test the configured workflows after the build. It's a must to have all test scenarios as well as reverse scenarios documented.

6. Workflows are not available by default when CRM On Demand is provisioned for you. You have to contact the customer care to enable the feature. When customer care sets up the workflow rule functionality, the **Workflow Configuration** link is visible in the Business Process Management section of **Admin Homepage**.

About workflows

After completing the ground work as mentioned in the previous section, you are well equipped to create workflows in the CRMOD application.

A workflow is made up of three components. These three components define and drive the functionality of any workflow. The components which comprise a workflow are listed as follows:

- **Rule**: The rule defines the conditions to be met to execute an action
- **Trigger**: The trigger defines the specific event that must occur for the workflow to get executed
- **Action**: The actions are the actual activities that a workflow performs.

Adding and modifying the workflows

The user of the application must have the necessary privileges to be able to create and manage workflows. Once the desired privileges are acquired, the user can attempt at configuring workflows in CRMOD.

To begin, go to **Admin | Business Process Management**, as shown in the following screenshot:

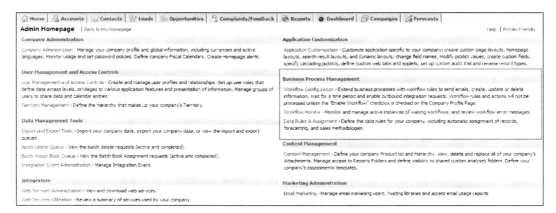

Click on the **Workflow Configuration** link to start configuring workflows. On clicking the link, you will be redirected to a page where the already configured workflows are listed. On this page, an option is provided to the user to create/modify a workflow. Follow these simple steps to create a new workflow:

1. Click on the **New** button on the title bar to create a new workflow rule; this button is shown in the next screenshot:

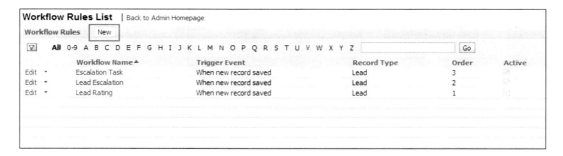

2. When the **New** button is clicked, a new page opens up where you are required to specify details related to the workflow such as **Workflow Name**, **Record Type**, **Trigger Event**, **Rule Condition**, and the **Active** status, as shown in the following screenshot:

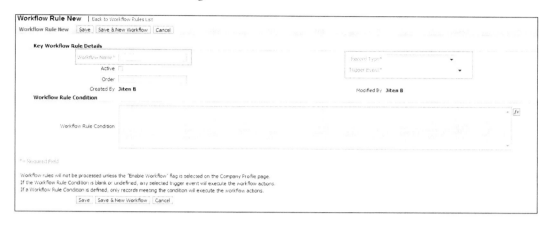

 After a workflow rule is created and saved, **Record Type** or **Trigger Event** on the rule cannot be changed. However, the workflow condition and order can be updated.

3. To create a new workflow rule by copying an existing one, click **Copy** on the workflow rule that you want to copy; refer to the following screenshot:

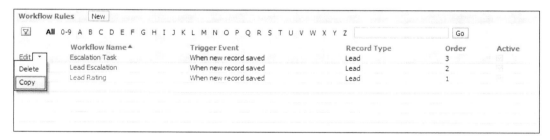

When you create a new workflow rule by copying an existing one, the values of **Record Type** and **Trigger Event** are retained from the original workflow rule and rest of the features are available for making any changes.

We will cover each aspect of these components used for creating a workflow in detail as we move ahead in this chapter.

Record types

While creating a workflow rule, almost all record types are available to choose from. Industry-specific record types are available only when an industry-specific edition is in use.

Mostly, a workflow rule is related only to a single record type. This implies that when a workflow rule condition is applied and assessed on the selected record type, the actions are also performed on the same record type.

An exception to this statement comes into the picture when **Trigger Event** is set as **After association with parent** or **After dissociation from parent**.

A classic example for this scenario is a contact record being associated with an account record. So, if the business need is to trigger a workflow whenever there is an association formed between a contact and an account, there will be more than one record type available in the workflow structure.

In this case, we set **Record Type** as **Contact**, **Parent Record Type** as **Account**, and **Trigger Event** as **After association with parent**.

In this case, both **Parent Record Type** and **Child Record Type** can be specified.

Refer to the following screenshot to visualize this scenario:

 Once a workflow rule is saved, **Record Type** on the workflow rule cannot be changed at all. Hence, think twice before making a choice and saving a new workflow rule to avoid cluttering the system with unused workflows. However, there is always an option to delete the workflow.

Trigger events

As the name suggests, trigger events are events that trigger the execution of the workflow. So depending on your business need, select the right trigger event. The way you choose the trigger events can make or break your business logic by either automating a manual process at the right instance or by creating havoc by setting off at a wrong instance. Based on the trigger event, the workflow rule conditions are evaluated (or if there are no conditions defined on the rule) and appropriate actions are taken if the condition is met.

Various available trigger events are as follows:

- **When new record saved**
- **When modified record saved**
- **Before modified record saved**
- **When record is deleted**
- **After association from parent**
- **After dissociation from parent**
- **When record is restored**

Note the difference between the **When modified record saved** and **Before modified record saved** events.

The **When modified record saved** event is the trigger event which triggers when an existing record is modified and thereafter saved by clicking on the **Save** button. Some of the actions that it can trigger are sending an e-mail, creating a task, assignment to a book, creating an integration event, and updating field values. The **Before modified record saved** event is the trigger event which triggers when an existing record is attempted to be modified and before it can be saved. So if you require a validation to be applicable on a particular field, this trigger event comes in handy, not allowing the user to save the modified record till the defined conditions are met. The only available action that can be invoked as a result of this trigger event is the **Update Field** action.

To sum it up, any of the following can trigger a workflow rule:

- Creating, updating, or deleting a record
- Associating or dissociating a record with/from another record

 Once a workflow rule is saved, the trigger event on the workflow cannot be changed at all. Hence make a careful selection so that you don't end up cluttering the system with unused and redundant workflows.

Refer to the following screenshot, which shows the available trigger events:

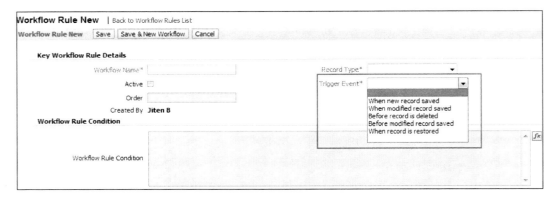

Workflow rule condition

A workflow condition defines a criterion which should be met for an action to take place. It is evaluated whenever a trigger event sets off. It is optional to have a workflow condition defined on a workflow rule. A rule with no condition indicates that the rule should be executed on *all* records of the designated type when the triggering event occurs.

To define a rule condition, click on the **fx** icon in the **Workflow Rule Condition** section of the page, as shown in the following screenshot:

On clicking the **fx** button, an **Expression Builder** window opens up. **Expression Builder** is a tool for defining and implementing business rules using expressions (operators, functions, fields, and literals that can be evaluated by CRMOD); this tool is shown in the following screenshot:

 A workflow rule condition can comprise 1024 characters at the most.

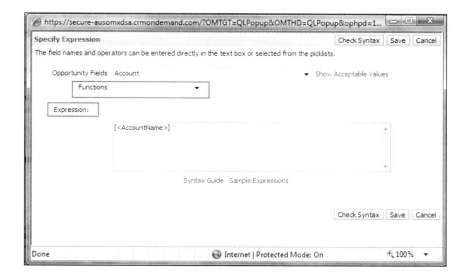

The **Expression Builder** tool is a clever and intuitive editor which helps us in building basic and advanced criteria/validations, which form a workflow condition. This condition is evaluated by the workflow engine to take the desired actions.

Let us try working with an example to further illustrate various components of a workflow. Consider a business scenario where it is required to intimate the sales representative's manager whenever a new opportunity is created by him. Let us break down the given requirement into various components of a workflow, as follows:

- **Record Type**: Opportunity
- **Trigger Event**: When new record saved
- **Workflow Rule Condition**: None (in this case, action will be performed every time the workflow is triggered)
- **Action**: Send e-mail to manager

Let us now go a step ahead and add a rule condition so that the action is performed only when the rule condition is met. The business scenario is now modified to sending an e-mail to the sales representative's manager when a new opportunity record is created and the opportunity reaches the **Closed/Won** sales stage.

So the applicable **Workflow Rule Condition** will be something similar to the following:

PRE('<SalesStage>') <> [<SalesStage>] AND FieldValue('<SalesStage>') = "Closed/Won"

The **PRE** function in **Expression Builder** returns the previous value of the specified field. The first part of this expression basically ensures that the workflow actions are executed only when the **Sales Stage** field is modified and the second part ensures that workflow actions are executed only when the sales stage is **Closed/Won**. This expression is shown in the following screenshot:

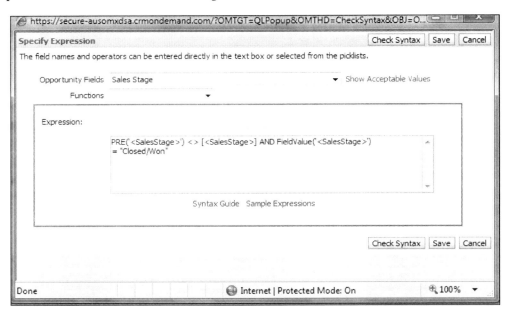

The steps to write this **Workflow Rule Condition** are presented in the following steps:

1. Select the **PRE** and **FieldValue** functions from the **Functions** drop-down menu.
2. Select the **Sales Stage** field.
3. Expand the validation as provided in the code snippet.

4. Check whether the syntax is valid using the **Check Syntax** button.

5. If you need any additional help on syntax or some sample expressions for reference, click on the **Syntax Guide** and the **Sample Expressions** links.

These steps complete the process of building a rule condition for any workflow. Writing advanced/complex rule conditions in CRM On Demand is a knack by itself and they can only be built with practice and experience over a period of time.

Actions

Actions determine the actual course of activities that will take place when a rule condition is met. A workflow without an action is just like a restaurant without a chef, where a framework is available but there is no one to drive it.

There can be multiple actions created for each workflow rule. However, the number of actions for each workflow rule is limited to a maximum of 25. An attempt to create more than 25 actions for a workflow rule will trigger an error message from the application.

Ordering of actions

When there are multiple actions defined for a workflow rule, a sequential order is followed to perform the defined actions starting from the action numbered **1**. Subsequent actions are performed after completion of the previous action. Click on the **Edit Order** button to order the actions.

The **Active** checkbox should always be checked in order to activate an action, or else it will not trigger at all! On the other hand, you can opt to uncheck the **Active** checkbox if you don't want a particular action to take place.

Various available actions will be explored in the upcoming sections.

Assign a Book

This action automatically assigns a record to a specific book/books if the workflow rule conditions are satisfied. For example, add a new UK-based user to the respective book based on his country/location. This, as discussed in the previous chapters, is to control the visibility of data across the application.

Refer to the following screenshot to visualize how this action can be configured:

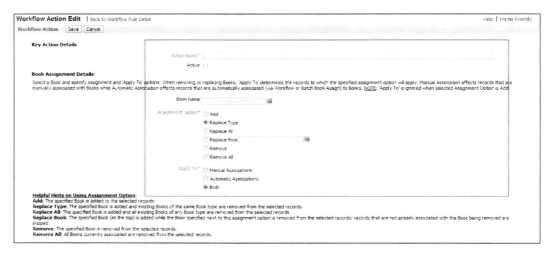

Provide a name for the action, select the book using the book lookup window, and specify the **Assignment Option** and **Apply To** options. Many **Assignment Option** values are available to choose from depending on the business needs. Refer the CRM On Demand help section at `http://docs.oracle.com/cd/E27437_01/books/OnDemOLH/index.htm?toc.htm?assigningrecordstobookshelp.html` for more details.

When removing or replacing books, the **Apply To** option determines the records to which the specified assignment option will apply. **Manual Associations** affects records that are manually associated with books while **Automatic Associations** affects records that are automatically associated to books; both handle all records that are either manually or automatically assigned.

Create Integration Event

This action triggers the creation of integration events and adds it to the predefined integration queues. Integration events are covered in detail in *Chapter 8, Web Services Integration*. For now, a brief introduction to what basically an integration event means is provided so that the usage of this particular trigger event can be understood and appreciated.

Integration event enables triggering of external processes when specific changes such as creating, updating, deleting, associating, and dissociating of records occur in CRM On Demand. The external processes can access the detail of the events in CRM On Demand through one or more integration event queues.

For example, let's consider a scenario where an external application has to be notified when the status of a service request in CRM On Demand is modified. You can create a workflow that executes when the above condition is met by adding an integration event to the integration event queue for the external program to read and perform required actions. Specific fields of the service request that are to be tracked can be defined as part of the configuration. The following screenshot helps to visualize how an integration event is configured:

Provide an appropriate name for the workflow action and select the integration queues to which the integration event will be written to. Once this action is created, you can use the configure option to specify the fields to be included/tracked in the integration event queue.

Create Task

This action creates a task if the workflow rule conditions are satisfied, for example, a follow-up task for a service representative.

Refer to the following screenshot to have a quick glance at the **Create Task** action:

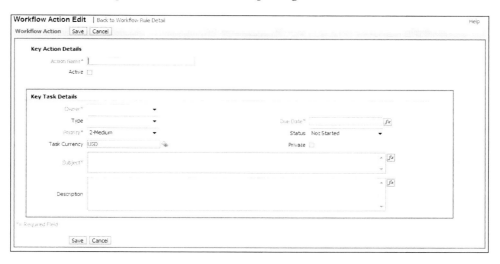

Provide an appropriate name for the workflow action along with other details such as **Owner** (who will own the task record), **Due Date** (the date at which the tasks fall due), **Priority** (priority of the task), **Status** (the default status with which the task has to be created), **Subject** (the subject line of the task), **Private** (turn on the private flag if you intend to restrict the visibility of the task to only the task owner), **Task Currency**, and **Description** of the task. A new task will be created in the system based on the values provided in the action. Refer to the CRM On Demand help-text reference at `http://docs.oracle.com/cd/E27437_01/books/OnDemOLH/index.htm?toc.htm?wftaskhelp.html` to understand the meaning and acceptable values for each field required for creating a task action successfully.

Send Email

This action sends an e-mail if the workflow's conditions are satisfied. The action will come in handy in the case of the example quoted earlier in the chapter, where an e-mail is required to be sent to the sales representative's manager when a particular rule condition is met.

Refer to the following screenshot to have a quick glance at the **Send Email** action:

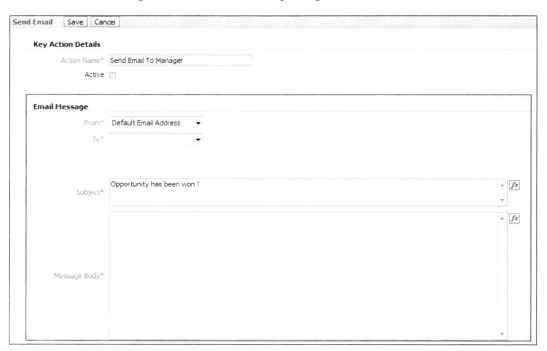

Provide a relevant name for the action. The **From** field contains the e-mail address of the sender of the e-mail, (for example, the e-mail address of the sales representative). There are various options to choose from; these are as follows:

- **Default Email Address**: support@crmondemand.com is the default e-mail address selected
- **Current User**: E-mail address of the signed-in user who triggers the workflow is selected
- **Specific Email Address**: Manually key-in the e-mail address or define the e-mail address using the **Expression Builder** tool (**fx**)

The **To** field contains the e-mail address of the recipients (for example, manager's e-mail address). The various options available are as follows:

- **Specific User**: Click the lookup icon to select the user
- **Relative User on Record**: Select the recipient from the list
- **Specific Email Address**: Specify the addresses manually or define the e-mail address using the **Expression Builder** tool (**fx**)

Multiple e-mail addresses are supported and accepted in the **To** field. To enter multiple addresses, a semicolon (;) is used as a delimiter to separate each e-mail address.

The **Subject** field contains the subject line for the e-mail. The available options are as follows:

- Enter free text in the subject line. For example, **Opportunity is in the Closed/Won stage!**
- Embed functions and field names in the text: **Expression Builder** can be used to embed a function or fieldname. For example, **A new %%%[<AccountType>]%%% account has been created**.

Enter text in the **Message Body** textbox for the e-mail as follows:

- Enter free text in the message body. For example, Hello Mr. John Doe.
- Embed functions and field names in the text. For example:
  ```
  Hello Mr %%%[<ContactLastName>]%%%
  ```

The **Message Body** field can contain a maximum of 2000 characters, including the percent signs before and after the expressions.

Update Field After Wait

This action is used to update a field on the record type that has triggered the workflow rule. There must be at least one active wait action that precedes the **Update Field After Wait** action on the workflow rule. This action is performed only when the defined wait period is over. CRMOD does not allow you to activate an **Update Field After Wait** action unless the action is preceded by an active wait action. The key is **Active**. So make sure that you check **Active** after you have created your wait condition.

You can create more than one **Update Field After Wait** action on a workflow rule, provided that at least one active wait action precedes the first **Update Field After Wait** action on the rule. Note that time to wait can be 0 seconds, so that the wait isn't really a wait at all, so be assured that this action will not slow down your business process.

Refer to the following screenshot to have a quick glance at the **Update Field After Wait** action details:

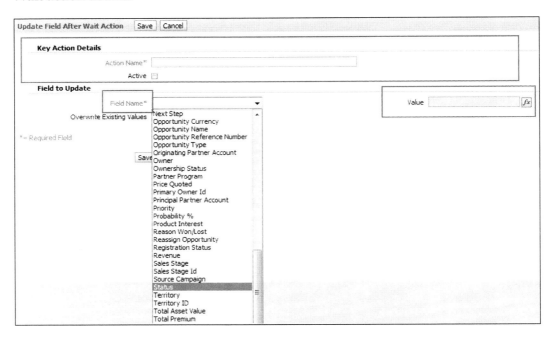

Also refer to the CRM On Demand help-text reference at `http://docs.oracle.com/cd/E27437_01/books/OnDemOLH/index.htm?toc.htm?wfupdatehelp.html` for additional details on applicable values for each of the above fields.

To illustrate the **Update Field After Wait** action, I would like to cite a classic example where the action comes in handy. Consider a new service request created in the system to register a complaint/issue by a customer. If the newly created service request (SR) is not assigned to any agent within a specified time (for example, within 1 hour), it should then be automatically assigned to the agent-supervisor, who in turn can manually reassign the SR to any available agent.

Now try implementing the requirement by using the action in question by setting the following values:

- **Record Type**: **Service Request**
- **Trigger Event**: **When new record saved**
- **Workflow Rule Condition**: Set **Owner** to **Null** (SR is not assigned to any agent)
- **Wait Action**: 1 hour
- **Update Field After Wait**: Update the **OWNER** field by assigning the SR to the supervisor

Update Values

This action is used to update a field value on a record when the workflow rule conditions are satisfied. The field value is updated when a record is changed.

Wait

This action delays the execution of subsequent actions on a workflow rule until the defined period is over.

Refer to the following screenshot to have a quick glance at the details of the **Wait** action:

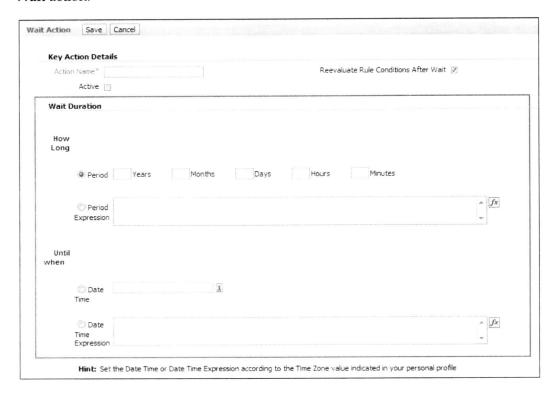

Provide an appropriate name to the action. **Reevaluate Rule Condition After Wait** is used to ensure that the trigger rules are executed again after the wait period to ensure the business rules are satisfied even after the wait period to execute the actions. To enable this feature, a checkbox needs to be checked while configuring a **Wait** action in CRMOD. This would reevaluate the rule condition again after the waiting period ends.

To understand this concept better, let us extend the example cited in the previous section where an unassigned SR is automatically assigned to a supervisor when the waiting period ends.

In the previous example **Trigger Event** is set to **New SR created** and the rule condition is **Owner is null**. If the **Reevaluate Rule Condition After Wait** checkbox is checked, then every time the waiting period ends (1 hour in our case), the rule condition defined on the workflow will be reevaluated. So after 3 hours, it will reevaluate the rule before assigning the SR to the supervisor as it is highly probable that in last the 3 hours, an agent would have got assigned to the SR.

Specify the duration of the wait in the **Wait Duration** section. There are multiple options available for doing so. Refer to the CRM On Demand help-text reference to explore the various options for defining a wait period at

```
http://docs.oracle.com/cd/E27437_01/books/OnDemOLH/index.htm?toc.
htm?wfupdatehelp.html.
```

Actions available by events

The trigger event on the workflow rule determines what type of actions can be created on the rule. So the available set of actions that can be created for a particular workflow rule is a subset of the entire set of actions we looked at in the previous section, depending on the trigger event you choose for the workflow.

The action that is available for all events is **Send Email**. The restrictions on available actions by each of the trigger events is understandable as there is no meaning in expecting an action on **Assign a Book** for the **Before record is deleted** trigger, since record itself is deleted in the system. For a complete list of applicable actions for a given event, refer to the CRMOD help-text reference at `http://docs.oracle.com/cd/E27437_01/books/OnDemOLH/workflowruleshelp.html`.

Ordering the workflows

Ordering a workflow means assigning it an order number when there are multiple workflows configured for the same event. On creation of a new workflow, the next unused order number is automatically assigned to it. The ordering of the workflow rules is based on record type and trigger events. This means that for a combination of the same record type and trigger event the order numbers must be unique for each workflow. This ensures that the workflows are executed in the right sequence, triggering the right actions when multiple workflow conditions are met.

It is quite possible that a workflow rule is judiciously created on a correct record type with an appropriate trigger event to accomplish a set of activities (actions) but when the right time comes, it does not do what it is supposed to do. This is a very common scenario that you will face when working with workflows. So instead of breaking your head over the workflow design and condition/action-expressions, you now know what needs to be checked first—the order of the workflow!

Let us consider a very simple example to illustrate the concept of ordering the workflows.

The objective of this example is that when a new account of type **Retailer** is created, an e-mail is sent to the manager and when a new account of type **Competitor** is created, the record is added to the **Competitor** book.

For this, we set the **Record Type** to **Account** and **Trigger Event** to **When New Record Saved**.

In this case, both the objectives are mutually exclusive in nature. Two different workflow rules are required to achieve the desired task. A different order number will be assigned to each workflow rule so that both can be invoked whenever a new account record is created and based on the type of account, desired actions are taken.

The flipside to this scenario is the invoking of a workflow rule which is dependent on successful task completion by a preceding workflow on the same record type and trigger event. In this case, it becomes critical to correctly order the workflows or else the dependent workflow will not be invoked at all.

For example, based on the type of SR created in the system, update the e-mail address field and send an e-mail notification to the supplied email address.

If the service request type is set to **Complaint**, then set **Update Email Address** to `complaints@abc.com`. If the service request type is set to **Enquiry**, then set **Update Email Address** to `enquiries@abc.com`.

In both cases, e-mail notification can be sent after the e-mail address field is correctly populated with the e-mail address. So the workflow for updating the e-mail address field based on the service request type should always precede the workflow used for sending out the e-mail as the e-mail address value will be picked up from the record on the basis of what was set by the preceding workflow action.

If the workflows are incorrectly sequenced then the workflow might not trigger at all.

Let us consider a scenario where a new workflow rule is created with **Record Type** as **Account** and **Trigger Event** as **When record is deleted** and there are two workflow rules with the same record type and trigger event combination existing in the system. In such a case, the new workflow rule will be assigned an order number of 3. You can change the order number anytime to reprioritize the workflows.

Refer to the following screenshot to see how the **Edit Order** button works:

Select the workflow that you want to reorder by clicking on **Workflow Name**, listed in **Workflow Rules List**.

On the **Workflow Rule Detail** page, click **Edit Order**. In the **Edit Workflow Order** page, click the arrows to change the order of the rule. Click **Save** to save your changes. All these are shown in the following screenshot:

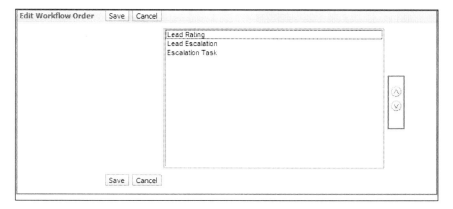

Deleting workflows

In today's fast-paced world, every business process evolves with time. If your business processes undergoes changes, it is highly probable that some of the existing workflows will become obsolete.

To address the same, there is a provision provided in CRMOD to completely delete the existing workflows and create new ones.

When you delete a workflow, all actions associated with the workflow are also deleted. Also, the order numbers on the remaining workflows for the relevant record type are automatically updated as necessary to ensure that there is no gap in the sequence of the numbers.

Refer to the following screenshot to have a quick glance at using the **Delete** button to delete a workflow:

Select the workflow that you want to delete from the list by clicking the **Workflow Name** link. In the record-level menu for the workflow, select **Delete**. Confirm that you want to delete the workflow by clicking on **Ok** in the **Confirm** dialog box. One can also delete a workflow directly from the workflow list on the workflow homepage without navigating to the record level details.

Active and inactive workflows

As discussed earlier in the chapter, the **Active** checkbox on the workflow must be checked to keep it in active state. Only if the checkbox is checked, will the workflow be invoked and related actions triggered.

If you want to temporarily make a workflow dormant, it is required to uncheck the **Active** checkbox. This would lead to deactivating the workflow till the time the checkbox is checked again. When a workflow is inactivated, any associated action on the workflow will not be triggered. This feature comes in handy when you don't want to perform any of the workflows to be executed when you load data into the system.

If you deactivate a workflow rule while an instance of a **Wait** action on the rule is in the pending state, then when the waiting period ends on the instance of the action, none of the remaining actions on the workflow rule are performed, and none of the subsequent workflow rules in the sequence of rules for the record type are triggered.

You can inactivate a workflow rule by unchecking the **Active** checkbox, either on the **Workflow Rules List** page or on the **Workflow Rule Detail** page, as shown in the following screenshot:

Workflow Monitor

Workflow Monitor, as the name suggests, is a tool for monitoring and managing instances of waiting workflows and reviewing workflow error messages.

In layman's terms, it will help you to take your workflow out of Limbo!

You can use **Workflow Monitor** to view instances of the workflow's wait actions that are in a pending state and instances of workflow actions that terminated unexpectedly on or after a wait action ended. The **Workflow Monitor** page shows two lists:

- A list of pending instances
- A list of error instances

This tool is shown in the following screenshot:

Pending Instances

The **Pending Instances** section, shown in the previous screenshot, contains the list of all workflow instances that are pending in the **Wait** mode. For example, you would have configured a workflow which is supposed to trigger an e-mail notification if new service requests remain unassigned without an owner for 48 hours. Now for every service request created without an owner, a workflow instance would be created and available in the **Pending Instances** section. These workflow instances would be moved out of this section after a waiting time of 48 hours. This section helps you to drill down on the pending instance, view the action details, and delete it if required. On deletion, any configured workflow action—for example, **Send Email**—will not be executed. This comes in handy to handle some ad hoc cases where you are sure that there is no use in further execution of the workflow instance.

Error Instances

The **Error Instances** section will help you to look into failed instances of workflow on or after any **Wait** action. If there are workflows which don't have any wait action but end up in an error, they don't appear in this section. They are generally shown as an onscreen error to the end user if the workflow is triggered on user actions such as create, update, or delete record, or in the log files if it is trigged due to data import processes.

A workflow can fail due to multiple reasons. For example, in the scenario that we discussed in the **Pending Instances** section where an e-mail notification has to be sent in 48 hours if a service request is unassigned to an owner, a workflow instance would have failed after **Wait**; maybe because the service request itself is deleted in the system or it could be a case where the workflow rules are not robust enough to handle all possible record field values, leading to errors in executing the workflow condition. If it is the latter case, then having a close monitoring of the **Error Instances** section will help you out to identify and fix these errors in workflow configuration, as they may not be noticed or reported by end users.

Deleting instances from the Workflow Monitor

Workflow instances can be deleted one at a time or a can be deleted as a batch of filtered list of workflow instances. The **Batch Delete** option is not available for error instances and generally these error instances are maintained in CRM On Demand for 3 months before the system automatically purges it.

Assignment rules

If a question were to be asked, "What is the primary purpose of your business", the most likely response would be "to create a customer". Thus, customer service is one of the greatest keys to your business success. It can literally make or break you. The reason is evident as your entire business, marketing, sales, and profits depend on your customers. As discussed earlier in the chapter, automating critical business processes and reducing the turn-around time for customer service plays an important role for any business. Till now, we got a chance to learn the concept of workflows and how vital it can prove to be in automating business processes within the CRM On Demand application. Assignment rules are one of the pillars of CRM On Demand. In this section, we will concentrate on learning and creating assignment rules to streamline and automate assignment processes in CRM On Demand.

About Assignment rules

Assignment rules are used to automatically assign records to the right people in the organization. Automatic assignment of records increases productivity and ensures that records are routed to the right people as soon as they are created/modified in the system. It also facilitates large volumes of records to be imported and automatically assigned, eliminating the need for manual assignment or bulk assignment.

Hold on!

Before you begin, ensure that the **Data Rules and Assignment** privilege is assigned to your role. Assignment rules can be complex, so it is always a good idea to document the business assignment rules. This is used for designing as well as for training the user community where the records are being assigned. Documenting assignment rules provides a framework and a reference point to understand how the workload is routed and managed on the basis of skill-set, product expertise, or demography. Some common scenarios are as follows:

- Sales leads are assigned to the regional sales manager based on the demography
- Newly created service request is assigned to the technical service manager based on the skill-set

Applicable objects

Assignment rules facilitate in the automatic assignment of leads, opportunities, service requests, and accounts to appropriate individuals, teams, and territories. This assignment is done based on the rules which can be set up in the CRMOD application. Note that the **Reassign Owner** checkbox should be checked wherever required (lead, opportunity, service request, or account) to trigger the assignment rule.

Defining a rule group

Rule groups are made up of rules, which, in turn, are made up of criteria.

A **rule group** is a set of rules that defines all the possible scenarios that should be considered when routing records to people. Multiple assignment rule groups can be created in the system; however, there can be only one active rule group at a time for a record type.

 It is a good practice to mark unused rule groups as inactive rather than deleting them as they can be used as a reference in future.

The following section details the steps involved in defining a rule group:

1. To create a rule group, navigate to **Admin | Business Process Management | Date Rules & Assignment**.

2. In the **Assignment Rules** section, click the link for the appropriate record type. A list of all of the rule groups that have been defined for your company till now appears.

3. Click on the **New Rule Group** button to create a new rule group, as shown in the following screenshot:

4. On the **New** or the **Edit** page, fill in the fields as mentioned in the following table:

Field	Description
Rule Group Name	Name of the rule group.
Active Rule Group	By default, only one rule group can be inactive. If you make one of the rule groups active, the other rule groups become inactive.
Unassigned Owner	A user in CRM On Demand to whom the records are assigned, if the system is not able to assign the record successfully to anyone.
Return E-mail	For lead and service request assignments, the system has a feature to send an e-mail notification to the owner on assignment of the record. The e-mail address specified here would appear in the **From** e-mail address of those e-mails.
Unassigned Account Territory	Similar to **Unassigned Owner**, but here it provides the facility to specify the territory to assign your records if the system is not able to find a matching territory with your defined rules.
Unassigned Opportunity Territory	Similar to **Unassigned Account Territory**, but applicable only for assignment of opportunity records.

A **rule** defines the criteria used to assign ownership of a record to the appropriate person. While defining a rule, it is important to bear in mind the order, that is, a correct order number should be assigned to every rule because if a record does not match the first rule, the next rule in the group is considered until a match is found. Conversely, if a rule is met, subsequent rules are ignored.

The following section details the steps involved in defining a rule:

1. To create a rule, navigate to **Admin | Business Process Management | Date Rules & Assignment**.

2. On the **Rules** title bar under the **Rule Group Detail** page, click **New**, which is highlighted in the following screenshot:

3. On the **New** or the **Edit** page, fill in the fields as mentioned in the following table:

Field	Description
Rule Name	Name of the rule.
Order	The sequence in which the rules have to be executed. The moment one of the rules in the rule group is successful the system doesn't execute subsequent rules.
Assign To Owner	The user to whom the record will be assigned if the rule criteria are met.
Assign To Territory	The territory to which the record will be assigned if the rule criteria are met.
Include Related Contacts	This field is applicable for account rules. Provides an option to assign the related contacts of the account to the same user if the rule criteria are met.
Include Team Assignment	This field is applicable for account and opportunity rules. Provides an option to include team members if the rule criteria is met.

The **rule criteria** is the information that is actually evaluated and used for assigning records. A rule criterion has the following three components:

- **Field**: The record field that will be evaluated
- **Condition**: How the value of the field is evaluated
- **Value(s)**: The text or number in the field against which a match is evaluated

For example, **Field** can be set as **Region**, **Condition** can be set as **Contains all values**, and **Value(s)** as **West**.

The following section details the steps involved in defining a rule criteria:

1. To create a rule criteria, navigate to **Admin | Business Process Management | Date Rules & Assignment**.

2. On the **Rule Criteria** title bar under the **Rule Detail** page, click **New**, as shown in the following screenshot:

3. On the **New** or **Edit** page, fill in the fields as mentioned in the following table:

Field	Description	Example
Field	The field to be evaluated.	**Region**
Condition	The condition that has to be used to compare the field value against one of the possible values defined in the rule. Note that the operations such as **Contains all values**, **Contains exact field value**, and **Contains none of the values** are not applicable for date fields. Similarly **Greater than or equal to**, **Less than or equal to** are applicable only for number fields; and the **Between** operator only for date fields.	**Contains all values**
Value(s)	If you have multiple values, then separate each value by a comma. If you have a comma in the value text, enclose the same using quotation mark and if you are using the `Between` operator use comma as a separator to specify the minimum and maximum field value.	**West**

 Note that if there are multiple criteria defined under the same rule, the system applies an `And` condition and the rule succeeds only if all the criteria are met.

Lead Conversion Administration

Leads are generated from trade shows, mailing campaigns, and other such marketing events. When such a lead matures, it qualifies to be converted into an account, contact, or an opportunity. This would typically trigger when a salesperson thinks that the lead has been well qualified and that there is a real opportunity, following the contact he had with the prospect. CRMOD application facilitates this conversion process.

Hold on!

Before you can utilize the **Lead Conversion** utility of the CRMOD application, make sure you have the required access and privileges assigned to your role. A role must have the following settings:

- The **CRM Marketing: Convert Leads** privilege
- Appropriate access-level settings for record types that allow you to convert leads

Converting a lead

When users convert a lead, they can do one of the following:

- Create a new account, contact, or an opportunity, which is linked automatically to the lead record.
- Link the lead record to existing account and contact records. Users select the records that they want to link to the lead while converting the lead.

Lead Conversion Mapping

Lead Conversion Mapping facilitates field mapping, after a lead is converted, for accounts, contacts, or opportunities. When users convert leads to an account, contact, or an opportunity, some values are carried over to the new/existing records by default. However, you can extend the amount of information that is carried over by mapping additional fields, including custom fields.

 Do not map Web link fields for lead conversion. The contents of Web link fields cannot be carried over to the new records when a lead is converted.

Hold on!

Ensure that your role includes the **Data Rules and Assignment** privilege to perform a lead conversion mapping.

Mapping fields for converting leads

To map additional fields when converting a lead, follow these steps:

1. Navigate to **Admin | Business Process Management | Data Rules & Assignment | Lead Conversion Administration | Lead Conversion Mapping**; this is shown in the following screenshot:

2. On the **Lead Conversion Mapping** page, select the fields that you want to map.

3. Use the **Default** button in the title bar, to revert back to default settings. Refer to the following screenshot to visualize **Lead Conversion Mapping**:

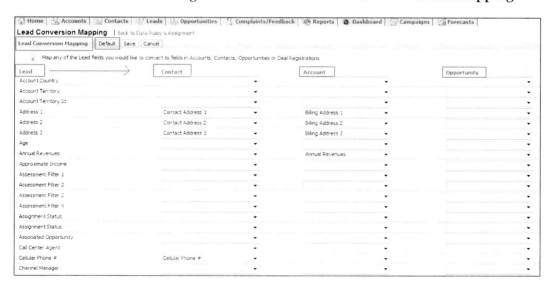

So let us now see how values in the mapped fields are carried over; they are explained as follows:

- On conversion of a lead, when users create a new account, contact, opportunity, or deal registration records, the values from the mapped fields on the lead record are carried over to the specified fields in the new record. According to the previous screenshot, when a **Lead** record is converted to a **Contact** record and an **Account** record, the value of the **Address 1** field at the **Lead** record will be populated in the **Contact Address 1** field of the **Contact** record and **Billing Address 1** field in the **Account** record.

- On conversion of a lead, when users link the lead record to an existing account, contact, opportunity, or deal registration records that they select when converting the lead, the fields in the existing records that already have values remain unchanged. Fields that are empty are updated with the value from the mapped lead field.

Lead Conversion Layout

Depending on the business model defined for an organization, a sales representative should be able to convert a nurtured lead into an account, contact, or an opportunity. However, if the business model demands, there should be an option to restrict the sales representative to convert a lead to accounts, contacts, and opportunity and just do a partial or customized conversion.

To address this need, the concept of lead conversion layout comes into the picture. This utility is used to define customized lead conversion layouts, which specify what options are available to users when they convert leads. Once the layouts are defined, they are assigned to user roles as per the business requirements.

Refer to the CRM On Demand help-text reference at `http://docs.oracle.com/cd/E27437_01/books/OnDemOLH/ldconvlayouts.html` to explore the list of configurable options available in the **Lead Conversion Layout** page.

The **Deal Registration** options are applicable only if your company is set up to use the Oracle CRMOD Partner Relationship Management Edition.

Depending on the options that you make available for a record type, the corresponding sections on the **Convert Lead** page are affected, explained as follows:

- If you do not make any of the options available for a record type, the **Convert Lead** page does not include a section for that record type.

- If you make only the **Do Not Convert to Account** option available for the **Account** record type, the **Accounts** page does not appear on the page.

- If you make only the **Do Not Convert to Opportunity** option available for the **Opportunity** record type, the **Opportunity** section does not appear on the page.

- If you make only the **Do Not Create Deal Registration** option available for the **Deal Registration** record type, the **Deal Registration** section does not appear on the page (this is applicable only in Oracle CRMOD Partner Relationship Management Edition).

Creating a lead conversion layout

To create a lead conversion layout, follow these steps:

1. Navigate to **Admin | Business Process Management | Data Rules & Assignment | Lead Conversion Administration | Lead Conversion Layout**; this is shown in the following screenshot:

2. In the **Lead Conversion Layout** page, click **New Layout**.

3. In **Step 1**, enter the name for the layout. Enter a description for the layout (optional). If you want this layout to be the default for all users, select the **Default Lead Conversion Layout** checkbox, as shown in the following screenshot:

 By default, the standard **Lead Conversion Layout** provided in Oracle CRM On Demand acts as the default lead conversion layout for the company unless another layout is marked as the default.

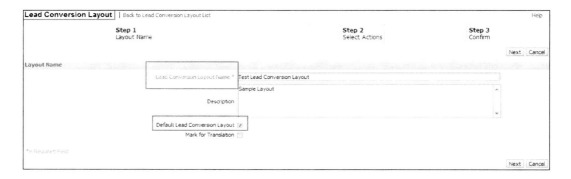

4. In **Step 2**, highlight the record type for which you want to select the actions (**Account**, **Contact**, or **Opportunity**) in the **Lead Conversion Record Types** section, and then use the arrows to transfer the actions you want to display on the page from the **Lead Conversion Available Actions** section to the **Lead Conversion Selected Actions** section. Repeat this step for each of the record types; this step is shown in the following screenshot:

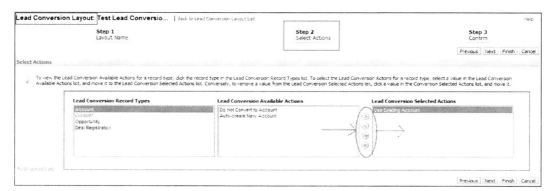

5. In **Step 3**, review your selections, and if necessary, return to **Step 2**. Select actions to change your selections. This step is shown in the following screenshot:

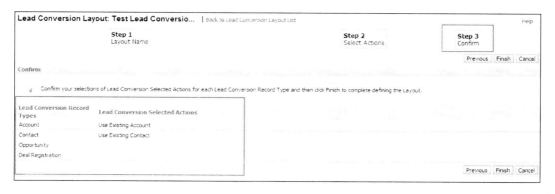

By customizing specific lead conversion layouts on the basis of record types and selecting corresponding actions, we can empower and control the user roles to convert leads differently in different scenarios.

Sales methodology

A very interesting saying in the world of sales goes like this: "sales process is to religion as sales methodology is to prayer". Sales methodology is the approach that you use within your sales process in much the same way that prayer is the approach you take within your religion.

An effective sales methodology is one that a sales organization has thought out clearly and provides it to its sales force. A consistent sales methodology helps you to enforce consistency within the sales force and track your progress against important milestones in your company's sales cycle. In this section of the chapter, we are going to learn about CRM On Demand's default sales methodology and the ways to configure and customize it according to the specific needs of the sales environment.

Sales process

In simple words, a sales process is a methodology adopted by any sales organization for selling its products or services. In CRMOD, a sales process is a collection of sales stages which provides meaningful visibility into the sales pipeline.

An organization may have one or more sales processes depending on the process they adopt towards selling different kinds of products and services. For example, Oracle as an organization may sell both products and services. The sales process to be adopted in terms of various sales stages for the product's line of business could be different from the services line of business and that is where configuration of multiple sales processes helps.

You can associate the sales process to the opportunity type or user's role; so depending on the opportunity type or role of the user creating the opportunity, the appropriate sales process is defaulted by the system automatically.

Sales stage

A sales stage is a step in a sales process towards reaching the final state of winning or losing the opportunity. Typically, the sales stages progress sequentially, though always not necessarily. The CRM On Demand system provides the facility to specify the sequence for each of the sales stages, an opportunity winning probability percentage for every sales stage, and set of activities that you can automatically create for users to perform when the opportunity reaches a given sales stage.

In addition to that, you can also define the mandatory fields in each of the sales stages as well as the steps to be performed by the sales user for each of the sales stages, along with any supporting documentation that he can refer to using the sales coach feature. The details of the configuration steps involved in it are detailed in the subsequent sections. Refer to the following diagram for a detailed analysis of the sales cycle:

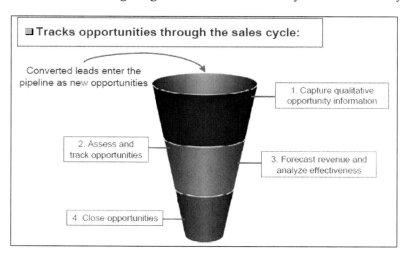

Opportunities enter the sales funnel when they are created individually or converted from a lead.

Setting up a sales stage

To set up the sales stages, follow these steps:

1. Navigate to **Admin | Business Process Management | Data Rules & Assignment | Sales Methodology | Sales Processes**.

2. Select **Sales Process Name** by clicking on the link in the **Sales Process List** page.

3. In the **Sales Stage** title bar, click **New** to create a new sales stage, or select **Edit** in the record-level menu of the sales stage that you want to edit.

4. On the **Edit** page, complete the required information. **Sales Stage Name** and **Order** are mandatory fields and cannot be left blank while setting up a sales stage.

The different types of field are explained in the following table:

Field	Description
Sales Stage	The sales stage name; a mandatory field.
Default Probability	The probability of winning the opportunity at this sales stage. A number from 0 to 100. The default sales stage **Own** has a probability of 100 and **Lost** has a probability of 0. The probability percentage specified here is defaulted when the opportunity moves to the sales stage. This percentage can be overwritten by the user.
Order	The order of the sales stage in the sales process. Set it properly so that it appears in the same order in the **Sales Stage** drop-down menu in **Opportunity**.
Description	Comments.
Mark for Translation	This is an optional field that you may have to select if you intend to translate the name of the sales stage in multiple languages. It gives a visual cue to remind you that you have to set the translated value of the sales stage for each of the languages that you intend to configure in the system.
Stage Category	A category under which the sales stage falls. A list of available predefined categories would be displayed here.

All these fields are shown in the following screenshot:

Once a sales stage is created, the following customizations can be defined for a sales stage:

- Mandatory fields
- Process coach
- Automated tasks
- Useful resources

We will cover each of these bullet points in detail to develop a better understanding.

Mandatory fields

Additional mandatory fields can be defined that are specific to a sales stage. Note that **Closed/Lost** and **Closed/Won** are system-mandatory sales stages and hence cannot be deleted or renamed from the sales process.

To add additional mandatory fields, follow these steps:

1. Scroll down to the specific sales stage by clicking on the **Sales Stage** link.
2. Click on the **New** button in the **Additional Required Fields** title bar.
3. Select the field from the list.
4. Enter the default value. It is advisable to review the onscreen tips while making a selection.

5. Save the record. Refer to the following screenshot to better understand these steps:

6. For example, If **Sales Stage** is **Initiation**, **Priority** field on the **Opportunity** record should become mandatory and the default value should be set to **High**, as shown in the following screenshot:

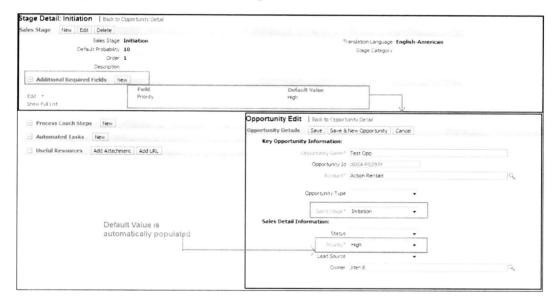

Process coach

The sales process coach acts as a guide for sales representatives, guiding them through each stage in the sales process. Using the process coach can help a sales team in ensuring that every sales stage is completed without missing necessary information.

To set up the coaching feature for a sales stage, follow these steps:

1. Scroll down to the specific sales stage by clicking on the **Sales Stage** link.
2. Click on the **New** button in the title bar of the **Process Coach Steps** page.
3. In the **Edit** page, enter **Order** number to control the sequence in which this information should appear. Provide a relevant **Step Name**.
4. Save the record, as shown in the following screenshot:

The **Process Coach for Sales Stage** page opens up when an employee clicks on the **Coach** button for an opportunity record. This provides a screenshot of the milestones and activities which should be addressed or completed while in this particular stage.

Refer to the following screenshot to visualize this concept:

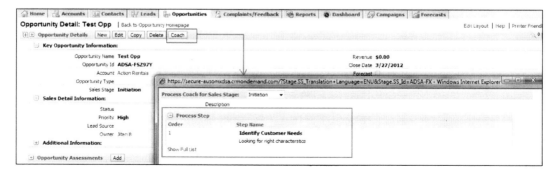

Automated tasks

Automated tasks can be used to automatically create certain tasks that are specific to a sales stage. These tasks will be created when an opportunity is in a specific sales stage and will appear in the employee's task list for following up. This acts as a to-do list for the employee. Sales representatives have visibility of these tasks for each sales stage. Follow these steps to create a task when an employee updates a sales stage:

1. Scroll down to the specific sales stage by clicking on the **Sales Stage** link.

2. Click **New** in the title bar.

3. On the **Automated Tasks Edit** page, enter the required information, which will serve as a template for the task. The task created is available on the **Opportunity Detail** page as well as in the relevant activity lists.

 Provide a number in the **Due Date** field to indicate when the task is due since the time it was created. For example, set **Task Created Date** as January 6, 2012 and **Due Date** as 7. Thus, the task will appear in the employee's task list as due on January 13, 2012.

4. For **Owner**, the following behavior applies:

    ° The task is created for every user having the role you select

    ° If no user fulfills the account team role, then the task is assigned to the opportunity owner

5. Save the record. Refer to the following screenshot:

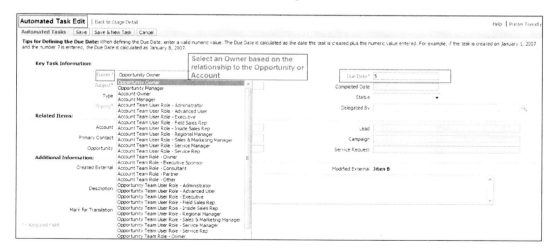

Useful resources

Useful resources are the additional information that can be used by a sales representative when dealing with an opportunity, in particular a sales stage. Useful resources will equip the sales representative well enough to handle the opportunity in a more complete and controlled way.

Various documents, templates, and other relevant information can serve as useful resources. This information is made available in the form of attachments and URLs.

The **Attachment Edit** section is shown in the following screenshot:

The attachments or URL linked to this sales stage can appear in the **Process Coach for Sales Stage** page from the opportunity record page for the employee to refer to, as shown in the following screenshot:

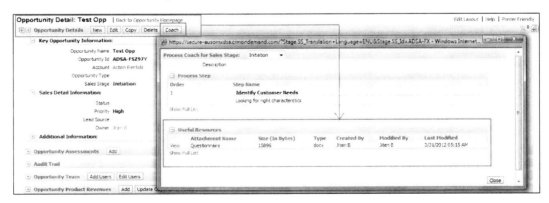

Sales category

As we have discussed earlier in this chapter, multiple sales processes, based on various factors, can co-exist in the CRM On Demand application. In turn each sales process can comprise of multiple sales stages. There can be a business need to consolidate the sales data across the sales stages belonging to different sales processes, for analysis and forecasting. Sales category is defined to achieve the same. Sales stage categories can be defined as stage 1, 2, or 3. Sales categories can be linked to specific sales stages across sales processes. Information related to different sales processes can be consolidated based on the sales categories for an accurate view of sales pipelines across different opportunities and roles. The next diagram gives an example of leveraging the CRM On Demand reports facility to build a pipeline analysis report on opportunities under various sales stages. As you can see, the **Revenue** and **Expected Revenue** (revenue multiplied by probability) columns are grouped by various opportunity sales stages defined in the system.

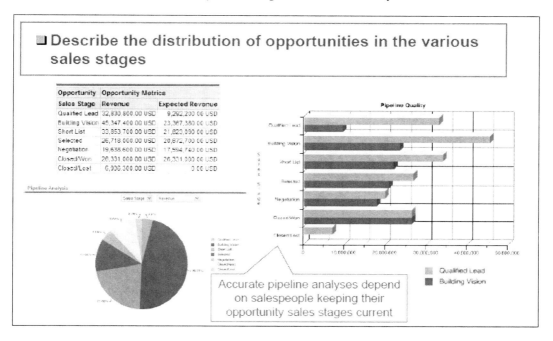

Setting up a sales stage category

Sales categories can be set up by following these steps:

1. Navigate to **Admin | Business Process Management | Data Rules & Assignment | Sales Methodology | Sales Categories**.

2. Click **New** for creating a new sales stage category or select **Edit** from the record-level menu for the sales stage category that you want to edit.

3. On the subsequent page, fill in the required information; this is explained in the following table:

Field	Description
Stage Category	Sales category name.
Order	The sequence of sales category. This sequence would be used when ordering sales categories in CRM On Demand reports.
Mark for Translation	It is an optional field that you may have to select if you intend to translate the name of the sales category in multiple languages. It gives a visual cue to remind you that you have to set the translated value of the sales stage for each of the languages that you intend to configure in the system.

Refer to the following screenshot; it shows the **Edit Sales Stage Category** section:

Administering forecasts

Forecasting is a self-assessment tool for any company. You need to keep checking the health of your business periodically by generating forecast reports and graphs to analyze the pulse of your business. It will lead to differentiating in just surviving and being highly successful in business as the entire organization planning and readiness depends on your forecast. It is a vital cornerstone of a company's budget. The future direction of the company may rest on the accuracy of your sales forecasting.

Setting up and administering forecasts effectively provides critical metrics for determining any company's sales effectiveness. In the CRMOD application, forecasts provide revenue-related information in the form of snapshots. Forecasts can be archived, which can serve as a reference in future.

CRM On Demand administrators can define when, how often, for whom, and what types of forecasts are generated. We will answer each of these questions in the upcoming sections.

When a forecast is generated, CRMOD sends an alert to the participating employees to review the forecast. The alert is posted on **My Homepage** of the employee for 2 days (this period can be extended by updating the **Expiration Date** field for that alert).

What type: Determining the types of forecasts

Forecasts can be based on any of the following:

- Opportunity revenue: Generates forecasts on the basis of the opportunity revenue
- Account revenue and contact revenue: Generates forecasts on the basis of revenue in revenue lines created under an account or a contact

How to choose the right type of forecasting methodology

If your company needs to forecast opportunity revenue, regardless of how much revenue is generated from individual products, then choose opportunity revenue forecasting.

On the other hand, if your company needs to forecast one-time or recurring product revenue for individual products or services, then choose product revenue forecasting.

You can use account or contact revenue if most of your business comes from existing accounts or contacts on a periodic basis in some form of repeat/replenishment orders.

When: Determining the forecast duration

Forecasts can display revenue projections for up to four quarters. By default, only the current quarter is included in the forecast. There is a provision to change the duration setting if you want multiple quarters to be included as part of the forecast. The current quarter is always included in addition to any future quarters in the forecast. So if three quarters are selected as the forecast duration, it will include the current quarter and the next two quarters.

For whom: Designating forecasting roles

You can select the roles that you want to include as part of a forecast definition. All users assigned to the selected role automatically become the forecast participants. Every forecast participant—who has a valid role defined in the user profile, is an active user, and also has a valid reporting hierarchy—is defined. Entire forecasts can fail if any of the forecast participants is not set up accurately.

The success and failure scenarios for forecast roll-up are presented in the following diagram. The first shows a success scenario where the forecast of individuals are rolled up to one person at the top of the hierarchy. The second is a failure scenario as there are two different branches rolling up to different persons playing the role of an executive.

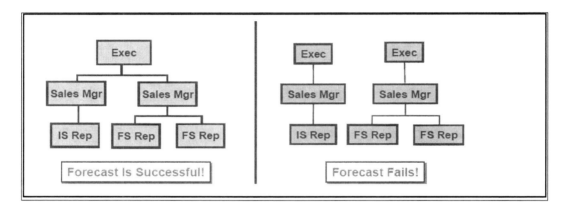

 In case of a failed forecast due to an improper reporting structure among the participants, an e-mail notification is sent to the primary contact (defined in the company profile) from customer support. The forecast is automatically generated when the reporting structure is amended.

How often: Frequency of forecasting

Forecasts can be generated on a weekly or monthly cycle. If you choose a weekly forecast schedule, you will be asked to specify the day of the week you want the forecast to be generated. If you choose a monthly forecast cycle, you will be asked to specify the day of the month. The frequency depends on your business need to do comparative analysis in the future of how the forecast evolved over a period of time for a given forecast period. Many organizations penalize sales teams for inaccurate forecasts either way (the actual value is either above or below the forecast).

Setting up Forecast Definition

A wizard will guide you through the steps of setting up your forecast. Follow these steps to set up the forecast definition:

1. Navigate to **Admin | Business Process Management | Data Rules and Assignment | Forecast Administration | Forecast Definition**.

2. Click **Update**.

3. In **Step 1**, check the checkbox corresponding to the forecast type that you want to generate, as shown in the following screenshot:

4. In **Step 2**:

   ° In the **Forecast Duration field**, select the forecast duration

    The duration of each quarter is determined by the fiscal calendar settings for your company.

   ° The **Create Forecast Snapshot Each** field specifies how frequently the forecast snapshot is to be created

   ° The **Forecast Snapshot Day** field, specifies the exact day of the month/week on which the forecast snapshot is to be created; these fields are shown in the following screenshot:

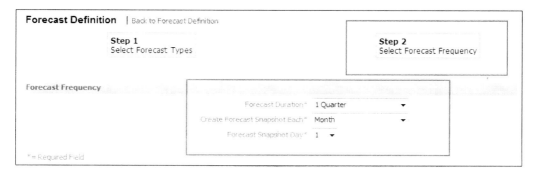

5. In **Step 3**:

- ○ Add the user roles for those users who are to participate in the forecast to the **Forecasting Roles** area.

- ○ There is an option for allowing forecasting for inactive users. Check the **Allow Forecasts for Inactive Users** checkbox. Forecasts for inactive users would be useful in case you haven't reassigned the opportunities of the users to other active users in the system.

- ○ Check the **Auto-submit forecasts for team upon manager submit** checkbox for allowing the manager to automatically submit forecasts for their reports. All these options are shown in the following screenshot:

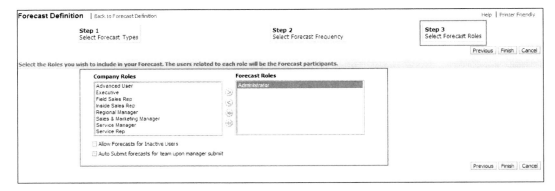

6. Click on the **Finish** button.

Updating and maintaining forecasts

An organization may require you to update its forecast definition to change the forecast frequency, or to add or remove roles, and so on. In addition, when certain changes are made to the user records, or if your fiscal calendar is modified, you must update the forecast definition so that it incorporates the changes.

To update a forecast with different settings, the administrator needs to click **Update** and go through the three steps of the **Forecast Definition** wizard. The option to update any forecast is available on the **Forecast Definition** page. The good thing is that after the forecast definition is updated, a summary of the update and a list of the updated participants are displayed on the forecast definition page.

Summary

In this chapter, we learned the importance of business process management and the key aspects of configuring BPM in the CRM On Demand application. We first defined the two most important ways of automating business processes in CRM On Demand using the **Workflow Configuration** and **Data & Assignment** pages. Then we covered each concept in detail with relevant business scenarios and examples. We also introduced the default sales methodology of CRM On Demand and the extent to which it can be customized by defining multiple sales processes, sales stages, and sales stage categories. In the last section of the chapter, we introduced forecasting, which is an important module as it facilitates measuring your sales performance and effectiveness. If leveraged efficiently, forecasting can really help in analyzing and projecting the sales of an organization.

Content Management 7

An organization is essentially an operation of knowledge, information, and data by the staff. When isolated data is organized we have information and when isolated information is organized we have knowledge. The goal of every business is, of course, to constantly accumulate or add to its knowledge in order to remain an effective organization; when the knowledge is represented or captured in a form that can be shared with and used by all the staff it helps increase the efficiency of the organization. Published or announced knowledge is **content**. The CRM organization will need to generate and manage its content regularly to be effective and efficient in its work.

A list of new customers in the past 15 days, a list of new customers in the past 15 days who were signed on Wednesdays or Thursdays, a Catalog of products that were offered for sale by the organization five years ago, a Catalog of products that are offered for sale by the organization for the next six months, and the list of standardized product names used by the organization, are all examples of content that can increase the effectiveness and efficiency of the CRM organization.

In this chapter we will learn about:

- Four types of content that can be managed in CRMOD
- The management of the four contents

By the end of this chapter you will be able to manage the Product Catalog and assessment scripts, manage access to reports and analytics folders, and manage the stock of attachment files in your CRMOD.

Content

There are four types of content that can be generated and managed in CRMOD:

- **Product Catalog**
- **Assessment Scripts**
- **Reports/Analytics Folders**
- **Attachment Files**

In the CRMOD Administration page, the **Content Management** section appears as shown in the following screenshot:

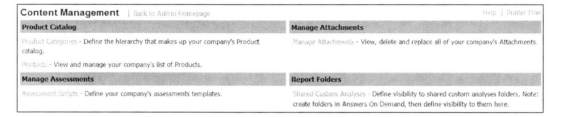

An effective CRM organization maintains a single catalog of the products produced by the business. Regardless of whether the business produces intangible services or tangible goods, salespersons and service persons can be more effective in the customer relationship management if there is a single catalog of products with which to communicate within and outside the organization. The product catalog is the content that needs to be centrally administered and maintained.

Evaluating leads, contacts, opportunities, and accounts through their life cycles is the normal workflow of sales and marketing organizations. Similarly, gathering service feedback from customers is a workflow of service organizations. The questions that constitute the evaluation scripts, and the feedback scripts, represent the business' knowledge about its mission and objectives. The assessment script is the content that needs to be centrally administered and maintained to be accessible to all users of the system.

Reports and analytics are usually written to provide answers to specific business-related questions. The business questions usually have different depths in terms of both quantity of data and the quality of answer expected, depending on the business role of the person asking that business question. An effective CRM organization ensures that each staff member has access to the maximum quality and quantity of information that relates to their specific role. Information overloads are as debilitating as information under supply. Separately, providing complete access to all of the business data to all the staff is an expensive process. For these purposes it is common to create a "folder" to contain reports that are relevant to specific roles, and restrict the access of users to these folders, thus ensuring all users have access to their most relevant information. Managing such report folders or content is necessarily a central function.

Attachment files or URLs are related information to data records in the CRM system. Users, based on their access profiles, gather and/or generate attachment files ("attachments" or "files") as part of the lead, opportunity, contact, account, and other records. Administrators may have attachment files as part of the broadcast alerts. Attachment files are typically used to store content that is otherwise not represented in the structured data records of the system. The stock of attachment files in your CRM system will need to be managed periodically for reasons of access control, relevance of the content, and consumption of network and storage resources. Access to the content within the attachment files is out of the scope of the CRM On Demand access controllers. So, for example, your organization may design to gather the attachment files from CRM On Demand and store them in a secured access-controlled server externally (which is provided with a seamless integration to CRM On Demand) or have a central user to manually apply password controls on attachment files, and so on. Content within some files may become outdated over time and therefore need removed from the system. Attachment files consume scarce network and storage resources, and therefore require centralized monitoring and management.

The administrative privileges related to content management should normally be the preserve of the main administrator user role and rarely activated to other user roles, for the changes in this part of the system are immediate and far reaching.

The product catalog

Every business has a set of products (goods and/or service) that provide it the reason to exist. No organization can exist that cannot articulate its productive potential. The product catalog is the list of products that are offered for sales and/or service by your business. The product catalog is the master/reference list that a salesperson or a service person would look up when transacting on opportunities, service requests, and other custom processes in your CRM organization (that are implemented in the CRM On Demand application) that relates to the products/goods that are offered by your organization to the world at large.

The product catalog at its simplest is a list of the names of the products. At the other extreme, it is a catalog that organizes the products by a commercial taxonomy, and carries comprehensive details for each of the products, including their physical, commercial, and business parameters. Some examples of such parameters are as follows:

- The current status of the product (alpha, beta release, production, and limited edition)
- Date of commercial release
- Date of production ending
- Legal terms in sale and service
- Minimum quantity of purchase
- Maximum quantity of purchase
- Place of manufacture
- Product code
- Shipping terms
- Type of pricing
- Minimum retail price
- The price lists for the product
- The relation to other products

A product usually has as many prices as the markets in which it is offered. While digitization of products and globalization of economies tend to reduce the number of markets to 1, in practice, the market is a negotiation between your business and the rest of the world economy.

Product category

An effective catalog normally organizes/groups the products into **product categories**. The categories may be organized in a hierarchy to better represent the lineage, classification, and other generalities of the actual products. An efficient product catalog posits the actual goods/services that are dealt by the business as products, and captures other abstraction surrounding those actual products as categories and/or commercial details of the products. In other words it requires the length and breadth of the CRM organization to agree on a common language to define/list the product names, the product categories, and the product attributes. Where this exercise is usually simple for a business that manufactures and sells, say, a single size, material and color of umbrellas, the real-world business of our times gives a lot of thought to defining its business, products, categories, and competitors, when designing its product catalog. In CRM On Demand, you would first create the records for each product category that have been defined for the catalog. If you have a hierarchy of categories, you would create the parent category first and follow it down to the child category. A record of a product category has a category name, its parent category (if applicable), and a description of the category, as shown in the following screenshot:

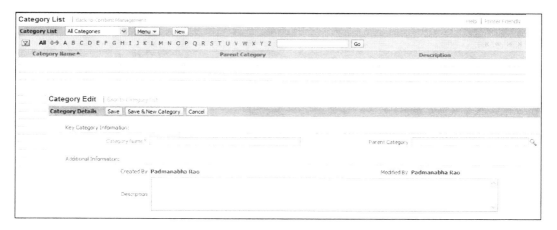

Product

A product once created cannot be deleted. You can remove/withdraw a product but never really delete it once it has been sold! This is true for the market and the same applies to the product record in CRM On Demand too. You remove a product from the market by not taking orders for it, and in CRMOD that is represented by the **Orderable** field on the product record. A product record that is not marked as **Orderable** (checkbox field = "Y") does not appear in the Product lookup field on the Revenue and other custom pages. It is not a good practice in the real market and correspondingly in CRMOD as well, to rename a product that has already been marketed. If you do need to rename, in CRMOD you should plan to update all the transactional records that are associated with the product record that has been renamed; not doing so would lead to incorrect forecasts, reports, and analytics.

A product can have a parent product and thus a hierarchy can be organized for the set of products. Normally you would need a hierarchy of products when you are selling/servicing components or parts as individual products in themselves.

A product catalog is the collection of product records. Before you can create records for each of your products you will need to know the attributes or characteristics or typology or fields to define, capture, and describe the products. The product management department of your business would usually have the list of attributes or fields that catalog all the products in your business. If the product cataloging attributes that are available in CRMOD out of the box do not suffice for your business, you can configure the additional cataloging attributes for the product record in the **Product Application Customization** section. The product is like any other object in CRMOD and the standard facility of object customization is available for it. The following screenshot shows the product object customization facility. Note the useful facilities such as **Cascading Picklists**, **List Access & Order**, and **Search Layout Management** that are available on the product object.

After you have finalized your product record page, including any custom fields and their layout, you would proceed to create the records for each of the products. You should note that a product name has to be unique and the **Orderable** checkbox is essential in populating the product catalog. The following screenshot shows a sample product record from a catalog:

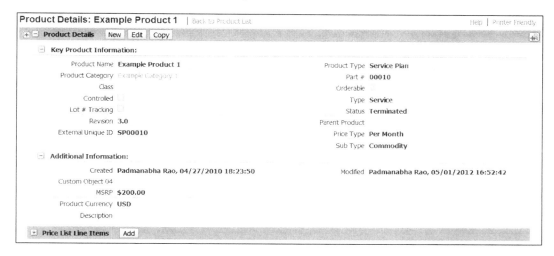

The product records can be imported in batch using the standard data import UI assistant.

Assessment scripts

You can configure assessment scripts for Leads, Opportunities, Contacts, and Service Requests. These objects are related in the CRM business process, and therefore the assessment filters are usually defined/captured so to resonate across the objects. CRMOD has a fixed set of four fields for assessment filters that are connected across the Lead, Contact, Opportunity, and Service Request objects. An assessment script however is specific to each object. You can have any number of assessment scripts for an object, however you will need to distinguish among the many scripts by applying mutually exclusive filters on them. Or, you may design a single script for an object that can be applied to all types of records of that object.

An assessment script has a unique name, its status as active or inactive, the filters to which it applies, the nature of questions (radio buttons, checkboxes, picklists), its decision tree, and finally the set of questions with their weights and sequence in the script. The following screenshot shows a sample assessment script:

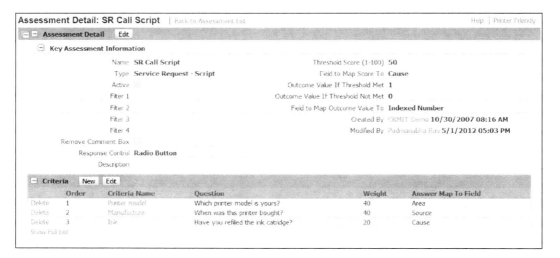

Assessments can be run on the same record, such as a Lead or Opportunity, multiple times. Different assessment scripts may be run on the same record multiple times, as long as the record meets the assessment filters of each assessment script. Every assessment, say of a Lead record, is stored separately and associated as a child record to the assessed Lead record. If you design multiple assessment scripts and if the various assessment records map their responses and/or final scores to the same fields on the assessed record, then subsequent assessments on that same Lead record would keep overwriting the previous values on those common fields on the Lead record.

The four assessment filter fields are the essence of the assessment scripting in CRMOD. You should not use those fields as any other prebuilt picklist fields in the object but plan and design to employ them for picklists relevant for assessment scripts regardless of whether you will implement assessments in your business process.

Assessments are available in the reports/analytics tables of CRMOD.

Reports/analytics folders

We saw in an earlier chapter that one of the privileges settings in the user role is that of whether that role has access to all the data in the analytics tables, independent of its specific accesses to the transactional tables. Reports and analytics are usually abstracts, summaries, dissections and scenarios, over the raw transactional data. From a functional perspective, in some organizations users and/or roles may have the training to build their own reports over the entire dataset of the company, some organizations may restrict reporting and analytics to their transactional data alone, and some others may define, pre-build, and provide a fixed collection of reports and analytics into a folder for each role. From a technical perspective reports and analytics, when they process large datasets and/or are utilized at high frequencies by many users, can consume significant computing resources, in which case governance of them becomes imperative. The Answers On Demand is where users build and access reports/analytics in CRMOD. Answers provides the facility to organize the content by folders. A hierarchy of folders can be maintained. In CRMOD, the administrator can govern access to the built reports and analytics, by associating the folders to user roles. Access to a parent folder implies automatic access to the content of all the sub-folders. A user role can be associated to multiple peer folders.

The Administrator role has access to all folders by default. Any role that is created by copying the Administrator role definition too begets this inherent property.

Do not copy the prebuilt Administrator role to create a new user role.

The following screenshot shows a sample listing of folders and user roles having access to them:

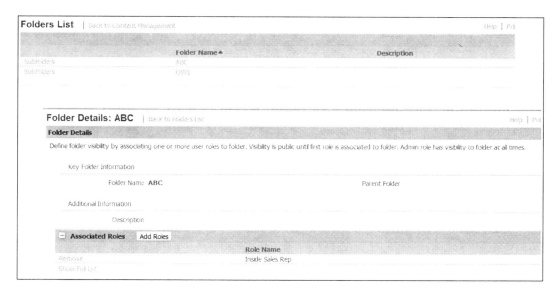

When you reorganize the folders, including creating new folders and renaming existing folders, you should revisit the folder accesses in order to refresh the access control. You do not need to refresh the access control when you add or remove content from the folders.

Attachment files

Attachment files can be associated by users to most objects in CRMOD. Attachment files represent unstructured data in the system. Such data may pose significant challenges to the business. Unstructured data can leak data outside the structured security controls. Files can consume scarce storage resources, if left unchecked and without a maintenance process.

For these requirements the administrator of CRMOD has a facility to view all the attachment files that are stored in the system in a single place, to study, monitor, manage, and maintain the files easily.

The list provides all the meta details of the attachment files loaded by users, including the file name, file extension, file size, the user name who uploaded the file, and the object to which the file is associated. The administrator can download individual files directly from the console. Separately, one can export the list of attachment files for offline analysis and decisions including purging, archiving, and replacements. Attachment files can be batch downloaded via the standard data export facility of CRMOD. Attachment files that are deleted can be restored similar to the restore facility available for transactional records.

Attachment files can be batch uploaded, as a file or URL, using the Web Services. See the chapter on Web Services Integrations for more information.

Attachment files cannot be associated to the Custom Objects 4 and above.

The following screenshot shows a view of the **Manage Attachments** section:

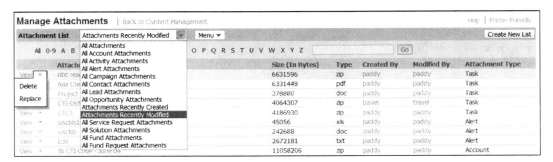

Summary

In this chapter we learnt that content comprises corporate knowledge items such as the product cataloguing attributes and the list of products, predefined reports and analytics, scripts to assess/evaluate CRM business data, and documents or files that users generate and associate to CRM business data. Maintaining the content is one of the main tasks of the administrator of the CRM system and this chapter explained the basics of the maintenance process in CRMOD.

8
Web Services Integration

Web services are all about standards-based integration between applications over the Web. The advantage of web service-based integrations over other means lies in the fact that web services allow you to integrate external systems without worrying about the technology/internal intricacies of other systems with which you integrate.

Web services are built on a core set of technologies, such as **Extensible Mark-up Language (XML)**, **Web Services Description Language (WSDL)**, and **Simple Object Access Protocol (SOAP)**. The primary scope of this chapter is limited to discussion of web services in the context of CRM On Demand, where we try to understand the integration capabilities of CRM On Demand that can help you to implement different types of integration between CRM On Demand and external systems followed by details on how to get started with CRM On Demand web services, list of services available, session management in CRM On Demand web services, design best practices in implementing web service-based applications, understanding web service limiters, and ways and means to monitor/handle web service limiters.

This book is not meant to go into the programmatic aspects of developing a web service program; for that you should refer to the reference material available on the Web.

CRM On Demand integration abilities

Information that CRM system requires might be scattered across multiple internal systems in any organization. Document management could be handled through the Microsoft SharePoint portal, order management-related tasks in your ERP system, employee-related information in your PeopleSoft application, customer financials in your FlexCube banking system, and so on. Bringing in this distributed information from across multiple silos into CRM—thus facilitating coherent search, access, replication, transformation, and analysis over a unified view of information assets to meet business needs—is a challenging task in implementing any CRM system. What kind of integration solution you need to adopt depends on your detailed integration requirements. To be able to select the right approach towards integrating these systems, arriving at the right answers for the following questions with your business/technology stakeholders is a good starting point:

- What is the business value expected from integrating these systems?

- To realize the business value and come up with a suitable approach, determine following points to arrive at the detailed integration use-case:
  - Understand the information that resides in the other system(s)
  - Understand the need for one way or bi-directional integration
  - Evaluate whether a batch integration would suffice or does it require a real time integration
  - Document out the role-based process workflow of users using the integrated applications
  - Capture the data structure and design elements of web-based frontend forms
  - Detail out the type of authentication and data security needs required by different roles for the integrated systems.

- Similarly, on the technology front, identify and document the following technical details:
  - Finalize the application development technology such as Java, .NET, and so on depending on your development team's skill sets.
  - Identify the right application server to deploy the solution. It could be an open source application server such as Tomcat or any of the paid application servers such as WebLogic, WebSphere, and so on available in the market.

○ Choose between the hub-and-spoke integration model and the point-to-point integration model depending on the complexity and number of systems integrated. Point-to-point will suffice if it is just between two systems and the integration use case is pretty simple. The hub-and-spoke model is preferred if the integration use case is complex and we are looking at integrating multiple systems.

○ Identify the frequency of data exchange between the systems.

○ Estimate the volume of data exchange that can happen between the two applications to design the application for better performance and scalability.

○ Evaluate the need for any special performance or error handling considerations such as minimal throughput transactions per second, special error logging format, e-mail notifications, re-run on failure scenarios, and so on.

If you have all the preceding information, then, as a next step, the following decision chart would come in handy to finalize the integration approach:

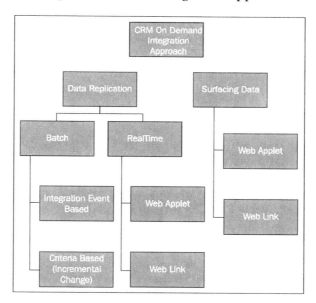

As you can see in the preceding diagram, there are two broad approaches possible. One is to do a replication of data from one system to another system to meet the integration needs and the other option is to surface the data of one system to another system without duplicating the data.

Transferring data between systems

This approach is the hardest between the two available options where required data entries are replicated in both the systems in real-time or batch mode. One of the most common reasons for the customer to opt for this approach is to run reports/analytics in CRM On Demand using data streams that come from multiple systems. This can be facilitated in CRM On Demand in the following two ways:

- **Data transfer at real-time**: When data has to be pulled in real-time from one system to another system during user interaction, this approach can be adopted; for example, for not only surfacing the account balance from financial information system to a call center agent in CRM On Demand but also persisting the latest retrieved account balance in CRM On Demand. The only disadvantage with this approach is that it can be time-consuming to retrieve the information in real-time and this can take a toll on the performance. This could be an ideal approach if the response time for retrieval of the projected load can be guaranteed by the target application with which you integrate. This can be achieved by using the following:

  - **Web applet**: Retrieve data corresponding to a record (for example, the latest account balance of all financial accounts of a customer from a core banking system), persist the data in CRM On Demand at runtime, and at the same time surface the data to the end user as a web applet in the **Customer Detail** page. Refer to the *Configuring Web links and custom applets* section for configuring a web applet in CRM On Demand.

  - **Web link**: It's similar to web applets, but the only difference is that it has to be executed by the end user by clicking the Web link whenever he needs the external system information. This is the preferred approach from a performance standpoint as it avoids putting unnecessary load on the other system. Refer to the *Configuring Web links and custom applets* section for configuring a Web link in CRM On Demand.

> Both Web links and web applets can also be leveraged to send data to external systems from CRM On Demand on loading or clicking the web applet or the Web link.

- **Batch**: This is suited for offline information exchange, where information in the systems is synced up on a periodic manner. Though the primary mode of integrating with CRM On Demand is through web services or the **Bulk Loader** utility, the way you integrate with other systems may be through different means such as web services, APIs, file-based exchange, and so on, depending on the capabilities of the other system. This can work in combination with real-time integration, where at the end of the day, a batch program can run and update the latest balance of financial accounts — from banking systems — for accounts where the balance is more than a day old. For batch-based integration, you can use either of the following approaches:

  - ° Integration events (for data to flow out of On Demand): Refer to the *Configuring integration events* section for more details. This approach is adopted if every change in the CRM On Demand system data has to be applied on the other system and applying periodic net change is not good enough. For example, assume that every time the status of the service request is changed to **Re-Open**, you perform some actions in the backend systems. When the number of times you perform **Re-Open** and the sequence of change in the status flow matters, using integration events is the suitable approach.

  - ° Querying records based on certain criteria: This approach is adopted when the requirement is to apply a net change (you aren't bothered about the number of times the status is changed and the sequence in which the status changes happen) in the other system. The set of incrementally changed data can be identified either through the timestamp fields (modified timestamp fields are available in every object in CRM On Demand) or using special fields that can serve as flags to identify the net changes to be applied on the other system.

Surfacing data from other systems

This approach comes in handy when your requirement is limited to the lookup/reference of data in one system by users of the other system, such as lookup of order status in ERP in CRM for the sales manager to respond to the status of their recent orders. This can be facilitated in CRM On Demand in the following two ways:

- Web applet: Retrieve data corresponding to a record (for example, orders that are created due to a successfully **Closed/Won** opportunity) as part of a web applet by calling the other system in real-time and surfacing the web applet without really persisting the data in CRM On Demand. Refer to the *Configuring Web links and custom applets* section for configuring a web applet in CRM On Demand.

- Web link: It's similar to web applets, but the only difference is that it has to be executed by the end users by clicking the Web link whenever he needs the external system information. This is a preferred approach from performance stand point as it avoids putting unnecessary load on other system. Refer to the *Configuring Web links and custom applets* section for configuring a web applet in CRM On Demand.

Configuring Web links and custom applets

In the following sections we will discuss in detail the steps involved in configuring a Web link and web applet—the two available options to surface data from external system in CRM On Demand.

Configuring a Web link

Adding Web link custom fields to CRM On Demand provides many new integration opportunities. A Web link is a custom field in CRM On Demand that can be placed in the CRM On Demand forms to surface relevant data either from an external application or from other CRM On Demand pages.

A good example of surfacing data from an external application is passing the account's address data to Google Maps for surfacing the account's address in a map. An example of surfacing data from another CRM On Demand page could be of surfacing a CRM On Demand report to present a list of open service requests for the account in the **Account** section.

The following screenshot presents the key parameters to be configured for a Web link. You can access this page by going to **Admin | Application Customization | Record Type Setup | Field Management System | Create Web Link Field**:

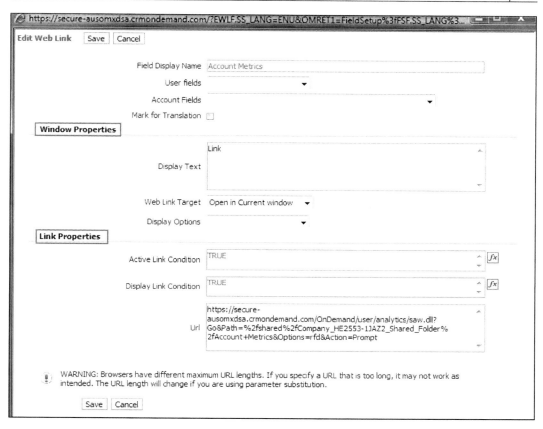

The key parameters to be configured are described as follows:

- The **Web Link Target** parameter controls how you expect the system to surface the external data when you click the Web link. You have an option either to surface the external page in the current window or in a new CRM On Demand custom web tab or in a new browser window.

- The **Display Options** parameter helps you to select whether you want to make this link available in the **Detail** page, the **Edit** page, or both. Note that in the **Edit** page, if you change the address and click the link to Google Maps, it would still take you to the old address.

- The **Active Link Condition** parameter helps to define a condition under which the link should be active. In the example, where we discussed Google Maps, you can make the link inactive, if account doesn't have any address information, by specifying a condition that account address fields are not empty. Similarly, **Display Link Condition** is a condition where only if it is set to **TRUE**, the link will be displayed in the page.

- The **Url** field is where you specify the external URL or link to another CRM On Demand page. In our example, this points to the external URL `maps.google.com` and the account's address fields **Address1**, **Address2**, **Address3**, **City**, and **Country** are passed as parameters for Google Maps to display the corresponding map. You can pick and choose the desired fields for the URL query parameter from the **Account Fields** drop-down menu or from the **User fields** drop-down menu depending on what parameters you have to pass to the external system.

Configuring a web applet

Custom web applets allow you to embed external web content at multiple places in CRM On Demand.

In the CRMOD application, the user can embed web content within the following pages:

- A record type's **Detail** page (navigate to it by going to **Admin | Application Customization | Record Type | Record Type Web Applet**; set **Location** as **Detail Page**)

- A record type's **Homepage** (navigate to it by going to **Admin | Application Customization | Record Type | Record Type Web Applet**; set **Location** as **Homepage**)

- **My Homepage** (navigate to it by going to **Admin | Application Customization | Global Web Applet**; set **Location** as **Homepage**)

- **Action Bar** (navigate to it by going to **Admin | Application Customization | Global Web Applet**; set **Location** as **Action Bar**)

The web applet properties that you would end up configuring are shown in the following screenshot; only the **Location** field differs, depending on where you embed the applet:

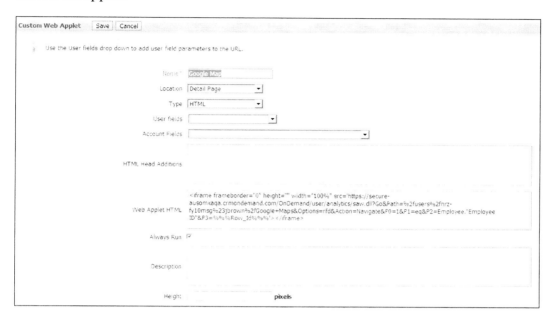

Different types of web contents can be surfaced in the web applets and these are listed as follows.

- **Feed**: Used to embed RSS feeds. For example, you might want to embed a news feed on **My Homepage**, Suppose you want the user's Twitter feed to be displayed in the web applet; you can configure the URL as `http://twitter.com/statuses/user_timeline.rss?id=%%%stTwitter_ID%%%&count=10`, where `stTwitter_ID` is a custom field in the **User Profile** page that captures the Twitter ID of the logged-in user.

- **HTML**: Used to embed HTML code. For example, embed web widgets from an external source such as Google Maps. For more information on how to use the HTML option, you can refer to `http://maps.google.com/help/maps/getmaps/plot-one.html`.

- **URL**: Used to embed the content available at the specified URL in an applet within CRMOD. The URL referred to here is the standard web URL and could point to your order management system to display the list of orders associated with the account that the user is viewing in the system.

As we had discussed in the previous section, you can pick and choose the desired fields for the URL query parameter from the **Account Fields** drop-down menu or from the **User fields** drop-down menu, depending on what parameters you have to pass to the external system. The **Always Run** field would instruct the application whether to run the code always in an applet or only when the user clicks the option to execute it. This comes in handy when you need to minimize the load that you put on the external system.

Configuring integration events

Integration events enable triggering of external processes when specific changes such as creating, updating, deleting, associating, and dissociating of records occur in CRM On Demand. The external processes can access the detail of the events in CRM On Demand through one or more integration event queues. For example, let's consider a scenario where an external application has to be notified when the status of a service request in CRM On Demand is modified. You can create a workflow— which executes when this condition is met—where it adds an integration event to the integration event queue for the external program to read and perform required actions using the integration event-related web service operations. You can also specify fields of the service request that are to be tracked as part of the integration event configuration, which helps you to read the modified values of the fields without performing an additional web service query.

You have to raise a service request to customer care to enable an integration event. Once enabled, navigate to **Admin | Data Management Tools | Integration Event Administration | Integration Event Queue Management** to configure it. Note that on an event, CRM On Demand cannot directly call an external web service, a JSP page, or an ASP page to pass the event details; you need a batch program to read the integration events stored in CRM On Demand integration event queue. The **Integration Event Administration** section is shown in the following screenshot:

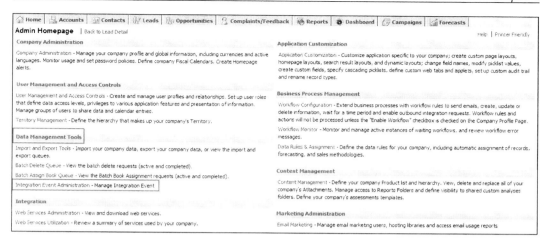

You can configure multiple queues here depending on your requirements. A queue may be used to track the changes in opportunities to integrate with your planning system and another may be used to track the change in the service requests status to an external engine that performs calculation adhering to service level agreement (SLA). The properties that need be configured while creating an integration event queue are presented in the following screenshot:

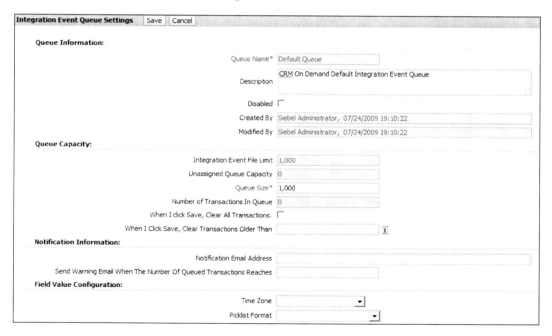

By default, you would have a queue by the name of **Default Queue** configured in the system; you can also configure any custom-named queue. The key parameters to configure the integration queues are documented at `http://docs.oracle.com/cd/ E27437_01/books/OnDemOLH/index.htm?toc.htm?createintegrationqueues. html`. When you configure workflows of integration events, you specify the queue name to which these integration events are sent. The name that you configure here is the name that you will choose while configuring workflows. As part of the workflow definition, you create a workflow by selecting the appropriate object, event, and condition under which the workflow should be triggered (for example, every time an account status is changed in the CRM On Demand system), followed by configuring an integration event queue where you direct the events to a named integration event queue. You can also configure the list of field changes in the account object that you like to capture as part of the event message.

You would consume these messages by invoking the integration event web services in your integration programs. The details of the service APIs available are presented in the following section. The steps involved in creating a workflow to capture the events in an integration event queue are as follows:

1. Create a workflow using the **Workflow Rule New** section, as shown in the following screenshot:

2. Configure an action of the integration event type using the section shown in the following screenshot:

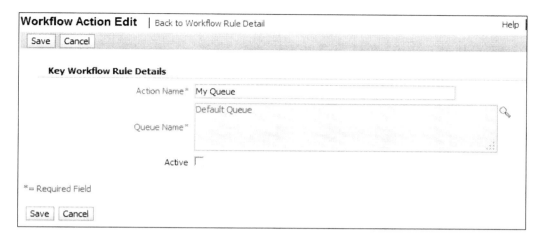

3. Configure the action you defined in the previous step to capture the following field changes:

Enabling CRM On Demand web services

To execute any of the identified integration strategies to meet your integration needs, you need web services in CRM On Demand to create, read, update, or delete information in CRM On Demand. When a new instance of CRM On Demand is provisioned, by default web services integration is made available for users playing the role of the administrator in CRM On Demand. To check whether your role has the necessary permission to work with CRM On Demand web services, select your role from **Admin | User Management and Access Control | Role Management | Edit your role| Go to the Step 4 | Privileges** to see whether the following two privileges are enabled:

☑	Integration: Web Services	Enable Web Services Access	Enable the ability to send Web services requests.
☑	Integration: Web Services	Manage Access to Web Services	Manage access to Enable Web Services Access privilege.

The **Enable Web Services Access** privilege provides you with the permission to perform web service functions in CRM On Demand, whereas **Manage Access to Web Services** provides your role flexibility to assign the **Enable Web Services Access** privilege to other roles configured in the system.

For the developers in your organization one of the key files that they would require to perform web service integration in any technology of their choice (Java, .Net, and so on) is the **Web Services Definition Language** (**WSDL**) file. The WSDL file contains all the required information, such as the endpoint URL to be accessed to perform a web service operation, the input and output message structure, and the list of operations exposed, for a developer to programmatically execute web service calls. The WSDL file can be downloaded by your developers from the **Admin | Web Services Administration** section by selecting the suitable object and hitting the **Download Custom WSDL** or the **Download Generic WSDL** button, as shown in the following screenshot:

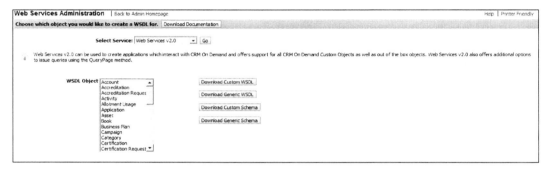

As you can see in the previous screenshot, there are two versions of services available—**Web Services v1.0** and **Web Services v2.0**. The former service is still available for clients who have compatibility issues; that is, developers who have developed web service-based integrations before Release 16 of CRM On Demand. In other words, you can say **Web Services v2.0** is a superset of **Web Services v1.0**; and a company planning to build new web service-based integrations should use **Web Services v2.0** instead of the former service.

In addition to these two versions, you can also find **Service APIs** and **Administrative Services** in the **Select Service** drop-down menu. **Service APIs** typically contains functions to perform user administration, as well as to query system and usage information.

Administrative Services contains functions to read the CRM On Demand metadata (configuration information) in XML format. The downloaded metadata can be used to programmatically update the configuration in new instances of CRM On Demand. This is very useful if you perform migration from one instance of CRM On Demand to other instances, such as from staging to production.

You would use the **Download Custom WSDL** button if you have customized the integration tags (field identifiers) for custom fields that you have created in the system as per your company standards, and you can use the **Download Generic WSDL** button if you haven't done any such changes and left the integration tag values to the default values set by CRM On Demand.

Integration tags are nothing but a unique identifier for a web service program to identify an object or a field in the CRM On Demand system. Unlike the **Display Names** field used while configuring the system, integration tags don't contain any special characters, blank spaces, and so on to adhere to the web service standards. Note that you don't have an option to change the integration tags for a standard, out of box fields provided by CRM On Demand.

Similarly, the **Download Custom Schema** and the **Download Generic Schema** options provide you with a facility to download the data structure of the object you have selected. Schema files are required if you use the integration event service in CRM On Demand, where via workflows any field changes to an object in CRM On Demand during various events such as creation, updation, and so on are captured in an integration event queue, which can be polled by your web service program using an integration event service for further processing.

A developer who has the knowledge of building applications using web services exposed by an external system would be able to understand how to programmatically call in the object-wise operations exposed by CRM On Demand.

Listing the available CRM On Demand web services

A list of the core services exposed via web services on any object in CRM On Demand is listed in the following table. Note that these are object-specific web service functions. For a complete list of objects supporting these queries go to the **Admin | Web Service Administration** section to review the same. With every new release of CRM On Demand, more and more objects are exposed via web services.

Method	Comments
Delete	On basis of the unique record identifier, this operation deletes the record in the CRM On Demand database.
Execute	This can be used to perform multiple operations (update, insert, and delete operations) on multiple records using a single web service query. Note that, though, you can perform different operations in a single query, the records should only be of the same object type.
Insert	This operation can be used to create a new record in CRM On Demand.
QueryPage	This operation can be used to fetch a list of records that meets the given query criteria.
Update	Updates an existing record in CRM On Demand on basis of the unique record identifier.

In addition to the broader understanding of the previously-mentioned key services exposed for every object, it is important to understand the usage of the following arguments that are sent as part of the many previous web service calls:

Argument	Comments
Echo	The Echo argument is applicable for web service functions such as Insert, Update, and Delete where it controls whether the web service calls should trigger integration event workflows configured in CRM On Demand or not. The default value is On, where it triggers integration event workflows; and if set as Off it doesn't trigger. This is basically used to avoid any recursive queuing in integration event queues where you have a need to differentiate between the update action performed by end users using web interface and programmatic updates.

Argument	Comments
ViewMode	The ViewMode argument determines the data visibility. The list of possible values for ViewMode is listed as follows: • Manager: Provides access to records owned by the current user or his subordinates or records where he is part of the record team. • EmployeeManager: This is the same as Manager, but provides access only to records where the user is part of the record. A team is not considered. • Sales Rep: Provides access to records where the user is part of the record team. • Personal: Provides access to only records that are owned by the user. • Organization: Provides access to all the records that the user has access to in the organization he belongs to. • Broadest: Provides access to all the records that the user has access to. This is the default access. • AllBooks: Similar to Broadest, but specifically meant for objects that have the books feature enabled, where by default it provides access to all books that the user has access to. • Context: Provides access to only records that fall under the user default book. For access to a specific book, you have to use the BookId and BookName arguments.
LOVLanguageMode	Controls whether processing for picklist values is done with **language independent codes (LIC)** or **language dependent codes (LDC)**.

Apart from the object-specific core services, CRM On Demand also exposes more services under **Service APIs** and **Administrative Services**. The **Service APIs** option typically contains functions to perform user administration as well as to query system and usage information. **Administrative Services** contains functions to read the CRM On Demand metadata (configuration information) in the XML format. A list of **Service APIs** is listed in the following table:

Method	Web service	Comments
DeletedItemQueryPage	**Deleted Item**	Gets information about deleted items. The items deleted could be either through standard web UI or via web services.

Method	Web service	Comments
DeleteEvents	**Integration Event**	Deletes events from an integration event queue. This facilitates deletion of events that are already processed by the integration program.
GetEvents	**Integration Event**	Gets events from an integration event queue. This provides an option to read events from the integration event queues.
GetMapping	**Mapping Service**	Gets a list of the display names of fields for a particular record type. This maps the display names with integration tags hence it provide a programmatic facility to fetch integration tags.
GetPicklistValues	**Picklist**	Gets lists of picklist values for a given picklist.
GetServerTime	**Time**	Gets the On Demand server time.
LoginHistoryQueryPage	**Login History**	Gets information about user login history.
MergeRecords	**Merge**	Merges records. Provide a facility to merge duplicate records, if any.
MetadataChangeSummary QueryPage	**Metadata Change Summary**	Gets a summary of changes to metadata.
SalesProcessQueryPage	**Sales Process**	Gets the sales process information.
SetPasswordAPI	**Password**	Sets the passwords of users who use the application.
SetSessionTimeZone	**Time**	Sets the time zone for a session.
UpdatePicklist	**Picklist**	Updates picklist values.
UpdateCascadingPicklists	**Picklist**	Updates cascading picklist values.
UserUsageQueryPage	**User Usage**	Gets information about web services utilization.

Administrative Services contain functions to read the CRM On Demand metadata (configuration information) in the XML format. This option provides a programmatic facility to read, update, create, and delete the configuration information in CRM On Demand. The list of configuration metadata that can be read, updated, created, and deleted is limited to **Access Profile, Action Bar Layout, Cascading Picklist, Custom Record Type, Custom Web Link, Custom Web Tab, Field Management, Homepage Layout, Page Layout Field, Page Layout Related Information, Picklist,** and **Role Management**. With every new release, CRM On Demand exposes more and more metadata via web services.

For additional details on web services, refer to the CRM On Demand web services guide available at `http://docs.oracle.com/cd/E27437_01/books/OnDemWebSvcs.pdf`.

Managing sessions in CRM On Demand web services

Establishing a valid session with CRM On Demand is a prerequisite to perform any of the web service functions listed in the previous section. A valid web service session helps On Demand to identify the user who is performing the web service action, thereby limiting the actions he can perform as well as the dataset he has access to. Sessions can be stateful or stateless. In case of stateful sessions, a valid session is obtained by performing a login query and the returned session ID is used for making subsequent web service queries, thereby establishing session continuity across all web service operations performed using the same session. In the case of stateless sessions, with every request, username and password tokens are passed, hence the requests are treated as discrete requests (stateless). In the case of stateless web service requests, CRM On Demand takes care of re-using the sessions in the server-side if a new request comes again from the same user.

Prior to CRM On Demand R16, stateless web services were not available. Only stateful web services were available and it was the developer's responsibility to ensure that the sessions were optimally utilized using a client-side session pooling mechanism to ensure that you don't exceed the number of limited sessions set forth by CRM On Demand. From R16, with stateless web service sessions in place, a stateless web service is considered the best practice to integrate with CRM On Demand. By default, the stateless web service is turned on for a new client getting a CRM On Demand instance. For clients using CRM On Demand prior to R16 and having now migrated to the latest version of CRM On Demand, stateless web service can be turned on by customer care by unchecking the **Web Services R16 Compatibility Mode** setting in the **Company Profile** page in Oracle CRM On Demand, as shown in the following screenshot:

CRMOD web service best practices

Some of the best practices in implementing CRM On Demand web service-based applications are listed in the following section. Ensure your development team takes care of adhering to these listed best practices.

It is recommended that you use batch operations to perform `Insert`, `Delete`, `Update`, or `InsertOrUpdate` operations as it optimizes the performance by reducing the number of web service requests. Typically, batch operations are used for data sync operations and a single batch has a limit of 20 top-level records per request. Note that even if a single record in a batch causes an error, the entire batch is not processed; that is, a batch of 20 account updates where one record contains an error will result in failure in the update of all 20 records.

Prior to R16, when stateless web service sessions were not in place, care had to be taken in managing the session use at the client-side by application developers. From R16 onwards, the recommendation is to use stateless web service as it takes the pain out from developers in managing the sessions. Hence, our recommendation is to convert your existing stateful applications to stateless at the earliest. But, if for any reason your applications were developed prior to R16 and are still using stateful web service sessions, ensure that the following best practices are adhered to:

- Always close sessions immediately after the web service operation if you are not going to re-use the web service session before the session timeout interval of 10 minutes. This would be a common scenario when you create stateful sessions that are specific to the logged-in user (using SSO token), where the user accesses via the web applets or web links, web service-based applications very sparingly (few times in a day) for his day-to-day operations.

- On the other hand, keep the sessions open and re-use them when the application process is likely to be used multiple times by the same user within the timeout period of 10 minutes. This is the recommended approach for all batch operations where multiple web service requests are executed in short time intervals, as well as when using real-time web service applications that the user accesses repeatedly, such as in a call center environment where the agent accesses the custom web service application for every call that comes in.

- When you are using a stateless web service, there is no need to create any sessions. You can pass the SSO token or user ID and password for every web service query and CRM On Demand uses a server side session pool mechanism to manage these web service requests.

- If you are using stateful sessions, then session pooling is an additional option that you can use to increase the performance of your application. In session pooling, you create a pool of sessions using a common **Admin** login with a hardcoded user ID and password stored at the application server and re-use the sessions for any web service requests coming from any end user accessing the web service applications. This is an option provided the end user data visibility doesn't matter, such as setting the status of all the activities of associated service requests as **Closed** when the user clicks a custom Web link to set the status of the service request as **Closed**.

 Note that you set the client timeout for any web service call to 10 minutes, to ensure that the client doesn't time out when the query is being processed by CRM On Demand.

If you are making complex web service queries containing filter criteria at the parent as well as the child record level (joins), the application performance might be poor. If you are facing this issue, then either go for multiple simple queries, or a combination of web service queries and soft filtering to improve performance. The right approach depends on the context of the usage, so there is a no single rule governing all cases.

Error handling and logging is key when developing a client application. Ideally, error handling/logging should provide the following information:

- SOAP requests/responses should be logged in debug mode to work with Oracle support to resolve any web service-related issue. Sometimes, just by looking at the actual SOAP request, we can identify the solution to a problem.

- Endpoints (server name, protocol) should not be hardcoded. Ensure they are kept in a configurable manner outside application code, making life easier in porting the application from one instance to another instance (for example, from CTE to production).

- Identify entry and exit of calls to On Demand web services to isolate CRM On Demand versus your application performance issues.

- A batch error could result from data errors or non-data errors such as network outage, session expiry, and so on. If an error is not data-specific, it is advisable to relogin and retry the web service call. If an error is data-related, one approach could be to split the batch into smaller chunks in a recursive manner so that records that don't have any data errors are processed without any issues.

- Ensure the way you designed your application takes care of several limiters that CRM On Demand has put in place to protect the system from various forms of denial-of-service attacks and incorrect usage. The delimiters are the limit on the number of sessions, request rate, request size limit, session timeouts, maximum records returned, and maximum objects in a web services request. We will discuss more about the applicable limiters in subsequent sections.

- CRM On Demand might not be available sometimes for scheduled maintenance and upgrades. The application should be able to deduct and handle these cases appropriately.

CRMOD web service allotment and limiters

On the basis of an exhaustive study conducted by CRM On Demand, Oracle has correlated some of the common performance issues faced by their clients with specific usage patterns. As CRM On Demand is widely sold to its customers in multi-tenant mode, a wrong usage of the system's resources by one of the tenants in a POD can create issues to other tenants connected to the same POD. To avoid this issue, CRM On Demand has enforced several limiters in the system, thereby reaping the following benefits:

- More predictable and consistent performance
- Reduced service requests and escalations at all levels of the business including sales, support, operations, engineering, and project management
- Clear service definitions and policies facilitating appropriate customer planning
- Enhanced SaaS hosting operations capacity planning
- Operational transparency, wherein customers have a more complete and holistic view of their implementation to drive user adoption initiatives

These limiters are set by Oracle under the three broad categories of storage allotments, web service allotments, SQL limits and peak hours for SQL timeout limits. These limiters change from time to time and also depend on the type of CRM On Demand instance such as single-tenant, multi-tenant, and so on. To know the applicable allotment values to your instance, raise a support request to Oracle.

Monitoring web service allotment usage

The subsequent sections detail the various options available in CRM On Demand to perform service allotment administration, setting alerts on hitting service allotments, and a list of sections available to monitor the service allotment usage effectively.

Administrating service allotment

There is a page in the CRMOD application to view and monitor the service allotments for your company. This section is used to view your current and historical usage of CRM On Demand services as well as to enable proactive alerts when you exceed the threshold values. To view service allotments, current and remaining usage, and configure alerts, navigate to **Admin | Company Administration | Service Allotment Administration**. This page is shown in the following screenshot:

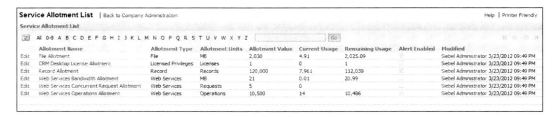

In the **Service Allotment List** page, you can view the following data for each service allotment of your company:

- The **Allotment Name** detail.
- The **Allotment Type** detail.
- The **Allotment Units** detail.
- The value set for the allotment by customer care.
- The amount of the allotment currently used.
- The amount of the allotment remaining.
- Whether an alert is enabled for the allotment. If the current usage exceeds the threshold value, an e-mail alert is sent to the defined recipients.
- The user who last modified the allotment data.

Setting alerts for service allotments

Scroll down on a service allotment to configure an alert. The threshold value should be specified for the system to send proactive alerts to the configured recipients when the service utilization exceeds the thresholds.

If alerts are enabled for a service allotment, the following defaults apply:

- **Alert Recipients**: The e-mail address of the primary contact for the company
- **Alert Threshold**: 70 percent of the allotment value

To set an alert for a service allotment, follow these steps:

1. In the upper-right corner of any page, click on the **Admin** global link.

2. In the **Company Administration** section, click on the **Company Administration** link.

3. In the **Service Allotment Administration** section, click the **Service Allotment Administration** link.

4. In the **Service Allotment List** page, click **Edit**.

5. In the **Service Allotment List** page's **Edit** section, complete the following fields:

   ○ **Alert Recipient**: Enter the e-mail addresses of the users who will receive a warning e-mail

   ○ **Alert Threshold**: Enter the percentage of the allotment value at which the alert e-mail will be sent

   ○ **Alert Enabled**: Select this checkbox to enable the sending of alert e-mails

Refer to the following screenshot, which captures all these details:

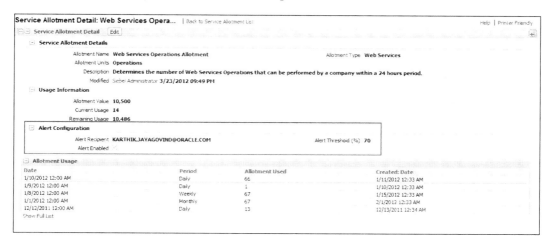

Service Allotment Usage History

From the **Allotment Usage List** page, you can review all the historical usage data about the allotments for your company.

Navigate to **Admin | Company Administration | Service Allotment Usage History**.

By default, the allotment details are listed in the following columns:

- **Date**
- **Period**
- **Allotment Type**
- **Service Allotment**
- **Allotment Units**
- **Allotment Used**
- **Created Date**

Refer to the following screenshot, where all these column names are shown:

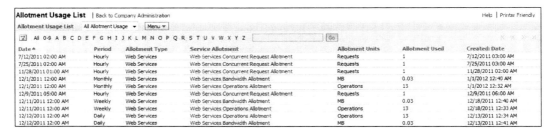

You can view allotment usages for **Daily**, **Weekly**, or **Monthly** periods, although this view varies with the allotment type.

Monitoring file and record utilization

As you can see in the following screenshot, the file utilization details can be viewed from **Admin | Company Administration | Service Allotment Administration | File Utilization**. It provides object-wise information on the number of files that are in the system, space occupied by the files, and the date at which the snapshot is taken.

By default, the current usage is displayed, but you can always view the historical usage using the **All File Usage** list from the **File Utilization List** drop-down menu, as shown in the following screenshot:

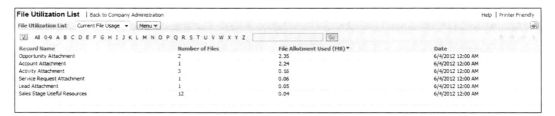

Similar to **File Utilization List**, **Record Utilization List** gives you information on the number of records by each record type in CRM On Demand database. This can be accessed from **Admin | Company Administration | Service Allotment Administration | Record Utilization**. By default, the **Current Record Usage** list is displayed and you can always view historical usage by selecting the **All Record Usage** list from the **Record Utilization List** drop-down menu; the **Record Utilization List** section is shown in the following screenshot:

Web Services Utilization

The **Web Services Utilization** section, available at **Admin | Company Administration | Service Allotment Administration | Web Services Utilization**, provides all the required information to monitor the usage of web services. The information available in this section is detailed in the following table:

Field	Description
End Time	The end time for the web service operation. It would be useful to compare this against your client-side logs to see whether there is any network latency that is creating a delay in the web service operation.
Entry Type	The application values are **Login**, **Logout**, and **Dispatch**. **Dispatch** is the common value for all calls other than **Login** and **Logout**.
Input Message Size (Bytes)	Size of the web service payload.
Operation	The web service operation performed.
# of Operations	Number of operations.
Output Message Size (Bytes)	Size of the web service output XML.

Field	Description
Session Id	The unique session ID for the web service request. Note that this doesn't match with the actual web service session that you get access to programmatically. This makes it difficult to debug any application performance issue.
Start Time	The starting time of the operation.
User Alias	The user who has executed the web service request.
Web Service Client Name	The web service client name. Comes in handy to differentiate between web service operations performed by multiple web service applications.
Web Service Name	The name of the web service.
Web Service Space	The namespace of the web service.

Summary

Thus, in this chapter, we learned about the integration capabilities of CRM On Demand that can help you to implement different types of integration between CRM On Demand and external systems followed by details on how to get started with CRM On Demand web services, a list of services available, session management in CRM On Demand web services, design best practices in implementing web service-based applications, understanding web service limiters, and ways and means to monitor/handle the web service limiters. In the subsequent chapters, we will discuss some of the prebuilt integration solutions available from Oracle and Oracle partners in the CRM On Demand space. Additional information about CRM On Demand web services, sample codes, and utilities can be found at the **Training & Support** link in your CRM On Demand instance under the **Web Services Library** section.

Reports and Analytics

9

The guru of the practice of business management, the late Peter Frederick Drucker, described business as asking the question of and knowing the answer to "Who is my customer?" The purpose of the transactional records that reside in your CRM system is to help improve your understanding of your individual customer, prospects, and the market. We record to research. The **Answers On Demand** service is a prebuilt and inseparable service of CRMOD. It is designed to deliver answers to the business questions of your users.

In this chapter, we will learn about:

- The Answers On Demand service
- Writing your own analytics and reports

By the end of this chapter, you will know about the service in CRMOD for reports and analytics, and the basics of writing reports and analytics.

The Answers On Demand service

A machine intending to efficiently answer business questions has to design for three things: namely, access to all the data generated by the business, the kind and form of business questions that might normally be asked, and most importantly, an interface for the user to ask the question and get the answer. A general modeling of such a machine is shown in the following diagram:

Each of the layers are technically-separated servers working in a hierarchy, as shown in the diagram.

The **data layer**, for Answers On Demand, is a set of all the fields of all the objects that are deployed in your CRMOD. The **business layer** is a collection or subset of objects that are thought of as functionally related and/or relevant for reporting and analytics. An example of a collection that is not normally functional or related is the opportunity and service requests data. Needless to say, it is possible for a business to actually relate an opportunity to a service request. The business layer is the functional and creative component that is defined by the data model and the universe of business questions in the given enterprise. The **presentation layer** refers to the representation and/or delivery of the information by the machine to the user.

Traditionally, the word "reports" refers to information that is presented in a fixed format to the user. The term "analytics" refers to information that is presented interactively to the user. Dashboards present a collection of reports and/or analytics, including analytical features over the collection. In this chapter and in CRMOD as well, for simplicity purposes, the term "reports" is used to imply both reports and analytics.

In CRMOD, working with reports and dashboards is possible by accessing the **Reports** tab and the **Dashboard** tab, as shown in the following screenshot:

Prebuilt reports

Oracle CRM On Demand is the only service in the industry that delivers a set of comprehensive reports, analytics, and dashboards out of the box. If you have adopted the model of CRMOD for your business processes, you will have all the normal reports and analytics that you might require, available right away from the second day of your inputting data to the CRM system. The analytical server runs the **Extraction-Transformation-Loading** (ETL) batch jobs on your CRMOD instance every night (in your local time zone), and therefore the analytics running on the historical subject areas will be available on the second day as soon as the first bit of transactional data is inputted to the system. It is as simple and powerful as that, and therefore you need to take the time to study these fabulous set of prebuilt reports, analytics, and dashboards that are present.

The following is a screenshot of the entire prebuilt collection for a visual reference. Each report is accompanied with a brief description to help understand what the report displays. As you can see, the reports are organized based on the standard model of CRM processes: namely, marketing, sales, and service processes. Additionally, there are reports for you to track the usage of the CRM system. These reports are organized under the **Usage Tracking** section.

Usage Tracking displays data about users; hence, access to these reports should be part of the general data access policies in your CRM organization. In CRMOD, access to the **Usage Tracking** section is therefore set out as a privilege while defining the user's role, separate from the general access to the other reports and data.

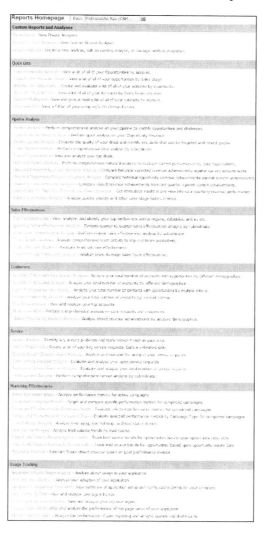

Interactivity

Reports answer specific questions about the business. A simple listing of data, or a "data dump" does not make a report. An intelligent report anticipates the form of questions that might be raised in a business, and offers interactivity to the user to pose the questions and get the answers. The collection of prebuilt reports in CRMOD ranges from simple lists to highly interactive reports that will meet most of the reporting needs of your users. These prebuilt reports are relevant if you are using the standard CRMOD out of the box. The next screenshot is of an interactive report, which shows the history of the opportunity pipeline along with a view from the various levels of the organizational hierarchy. A user can select the range of the opportunity closed date and the manager level of that data as the filters for the data, and then select what he wants to see in that data against a timeline, for example, a simple count of the opportunities, or a sophisticated metric of the average days spent in each sales stage.

A detailed description of the individual reports in the collection of prebuilt reports is out of the scope of this book. We encourage you to get to know these reports individually by using them. There is no better way to learn about them than by actually working with them. You need to ensure that there is sufficient data in the system that will populate the reports.

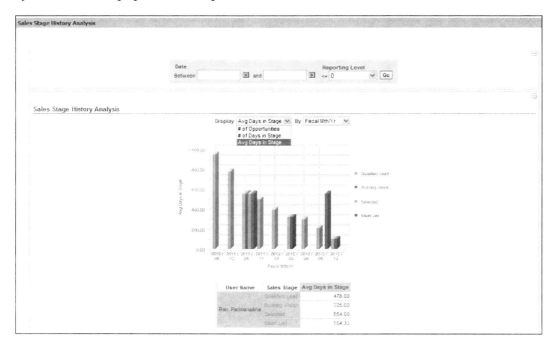

The prebuilt reports are delivered by a closed folder in the Answers On Demand service of your CRMOD; this means you cannot customize the reports. You can copy them, modify them, and save them as your custom reports, but you cannot change the content, listing, and organization of the collection of prebuilt reports that appear in the **Reports** tab. The entire collection of prebuilt reports is in a single folder and you can provide access to this folder to individual users by allocating a specific privilege to them. Note that the reports folder access that we learned about previously does not apply to the prebuilt folder.

Prebuilt dashboards

We learned the definition of a dashboard at the beginning of this chapter. The CRMOD is the only service in the industry that offers dashboards out of the box. Similar to prebuilt reports, dashboards too are comprehensive and are based on the standard CRM model. The following is a screenshot of the **Dashboard** main page:

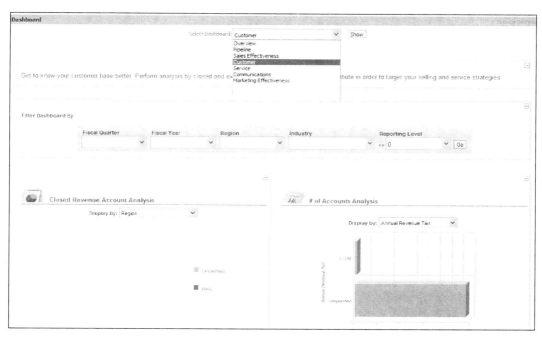

The user selects a dashboard and clicks on the **Show** button to view the dashboard. Similar to prebuilt reports, the best way to get to know about the prebuilt dashboards is to click on each of them. The prebuilt dashboards cannot be modified. You can build new, custom dashboards, all of which would appear in the same **Select Dashboard** drop-down menu, with a clear separation between the prebuilt dashboards and the custom dashboards. This separation could get a bit difficult for user adoption, as every user will see the entire drop-down menu, and therefore highly-customized dashboards that are specific to a user role would need some user training along with using proper naming conventions.

> The **Select Dashboard** drop-down menu items can be hidden using JavaScript; however, note that, as with any use of JavaScript, the maintenance cost also increases gradually. Hiding a dashboard is generally not a normal requirement, so you should review any such requirement thoroughly to check if the fundamental requirement is merely for data access or for viewing a mere dashboard.

Writing a report

When you customize CRMOD at the business or data layers to any extent—small or big—you will have concomitant requirements for reports that you would not find in the collection of the prebuilt reports. We will briefly look at the elements of writing a report. A detailed study of the Answers On Demand service that comes out of the box with CRMOD is out of the scope of this book. The CRMOD Answers is a complete reporting system. There are some very good reference books on the market that are focused on the art of getting custom reports from CRMOD Answers.

There are only three steps to write a custom report, which are as follows:

1. Create a folder for the custom report. A folder can hold as many custom reports as you want it to hold. A folder is part of a folder tree; you can build a tree of any length and depth you want.
2. Select the appropriate primary **Subject Area** option for the report.
3. Build the report.

We will look at each of these steps extensively in the remaining sections of this chapter.

For those who write custom reports, the door to use the Answers On Demand service is the **Design Analyses** link found in the first section of the **Reports** tab. There is absolutely nowhere else to go when writing custom reports; we agree this can be quite a disconcerting idea when you consider that this software is otherwise rife with a web of links all over the system. Please click this low-profile, high-value hyperlink now if you have not already done so.

Report Folders

The **Design Analyses** page can be viewed as containing two facilities when read from the top of the page.

The top half of the page is the semantic repository — the business layer of the analytics system, or the "categories" of business questions that your CRM organization might pose. This is the section where you create new analyses.

The bottom half of the page is the presentation repository — the presentation layer of the analytics system, or the catalog of reports. Here, you would edit the existing reports and reorganize/organize them with report folders. Expectedly, therefore, you will find two facilities in the catalog: namely a facility to edit/modify the existing reports and a facility to manage the reports folders. You can see these two sections labeled as **Open Existing Analyses** and **Manage Analyses**.

Manage Analyses

The next screenshot is of the **Manage Analyses** section that appears after you have clicked on the **Manage Analyses** button in the **Design Analyses** page.

You can create, rename, copy/move, and delete folders and subfolders. You have to scroll down on a folder to navigate to its subfolder structure.

You will want to adopt a reasonable convention for naming the report and the report folders. It is recommended that you deeply nest the report folders. The **Description** field for the reports should be used promptly as it will be useful when the number of users increases.

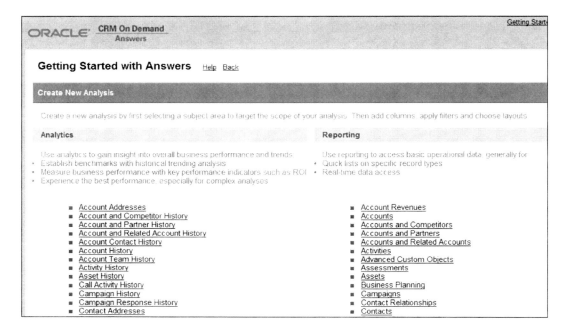

 When you have renamed or moved an existing folder that contains reports, which in turn contain links to other **Narrative** reports (narrative reports will be explained later in the chapter), then remember to update those links manually with the revised URL.

Open Existing Analyses

The next screenshot is of the **Open Existing Analyses** pop-up window that appears after you have clicked on the **Open Existing Analyses** button in the **Design Analyses** page.

In the pop-up window, you will find the entire tree of all the prebuilt and custom folders; you can then navigate to the report that you want to modify. You have to click on a folder to display its subfolder's structure. When you click on a specific report, CRMOD Answers will display that report in the design palette. You can then proceed to edit that report as required and finish the edit by clicking on the **Finish** button provided in the design palette.

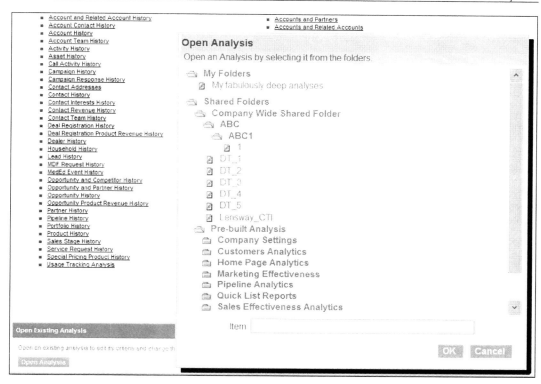

Subject Areas

Having created the folders for the new custom report, let us proceed and create our report. The first step in creating a report is to understand the concept of a subject area. The subject area refers to a collection of data tables that are conceptually related to each other. An example of two data tables that are, traditionally, not related conceptually in CRM practices (yet) are the opportunity and service request data tables. Subject areas organize the data for reporting, in ways that follow the business' processing of those data. For example, you would find a subject area that brings together the data tables of contacts, service requests, activities, and accounts.

The second step to create a report is to understand that analyses are usually of two types. Analyses may draw on real-time data, giving answers to real-time questions; these normally go by the name of **Reporting**. Analyses may also draw on historical data, giving answers to historical questions; these normally go by the name of **Analytics**.

A business system would normally be designed to separate its reporting and analytics facilities for at least two reasons. The demand for these two services is not the same intra-day, intra-week, intra-month, intra-quarter, intra-year, intra-decade, or intra-century. To supply these two services significantly, different technical resources are required. CRMOD follows the industry practice and therefore you would find that in the **Create New Analysis** section, there are two subsections: namely **Analytics** on the left-hand side and **Reporting** on the right-hand side, each of which lists the subject areas that are available out of the box. Subject areas are business constructs and CRMOD does not provide facilities to customize the subject areas or create new subject areas.

[When creating a report, it pays to think thrice before you click.]

The following is a screenshot of the subject areas in CRMOD Answers. When you click on any subject area, you have begun creating an analysis:

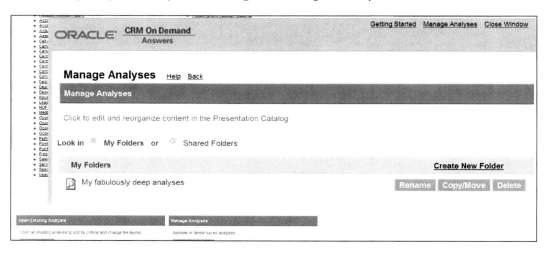

The content of a subject area is a data table. You should check every subject area that is available in Answers by clicking on it, and study its contents to learn the collection. When you click on a subject area, Answers displays the report design page. The design page has two parts to it: namely, the left-hand side that displays the subject area's contents and the right-hand side that displays the canvas and palette to build the report. In the next section, we will learn the main elements of building a report. The following is a screenshot of the contents of sample subject areas:

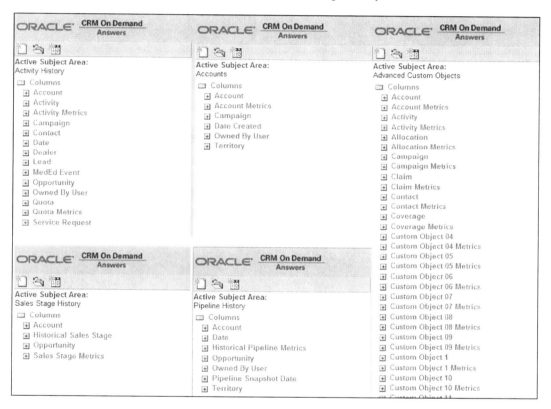

Building the report

In CRMOD Answers, a report is a definition, or a command, to the system. The report defines or commands which columns to gather from the database, what filters to apply for the data from those columns, and how to present the filtered data to the user.

When you build a report, you are building the definition or command. CRMOD Answers lays out an intuitive design page for you; this is displayed in the following screenshot:

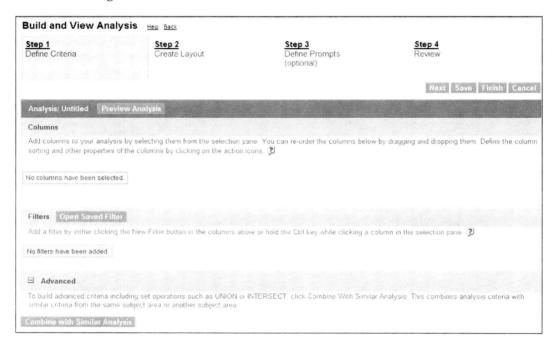

There are four actions or steps to build an Answer:

1. **Define Criteria** (define the columns and filters).
2. **Create Layout** (define the presentation of the data).
3. **Define Prompts (optional)** (define the presentation of the data).
4. **Review**.

Define Criteria

You can define columns for the Answer by clicking on the column from the subject area on the left-hand side of the design page. The columns will align themselves from left to right in the sequence in which you click the column. You can realign the columns by using the drag-and-drop method (use your mouse). There is no limit to the number of columns that you can put in the definition. The more columns, obviously, the longer it will take the system to build the report when the user clicks to generate the report.

When you wish to generate a transactional report, put the RowId column of your primary table as the first column. When a user clicks on the report to generate the report, Answers begins gathering the data in the sequence of the columns, and therefore having the indexed RowId column helps in reducing the time taken to gather the data. The RowId column can be hidden from presentation, if you need. Adding the RowId column is not advisable in all cases. When a report is pivoted on a list of values or metrics, adding the RowId column should be avoided.

Every column that you add gets displayed in the **Columns** section with two pieces of information. The first information is in the blue-colored bar (**Activity**), and it states the name of data table where the column exists. The second is the grey-colored box, which contains six pieces of information in all. The first of the six pieces of information is the column name. In the following screenshot, we can see that the data table is named **Activity**, commonly, for all the three columns with column names **Activity ID**, **Activity Type**, and **Priority**:

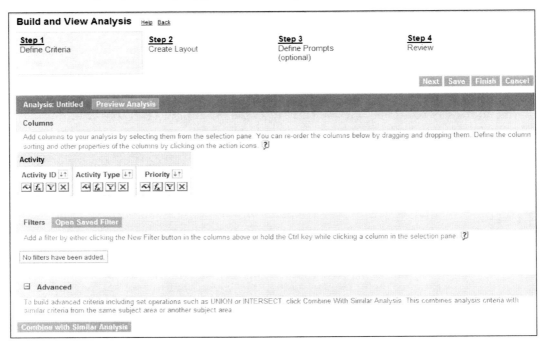

After the column name, there are five more pieces of information (or properties) in the grey-colored box, and these are large information sets in themselves and therefore are represented by five small square buttons with icons on them.

The button that is on the right-hand side of the column name is used to sort the order of the data in that column. The downward-facing arrow indicates a descending sort, and the upward-facing arrow indicates an ascending sort. When both the arrows are visible in the screenshot, it implies that the data is unsorted. This button is a toggle button, so repeated clicking of the button will cycle through the descending and ascending indicators.

The four buttons below the column name, from left to right, are used to:

- Format data and columns
- Transform, perform calculations, and work with other formulas on each row of that column
- Filter the data of that column
- To remove a column

When you click on the button that is used to format the columns (the button immediately below the data table name), you will see the **Column Properties** pop-up window as shown in the following screenshot; this window comprises the **Style**, **Column Format**, **Data Format**, and **Conditional Format** tabs:

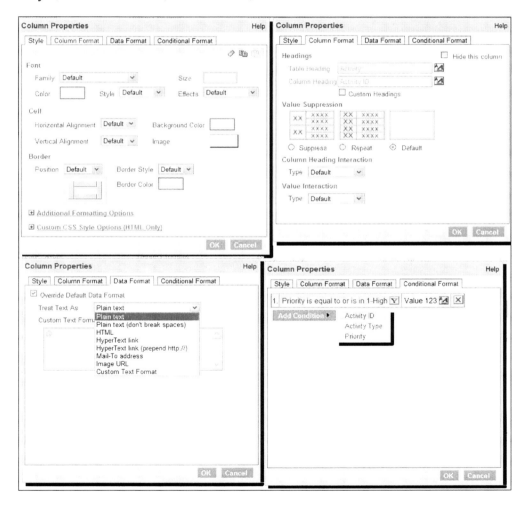

When you click the **Filter** button, you will see the **Create/Edit Filter** pop-up window as shown in the following screenshot. On clicking the **Formula** button, you will see the **Edit Column Formula** pop-up window, which is also shown in the following screenshot. CRMOD Answers provides a comprehensive collection of functions to meet the most complex of transformation and computation requirements:

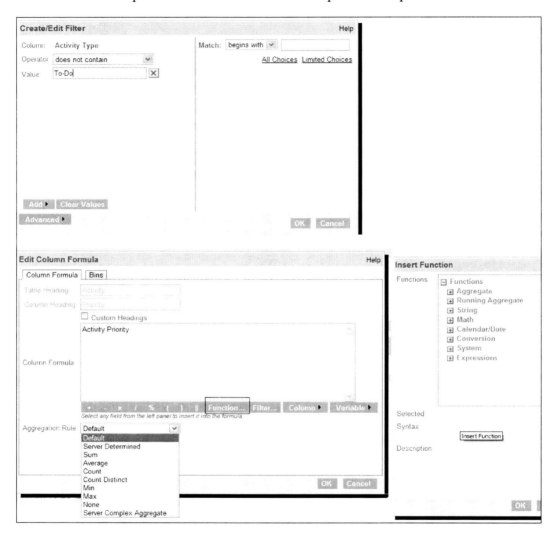

 To add a column filter without displaying the column itself, press the *Ctrl* key and click the column. This brings up the **Create/Edit Filter** box directly.

Create Layout

Clicking on the **Step 2: Create Layout** button on the top of the design page will display the layout section. A layout holds many views of the data.

CRMOD Answers provides a collection of views to the users from which they can select for the presentation of the data. The set of views that are available is prebuilt and you cannot add views to the set. The set of available views are **Title**, **Table**, **Chart**, **Pivot Table**, **Column Selector**, **Gauge**, **Funnel Chart**, **Ticker**, **Static Text**, **Active Filters**, **Legend**, **Selector**, **No Results**, and **Narrative**.

By default, an Answer normally has at least two views, the first view being the **Title** view, usually at the top of the layout; followed by the actual data displayed in the selected view. An Answer layout may have zero views; for example, when an Answer is specifically designed to be used as a filter within other Answers.

The following screenshot shows two sample views (**Title** and **Table**) added to the layout. If you want a different view, then choose from the **Add View** menu in the tab. You can choose to delete the original **Table** view or the **Title** view; you can also edit the existing views from this tab.

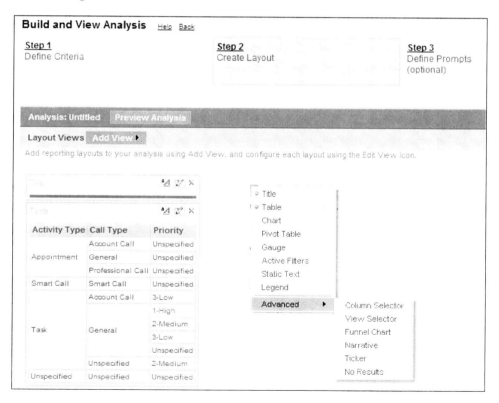

Define Prompts

The third step in building a report is an optional step and its use depends on the report. When your requirement is to present a further interactive filtering feature to the user, you would define those as **Prompts** in this step. These prompts appear as filters to be selected/defined by the user, after the user clicks on the report to generate the report. The following screenshot shows the **Prompt Properties** section that can be used to define the prompt properties defined by you at the time of building the report:

Summary

In this chapter, we learned about the Answers On Demand service that is integrated in CRMOD. We learned the definitions and the uses of the **Report**, **Analytics**, and **Dashboard** options. We also learned about the features of Answers On Demand, including its set of prebuilt reports, dashboards, and the facility to write custom reports. We learned the basics of writing custom reports including the concepts of subject areas and report folders. In the next chapter, we will look at the support services available for CRMOD.

10
Leveraging CRM On Demand Data and Integration Tools

To make sound business decisions, an organization must establish a solid data foundation. This foundation must combine both current and historical data values from multiple disparate operational systems in order to identify trends and predict future outcomes. Data integration involves combining data residing in different sources and providing users with a unified view of these data. When using an enterprise packaged solution such as CRM, data integration becomes a key to deliver complete, accurate, and consistent information in a timely manner. CRM On Demand facilitates data integration and migration with the help of out-of-the-box import/export functionality, data loader, configuration migration tools, and web services.

In this chapter we will discuss the data loader and configuration migration tool, which are helpful for CRM On Demand administrators.

In addition to the above facilities available for Administrators, CRM On Demand also provides a simple utility for the end users to import their contacts from excel/CSV files. Similarly for the end users to work effectively and stay ahead of the competition in today's demanding business environment, they require a flexible and convenient solution that delivers essential information regardless of where they are working. To address this need CRM On Demand offers the following suite of tools:

- Offline Client
- **Personal Information Manager** (**PIM**) **Sync** for outlook integration
- Mobile CRM
- Widgets to embed CRM On Demand data in external portals

This chapter also discusses these great utilities, which a CRM On Demand administrator should be aware of as they are of interest to end users.

Accessing CRM On Demand data and integration tools

The data and integration tools available in CRM On Demand can be accessed from the **My Setup** link that is seen at the top-left corner after logging in to CRM On Demand. The section has two links. One is **Data and Integration Tools** where most of the tools that we talked about in the introduction section are available and the other link **Embed CRM On Demand Content** contains sections that facilitate embedding CRM On Demand lists, reports, message center, and so on, in an external application such as Google or in your corporate intranet website:

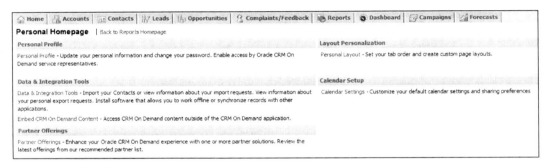

Importing your contacts

The import assistant helps you to add or update existing contacts in CRM On Demand. Depending on your role, the number of contacts you can import can vary. End users can import up to 2000 contacts at a time from a comma-separated value (.csv) file and administrators can import up to 30,000 contact records at one time, with a maximum file size of 20 MB.

To access the import utility, navigate to **My Setup** | **Personal Homepage** | **Data & Integration Tools** | **Personal Import and Export Tools** | **Import Your Contacts**:

Performing the task of importing contacts is a three-step approach. The details on each of the steps involved is presented in the following sections.

Step 1 – choosing your data file

In this step, apart from selecting the data file that you are going to import, you also select some of the key parameters of the import process. The parameters involved are detailed below.

Select the field that identifies the record in your file uniquely in the CRM On Demand system. This could be an "External Unique ID" of an external system from where you are importing the contacts or the "On Demand Row ID", which is the unique identifier for records in CRM On Demand (typically used when you want to update the already existing records in the system), or CRM On Demand predefined fields which are first name, last name, e-mail ID, and work phone number.

Next you should let the system know what it should do if there are records already present in the system that match with the records in your import file. The options that you have are either to create additional records even if the duplicates exist or not to import the duplicate records or to overwrite the duplicate records with the information that is available in the import file.

You also let the system know what to do if the record identified by the unique identifier doesn't exist in the system. You could either create the new record or not create the new record.

Specify what to do if the associated information is not present in the system. In the case of contacts, let us say the associated account of the contact is not present in the system, you have an option either to create a new account or not to create a new account. As far as contact import is concerned you have an option only to associate the account as part import process.

The rest of the parameters are related to letting the system know the date/format of date fields that you are importing, file encoding type, the field de-limiter (CSV or semi colon), and the level of error logging to be performed.

The last parameter is to select the file that you would like to import.

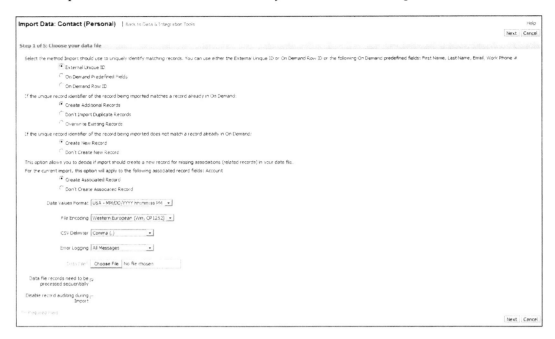

Step 2 – file validation

On moving to step 2, the system will validate the file that you are trying to import and provide warning/error messages if any. If there are any errors in the file that you have uploaded, you may not be able to proceed further unless you upload the file, fixing all the specified errors. In addition to the above, in this step you will specify the data mapping file that has to be used to map the columns in your import file against the **Contact** fields in CRM On Demand. If you don't have one, you can skip this step as in the following step the system provides an option to perform the mapping. At the completion of the import process, the system generates a mapping file. The generated mapping file will be available in CRM On Demand under data import logs for your future use.

Step 3 – mapping your fields

In step 3 the system will automatically pick up the fields in the first row in your import file and provide you a facility to map against the contact fields. It is important that you map all the mandatory fields as otherwise your import process will not work.

Once you are done with the above, the system validates the mapping to ensure all necessary fields are defined in the data file, and mapped to the contacts fields in CRM On Demand. In the next step it provides an indicative time that the system will take to perform the import process as well as the link from where you can monitor the import queue. On clicking on the import queue, you will be taken to the following page where a status "Completed" means that your import process is executed. You can drill down the import request to download the error log file, mapping file, and data file you have imported. If there are any errors in your import, you can fix the errors and start re-importing it again following the same steps. The error log file generated by CRM On Demand is pretty straightforward with reasons for failure in importing the data in record-wise format. This provides an easy option to fix these errors and re-import the data again. The imported contacts can be viewed under the **Contacts** tab in CRM On Demand:

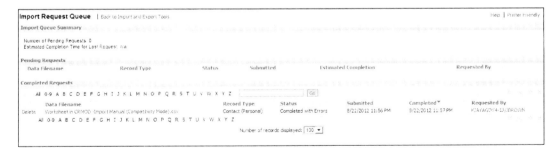

Oracle Offline On Demand

Oracle Offline On Demand is an Excel-based utility that allows you to view, add, modify, and delete your CRM On Demand data locally in your laptop/desktop without Internet connectivity. Whenever you have access to the Internet you can upload the modified information to CRM On Demand to make it available for online access to all users of CRM On Demand. It is an Excel-based utility that runs on Windows XP or Windows 7 and supports only Microsoft Excel 2003, 2007, or 2010. Installing the offline On Demand is pretty simple as it is essentially an Excel file that is available for download at **My Setup | Data & Integration Tools | Oracle Offline On Demand**.

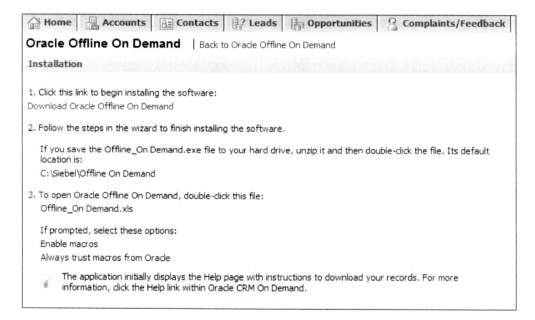

If you open the downloaded Offline On Demand, by default stored under `c:\Siebel\Offline On Demand`, the homepage looks like the one in the following screenshot. You may get a security warning from Excel saying "Some active content has been disabled". If you get one, click on the **Options** button next to it and select the **Enable this content** option to ensure the solution works properly in your system.

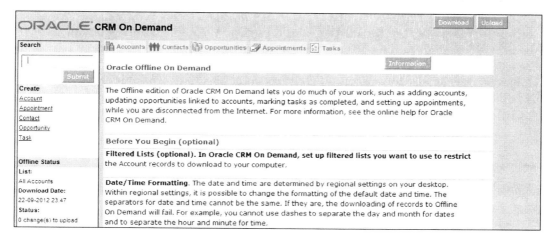

The homepage provides you a whole lot of detailed information on how to download the data in your Offline On Demand, how to add new records, update existing records, upload the updated information, tips to search records in the system, and resolving conflicts, if any, on uploading the information back to CRM On Demand when you have access to Internet connectivity. Do review this information carefully before you start using the application. The subsequent steps would detail some of the key steps such as downloading data, modifying/creating new data and uploading the modified information back to CRM On Demand.

Downloading data into Offline On Demand

On click the **Download** button in the Excel, the Excel prompts you to sign in with your CRM On Demand user ID and password to access On Demand and download the accounts, contacts, opportunities, tasks, and appointments information. The filters for download are either by **Account**, **Contact**, or **Opportunities**. Depending on the selection of **Primary** record type, all applicable lists for your login under **Accounts/Contacts/Opportunities** would be displayed. On selecting one of the lists, the system downloads all related information for the selected object. For example, if you have selected **Contacts** (as the primary record type) and **All Contacts**, the system downloads all contacts you have access to in the system, associated opportunities, and accounts. Depending on your selection under the **Additional Information** section, it would download the applicable appointments and tasks information too.

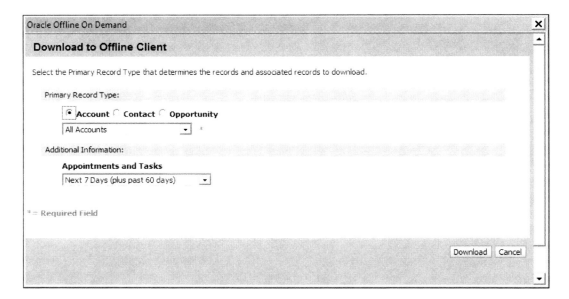

 The volume of data that you can import is restricted at a maximum of 250 accounts or 750 contacts/opportunities records. The download may take some time to complete depending on the total volume of records imported.

Adding/updating data in Offline CRM On Demand

Once the download process is complete, the Excel sheet looks almost like your Online CRM On Demand with required tabs to view, update, and create your accounts, contacts, opportunities, tasks, and opportunities data. Please note that Offline On Demand is restricted to offline access of contacts, opportunities, tasks, and opportunities data only and doesn't support any custom objects or other standards objects configured in the system. The following screenshot presents how the offline On Demand looks after successful download of records in your Excel:

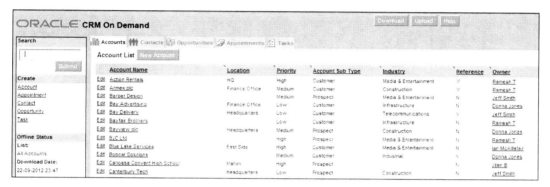

Excel provides you a facility to search any of these downloaded records using the **Search** option in the left navigation bar, create new records, or use the **Edit** link before each of the records to edit and update the information. Note that unless you perform the **Upload** action, the information will not be available in CRM On Demand for access by others. The layouts of the view/edit page would reflect the configuration setup in CRM On Demand at the time of download. The system would also perform the basic validations that you have defined at the field level in CRM On Demand.

Uploading Offline On Demand data to CRM On Demand

You can upload the modified information in your local system by clicking the **Upload** button. On successful upload, the system pops up a message, as shown in the following screenshot:

The system tells you that your information is uploaded successfully and further changes to the data that was downloaded in the past are not possible. If you intend to perform more changes, you have to select the **yes** option to download the up-to-date information in CRM On Demand. If you don't intend to do any further modifications in the Offline On Demand, you can select **No** but make a note that you cannot edit or add new records in the system unless you refresh Excel with fresh data from CRM On Demand. You can always download it using the standard **Download** button too.

Oracle PIM Sync On Demand

PIM stands for **Personal Information Manager** and Oracle PIM Sync On Demand facilitates synchronizing your appointments, contacts, and tasks in CRM On Demand with the ones that you have stored in your e-mail client. It supports Microsoft Outlook 2003/2007/2010, Palm OS 4.1.2/4.4.4, and Lotus Notes 7.0.4/8.0.2/8.5/8.5.1/8.5.2. PIM sync can be downloaded from **My Setup | Data and Integration Tools | Oracle PIM Sync On Demand** section. On installing and running the PIM sync, it prompts you to enter your CRM On Demand username and password and displays options to perform the application setup:

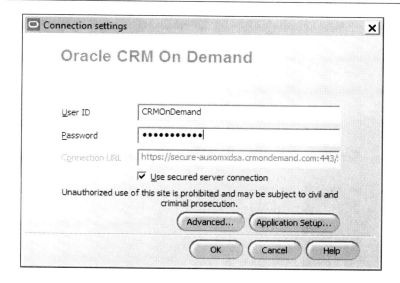

The application setup basically provides you information on what objects you like to sync up, such as **Contacts**, **Appointments**, and **Tasks**:

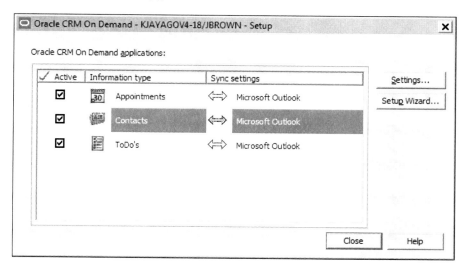

For each of the objects you can select the Setup Wizard to perform further configuration. The key configuration steps are basically to let the system know whether you like to perform a one-way sync from CRM On Demand or bi-directional sync between CRM On Demand, your e-mail client followed by the frequency at which the sync has to be performed:

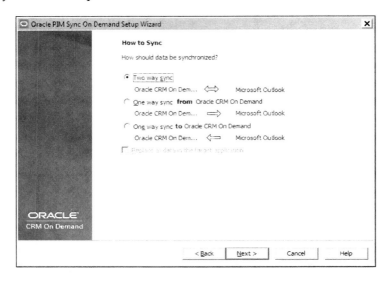

You can either opt for a manual sync or automatic sync at periodic intervals by selecting the appropriate options. Note that this can be different for each of the objects such as contacts, tasks, or appointments.

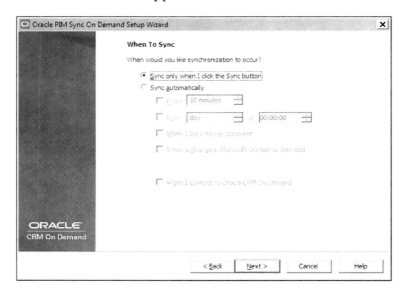

On successful completion of the previous step, the application is all set to synchronize the data in between your email client and CRM On Demand. The advanced setup in the first screen provides you an option to specify Internet connectivity options if your organization requires proxy setup to connect to CRM On Demand. Make a note that PIM sync was recently discontinued by Oracle. Though the product is available for download and use, if you encounter any issues, Oracle support would not be able to help you:

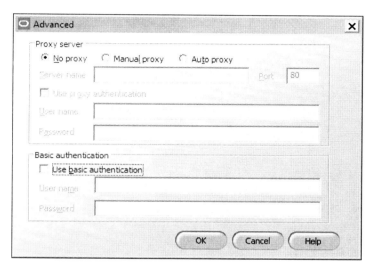

Oracle Outlook E-mail Integration On Demand

Oracle outlook Email Integration On Demand provides you a facility to upload the emails in your Outlook to completed activities in CRM On Demand. The completed activity can be associated to the relevant Account, Contact, Lead, Opportunity, or Service Request records in Oracle CRM On Demand. Note that this tool is available only for Outlook versions 2003, 2007, and 2010 and supports only Windows XP or Windows 7. The tool can be downloaded from My Setup | Data and Integration Tools | Oracle Outlook Email Integration On Demand.

The installation of Oracle OEI On Demand adds the **Add to CRM On Demand** button to your Microsoft Outlook toolbar:

To start using Oracle OEI On Demand, select any of the e-mails in your Outlook and Click on the **Add to CRM On Demand** button in Microsoft Outlook. On the Sign-in page, enter your Oracle CRM On Demand login and password. A task completion form, as shown in the following screenshot, should appear:

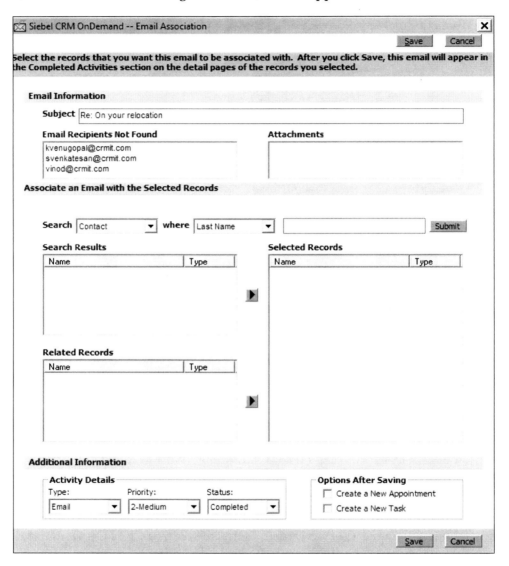

In the task you can search and select the relevant contacts, accounts, opportunities, leads, and service requests that you want to associate to your selected e-mail. If you don't find them you can right-click on the e-mail addresses that are displayed to create new contacts/leads in CRM On Demand. Though by default the status of the activity is set as **Completed** you always have an option to change the type, status, and priority at the bottom of the task window. You also have an option to create a follow-up task or appointment if required, to facilitate any post-follow up action on sending/receipt of an e-mail. When you are composing a new e-mail, the same action can be invoked using the **Send and Add to CRM On Demand** button that appears in the new e-mail composer screen:

Thus the Outlook Email Integration plug-in provides a nice facility to tag all relevant information in the form of e-mail, with associated records in CRM On Demand, without a need to perform them manually by logging into CRM On Demand saving your users precious time.

Oracle data loader

Oracle data loader is a command-line utility that helps you to create/update records in CRM On Demand. The command-line utility can be scheduled to run periodically, thereby information flowing from an external system on a periodic basic can be uploaded to CRM On Demand automatically without any manual intervention. Data loader performs better than the import assistant and is suitable for high volume data upload to CRM On Demand. The tool is essentially a collection of Java programs and can be downloaded from **Admin | Import and Export Tools | Oracle Data Loader On Demand**. Detailed explanation of the usage of the tool can be found at Oracle CRM On Demand Documentation Library available at `http://docs.oracle.com/cd/E27437_01/homepage.htm`.

Oracle Migration Tool On Demand

As discussed in earlier chapters, Oracle provides multiple CRM On Demand environments for the benefit of the customer and application administration team—CTE, Staging, and Production. Each of these environments is meant to be used during the entire lifecycle management of a project. For example, the development team might choose the staging environment as a test-bed for building a complex integration and set of configurations in preparation for a roll-out. The same set of changes has to be replicated in the production environment after being tested for the end user to use. To optimize this exercise, Oracle provides the Migration Tool utility. The Oracle Migration Tool On Demand client is a command-line based utility, which eliminates having to manually reproduce customized configuration data from one Oracle CRM On Demand environment to another, for example, from a customer test environment to a production environment. The Oracle Migration Tool On Demand client allows you to extract and import specific configuration data to your computer interactively, or in batch mode.

The list of configuration items that can be exported from one instance of CRM On Demand to another instance continuously evolves from one version of CRM On Demand to the next and as of Release 19 most of the configuration items identified below can be migrated automatically, saving considerable manual effort:

- Home page layouts, Page layout and Action bar layout, Related information layout
- Picklists and Cascading Picklists
- Custom applets, web tabs, and web links
- Custom record types, Field management definitions
- Access Profile and Role management
- Sales management template, and workflow rules and actions

The tool can be downloaded from **Admin | Data Management Tool | Import and Export Tools | Oracle Migration Tool On Demand**. The user of the tool requires the following privileges to execute the tool:

- The **Data Management: Import** privilege and **Data Management: Export** privilege are needed to download the Oracle Migration Tool On Demand client
- Enable the Web services access privilege to run the Oracle Migration Tool On Demand client

Detailed explanation on the usage of the tool can be found at the Oracle CRM On Demand Documentation Library available at `http://docs.oracle.com/cd/E27437_01/homepage.htm`.

CRM On Demand Connected Mobile Sales

Oracle CRM On Demand Connected Mobile Sales helps you to access Oracle CRM On Demand on your mobile device, keeping you connected to your data. Oracle CRM On Demand Connected Mobile Sales can help you to customize the mobile application without having to write any code, leverage existing Oracle CRM On Demand customizations. The steps involved in provisioning Oracle mobile sales assistance are as follows:

- Administration privileges in Oracle CRM On Demand to enable Oracle CRM On Demand Connected Mobile Sales.

- Valid subscription for Oracle Mobile Sales Data Access. This requirement enables Oracle CRM On Demand Connected Mobile Sales to exchange data with Oracle CRM On Demand.

- Configuration of specific privileges in Oracle CRM On Demand.

- Using Application Composer to make available record types and fields to users of Oracle CRM On Demand Connected Mobile Sales.

- Installation of Oracle CRM On Demand Connected Mobile Sales on mobile devices.

Detailed explanation of each of the above steps can be found at the Oracle CRM On Demand Documentation Library available at `http://docs.oracle.com/cd/E27437_01/homepage.htm`.

Oracle CRM On Demand Connected Mobile Sales runs on Apple iOS and BlackBerry devices. For the specific list of supported devices, see the Oracle CRM On Demand System Requirements web page at `http://www.oracle.com/us/products/applications/crmondemand/system-requirements/index.html` and scroll down to the heading for Oracle CRM On Demand Connected Mobile Sales System Requirements.

Accessing CRMOD content outside the application using On Demand Widgets

The focus of this chapter has been on accessibility of information, anywhere and anytime. Logical extension to this is to make the CRM data available outside the CRMOD application. For example, **Accounts** or **Contacts** can be included within other web portal applications such as iGoogle or MyYahoo to incorporate content or RSS feeds. On Demand Widgets provide this flexibility to embed CRMOD's content outside the application.

Oracle CRM On Demand provides you with HTML code that you can use to embed a number of On Demand widgets in desktop applications that support Web widgets. You can also embed Web widgets in portals, or in any standalone Web page. A Web widget is a portable piece of third-party code that can be embedded in HTML. If your company administrator has made this feature available to you, HTML code that you can use to embed On Demand widgets in other applications is provided on the **Embed CRM On Demand Content** page in Oracle CRM On Demand:

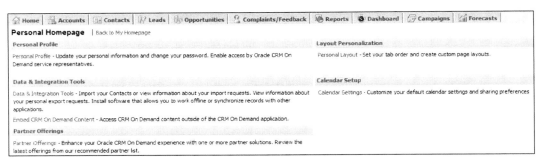

When you successfully embed this HTML code in your application, an Oracle CRM On Demand Sign-in window appears. Then, you can enter your sign-in details to access your Oracle CRM On Demand Favorite Lists, Message Center, and so on. You can open Oracle CRM On Demand in a new browser window by clicking on **Open Application**.

The list of widgets available in CRM On Demand are listed as follows:

- **Favorite Lists Widget**: This On Demand widget displays your favorite Oracle CRM On Demand lists; for example, All Opportunities, My Accounts, and so on.

- **Message Center Widget**: This On Demand widget allows you to access messages received in Oracle CRM On Demand without requiring you to first sign in to Oracle CRM On Demand.

- **Reports Widget**: This On Demand widget displays reports created in Oracle CRM On Demand.

- **Simple List Widget**: This On Demand widget displays a one-column list of shortcuts to Oracle CRM On Demand records. For more information on embedding the Simple List Widget, see *Embedding a Simple List Widget*.

The different types of widgets that are available in CRM On Demand are accessible on the following screen:

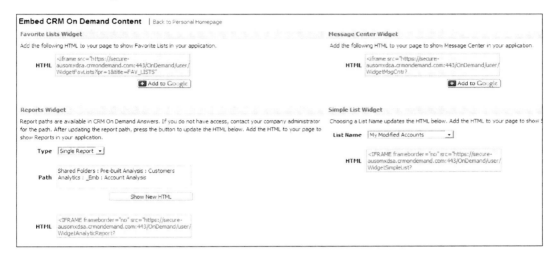

For widgets and Message Center, the HTML code required to surface the CRM On Demand content in an external web application can be copied directly from **My Setup | Embed CRM On Demand Content | Favorite List Widget (HTML) or Message Center Widget (HTML)**. The code for favorite lists looks like the following:

```
<iframe src="https://secure-ausomxdsa.crmondemand.com:443/OnDemand/
user/WidgetFavLists?lpr=1&title=FAV_LISTS" style="border:0px;pa
dding:3px;margin:0px;overflow:hidden;width:350px;height:220px;"
frameborder="0" scrolling="no"></iframe>
```

To embed reports or dashboards, first specify the path of the report under the **Path** section. The report path can be obtained from **Reports | Design Analysis | Open Analysis** where when you select a specific report, the path of the report would be shown under the **Item** field, as shown in the following screenshot:

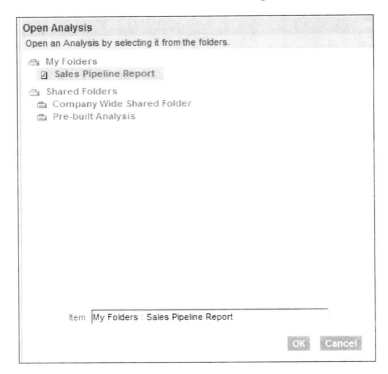

Copy and paste the path shown under **Item** to the **Path** under the report widget section, and click on the **Show New HTML** button to generate the new HTML that can be embedded in an external web application. In the case of Simple List Widget, on selection of the appropriate list, the HTML code changes automatically and can be embedded in an external web application. Thus CRM On Demand provides easy ways of surfacing your CRM On Demand in external web applications.

Summary

In this chapter we learnt the scope of integrating and migrating data which resides in the CRMOD application with other applications by using various utilities provided by Oracle. These include the in-built Import-Export utility, Oracle Offline On Demand, PIM Sync utility, Oracle Outlook Email Integration On Demand utility, Oracle Data Loader On Demand, Migration Tool, CRM On Demand Connected Mobile Sales Utility and On Demand Widgets. In the next chapter we will discuss the Help & Support Ecosystem component of CRM On Demand.

11
Help, Support Ecosystem, and Features in New Releases

When you are working with Oracle CRM On Demand, there are many ways in which you can get help. This chapter addresses some of the most popular channels and how they can be utilized to get support when you need it the most.

When you log in to Oracle CRM On Demand, the top-right corner shows many menu items. Two of them are of interest to us in the context of help and support:

- Training and Support
- Help

Towards the end of this chapter we will also discuss some of the new features of recent CRM On Demand product releases and relevant knowledge base materials available over the Web to explore them in detail.

Training and Support

This is primarily the self support area for CRM On Demand users, **Training and Support Centre**. This opens in a separate popup, so that you can continue working in your CRM system, while keeping this as a handy reference tool.

The homepage of your **Training and Support Centre** shows various options, such as the following:

- **Application Alerts**: This shows the status of various CRM On Demand components (**Service Availability**, **Web Services**, **Analytics**, **Assignment Manager**, **Email Marketing**, and so on) from your staging or production servers

- **My Oracle Support**: This is an area for you to log service requests and track them to completion (more on this later)

- **Best Practices**, **Expert Solutions**, **Articles**, and **Communities**

- **FAQs** and **Support Policies**

- Access to CRM On Demand Documentation in full: You may view the documents or download them as PDF, for offline access and reference

- Links to download CRM On Demand add-on applications, and useful templates and tools

- **News & Events**, **Release Info**, Access to CRM On Demand web services documentation

- Feedback/contact Oracle

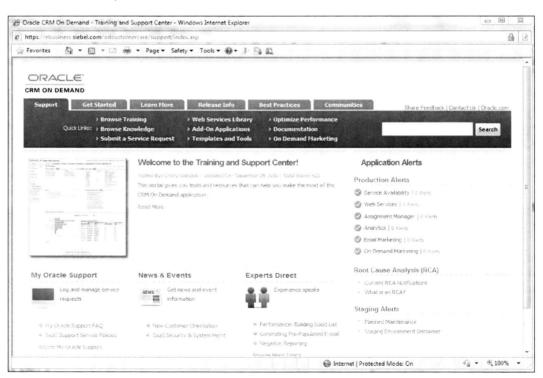

All articles you read in this area are constantly updated. This means that even if a CRM On Demand release changes, you are just a click away from the latest documentation. It may be very convenient to download a local copy of the entire documentation, but do remember that this is a SaaS solution, and hence, online help is the final source of truth.

For those who want to enjoy the best of both worlds, Oracle releases PDF versions of its online documentation very frequently. Visit this area to view and download them after every major release.

If you find a document useful, or feel it is not helping you much, use the **Rate This Article** option provided on every page to give your feedback to the support team. You can also hit the **Share Feedback** link to write to Oracle directly.

Help—CRM On Demand usage manual

This link provides the complete help manual for CRM On Demand users. As earlier, you may browse through the topics online, or download an offline PDF version.

CRM On Demand online help is split into convenient chapters such as *Getting Started, Calendar and Activities, Sales, Marketing,* and so on. Once you click a chapter, you can browse through the subtopics and articles:

All the help articles are presented with detailed explanations, screenshots, and links to related articles. You may print an article or jump to a PDF version at any time.

In addition to browsing chapters, subtopics, and articles, you can even read this help documentation as a book. The previous and next buttons on top of each page will help you navigate between pages.

Another useful option is the **Index** tab. This gives an exhaustive list of all topics in this help manual, similar to a book's **Table Of Contents** page.

Let us say you wanted to read about a particular point, but it seems to be missing in the chapters, subtopics, and articles. You couldn't even find it in the **Index** page. What do you do?

The best option is to search for it. CRM On Demand help provides a very robust and powerful search engine where you can type one or more keywords and get only those articles related to them. This is probably the most widely used feature in the "Help" area, and is shown as follows:

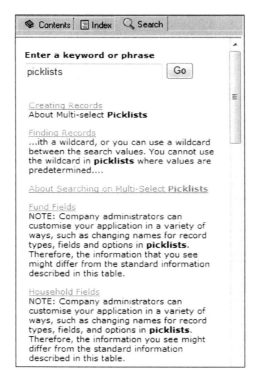

Support portal

CRM On Demand help manuals and documentation are useful to a large extent. However, when you are facing a serious issue, or want to achieve something new that the system doesn't seem to support, it is advisable that you log a service request with Oracle.

For this, you need to access the Oracle support portal first and become a member. Registration is free and takes just a few clicks.

Typically, you will be accessing the support portal via `http://support.oracle.com`. If you want to confirm, just hit the **Training and Support** link in your CRM On Demand window and then click on the **Submit a Service Request** link.

Now, you will be accessing a home page called **My Oracle Support**. This provides you various options such as user registration, login, training videos, FAQs, and so on. You can even choose the language in which you want to receive support.

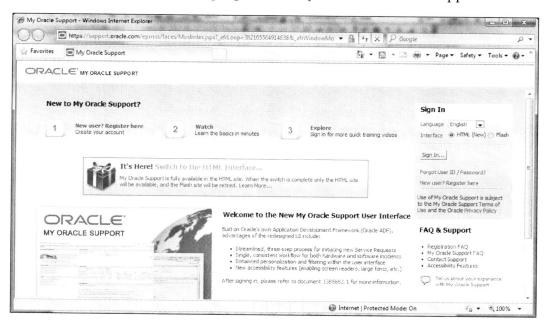

The first time you this page, you need to register yourself as an Oracle support user. This involves filling a form and confirming your e-mail ID. Within a few minutes, you are ready to go.

After your registration is confirmed, click on the **Sign In...** button, which will ask you for your username and password. Enter these details and access the homepage of your support portal.

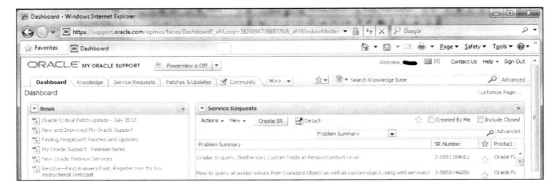

This page displays all your Service Requests as a snapshot. You can click on the **Create SR** button to log a service request, or search and browse through the knowledgebase, patches and updates information, and so on.

For almost all users, **Create SR** button is disabled when they access the support portal first time. This means they can't log a service request about the problem they are facing.

To enable this button, you need to ask your CRM On Demand administrator first. They have to link your Oracle support portal ID with your company CRM On Demand instance. Once this is done, you can start logging in service requests.

Before creating the service request

Search the knowledgebase fully, before creating a service request. Someone else might have faced this problem already and Oracle would have written a knowledgebase article that can solve your issue immediately. Do thorough research and confirm that your issue is unique and needs a new service request.

Even after you click on the **Create SR** button, Oracle still gives you a list of knowledgebase articles that are written for the problem area you have chosen. You can read them before finally creating the Service Request.

In order for Oracle support to go in and have a look at the problem you are experiencing, the support team will need to get into your system first. Instead of sharing your username and password with Oracle support, you can provide access to the support personnel to log in and troubleshoot using your login by turning on **Sign-In Access**, available at **My Setup | Personal Profile | Sign In Access**. The start and end date for sign-in access can be set in accordance with the needs of the service personnel. Post the end date of sign-in access, so support personnel cannot impersonate you.

Creating a service request

When you are creating service requests, there are a number of details you need to take care of:

- Provide a crisp summary and description about the problem you are facing. Don't leave any room for miscommunication and explain the context in the clearest possible way.

- Be sure to mention the object's name where the issue is occurring (sometimes it may have been renamed), what the exact field names are in the system (not the field name that you know internally), and include the exact layout or workflow's name, if there is something occurring with the layout or workflow. This may sound very obvious to you, but remember that someone who does not know your system intimately is going to enter your application now, and they need to find their way around using your description. Make it as exact as possible.

- Choose the right product, version, and problem type. Don't choose some default values or skip these fields. This ensures that your service request will be assigned to the correct skilled support engineer.

- If your issue covers multiple areas, it is advisable to expedite your issues to create separate service requests for each area. For example, one for administration and one for reporting. In this case, the reporting issue will go to a reporting expert and the administration issue will go to an administration expert. If you choose not to do this initially, you will most likely find Oracle support asking you to do so, and thus the longer it will take for your issue to hit the corresponding experts' queues.

- Provide a brief description of the test scenarios you have already carried out and the results you are seeing. If you have some error codes to report, specify them here. If you have any additional files (screenshots, XML files, log files, and so on), attach them.

- If you have set up delegated admin (recommended), include a note that you have done so, mentioning until what date and which login the delegated admin access is set to.

- Choose the right severity; on a scale of 1 to 4, how severe is your problem? This helps Oracle to prioritize their tasks and provide optimal support.

- On the last page of the **Create SR** wizard, make sure your e-mail address and phone number are correct. The support engineer working on your issue may want to speak to you to understand the issue better, and in that case, a wrong phone number will delay the possible resolution.

- If you are logging the request on behalf of someone else, check whose phone number/e-mail is mentioned in the service request. Make sure this is the best person who can talk to the support team and resolve the issue at the earliest.

Once your service request is created, you will be given a unique Service Request Number. This has to be used in all your future communication with Oracle.

For example, you may use this number to search for the current status of your service request in the support portal. If you are calling an Oracle call center (telephone support), they will ask for this number before providing any further help.

You can find Oracle's telephone support numbers in your **Training and Support** area, under the **Contact Us** link. For most countries, toll free numbers are provided so that you don't have to pay anything for the phone call. If your country is missing from this list, use a nearby country's phone number, or support portal.

Once a service request is created, how long will Oracle take to resolve it?

This purely depends on the issue. However, there are certain benchmarks you can assume:

- By default, your CRM On Demand sales agreement with Oracle has a **Service Level Agreement (SLA)**, which clearly mentions the expected response times.

- You can sign up for additional support too, from Oracle.

- Also, there are additional disaster recovery services available. Refer to the CRM On Demand website for the latest pricing information for these services.

There are certain things Oracle Support won't do. For example, they won't act as consultants. If what you are asking to do is a typical admin task or report that is a skill and can be obtained through Oracle training or engaging a consultant, Oracle support will direct you down that route. They may assist you as a one-off case, but ultimately you will need to have skilled resources in house for these activities.

Oracle support analyzes all the issues, errors, complexities, and testing bugs before they are forwarded to product engineering. After this you will be informed about the solution decision, and by when (which patch/release) you can expect it.

Support forums

Oracle CRM On Demand has a huge community of end users, business analysts, configurators, developers, integration experts, and more. In addition, there are Oracle engineering, sales team members who have a lot of experience in building/selling CRM On Demand. These people will have seen virtually every possible business case and technical issue, and will have practical tips, tricks, and best practices. This is another rich support channel that you can tap into.

To access the CRM On Demand forums, you need to click on the **Community** link in your support portal. This opens in a separate window and provides options such as **Communities/Groups**, **News/Announcements**, and **Discussions & Documents**.

Once you are in the community portal, you can start searching for discussions of interest to you, follow them, post responses, create new discussion threads, and more.

As you start using these forums actively, you can start contributing by providing tips and tricks to other users. Every time you help your community users, you gain points. These can be accumulated and you can become a CRM Guru!

In addition to this, the community portal also allows you to write/upload reference documents for other users. This is similar to help manuals, the product documentation we referred to earlier, except that they are contributed by the community.

To summarize, the community portal is a social channel for getting CRM On Demand support. When you build a good network, this may be the fastest way to learn and get help.

Release notes

Oracle CRM On Demand constantly evolves by fixing bugs, issues, and adding enhancements. As a customer, you can get to know about all these by referring to the latest release notes.

You can access the release notes information from the **Training and Support** menu item. In the new popup that opens, click on the **Release Info** tab and it will display the latest version of release notes, system requirements, and other resources.

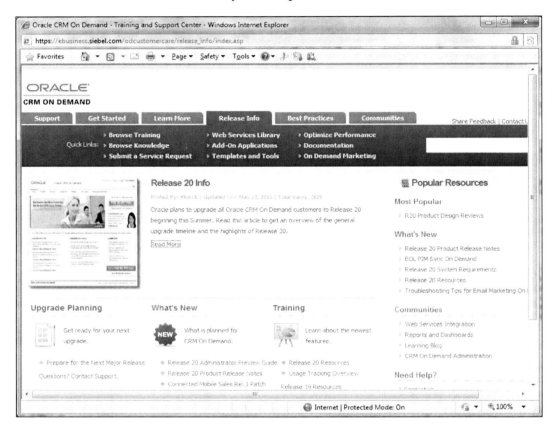

In the same page, you can also view the older release notes, and read up on what has changed in this release.

Product enhancements

In addition to service requests, you can also log enhancement requests on Oracle CRM On Demand. The procedure is the same as for a service request, but you should select the type as **Product Enhancement**.

When an enhancement request is logged, Oracle will assign it a unique ID and keep it in the pipeline. When more and more customers are asking for the same enhancement, product management picks those features for the next release.

If you want to know what features will be present in the next CRM On Demand Release, you need to follow Oracle's Release Pipeline/Roadmap document, which is released annually. You can also request this via a service request.

Release upgrade activities

When Oracle makes a new release of CRM On Demand, there is a certain process every customer-side administrator should perform. This is to ensure that the new version is fully tested before being exposed to their end users.

Normally, Oracle informs all the customers about a new release, via their notification e-mail. However, there is no assurance that those alert mails are going to the right person in your organization.

This happens because, during the sales process, Oracle reps set the notification information with whatever data they have at that time. Most likely, this will be the e-mail ID of the project sponsor in charge of buying the application.

This means, every time there is a new CRM On Demand Release, this (non technical) person gets the e-mail and ignores it because they don't understand the possible impact. On the flip side, the administrator who is actually implementing or maintaining it will never get a mail, and this can cause serious trouble.

To avoid such issues, make sure you are on the Release notification list. This can be done through the following steps:

- **My Setup | Personal Profile | Personal Information | My Profile | Personal Detail | Edit**
- Check the **Contact Preferences** checkbox
- Make sure **Always Send Critical Alerts** is selected
- Save the preferences

This ensures you will get an e-mail for every new release. Once you see the e-mail, you need to follow a three-step process:

1. Oracle plans for the new release, sends the notification to the administrator(s) of your CRM On Demand instance about when the release can be expected, in which instance(s) it will be enabled, and what changes (if any) need to be taken by you to adopt to the new version.

2. Migrate the staging environment, doing an end-to-end testing of all CRM On Demand pages, including integrations and making modifications, if necessary.

3. Migrate the production environment.

While testing the new release, if you face any issues, you will need to follow the same standard support portal service request process. Oracle will provide solutions to take care of these upgradation problems.

> Your issues may not be addressed immediately, especially if you are in a multitenant CRM On Demand environment. Oracle will definitely solve all the generic product issues that every customer is facing, but if you are facing an issue related to your customization or integration, then that will be given a lower priority. Until it is resolved, you may have to look for workarounds, so that your production users are not affected.

New features in recent releases of CRM On Demand

Throughout this book we have focused on the core sales, marketing, and service features of CRM On Demand that are very crucial for a successful CRM On Demand deployment. Saying that, we also understand the importance of you being aware of some of the cool features that are introduced in new releases of CRM On Demand.

We started writing this book when CRM On Demand release 18 was on the market and today the latest version that is provisioned for new customers is release 21, and existing customers are migrating in an incremental manner to release 21.

On average Oracle makes one release every six months and add-on innovation packs (incremental enhancements) every two months. Most of the features of new releases of CRM On Demand fall under the following broader sections:

- Usability-related enhancements
- Improved access to CRM data through a wider variety of channels such as tablets, mobiles, desktop applications, and so on
- Core functional enhancements
- Automation/reports and dashboards-related enhancements

I have summarized some of the notable new features in Release 19, 20, and 21 of CRM On Demand in the following section under the previous broader areas and towards the end added some references and pointers on the Web for you to explore them in detail.

The usability enhancements made by Oracle in recent releases are noteworthy. A few of them that caught my attention are listed as follows:

- When you access predefined lists in CRM On Demand, you don't have an option to check the total number of records being listed across multiple pages. Recently, CRM On Demand provided a cool feature to display the number of records retrieved by the list.
- You can search in the lookup windows on the basis of the pre-defined lists that are configured, making search and lookup a lot easier.
- Similarly, as an administrator you now have an option to display the related applets in a list mode or tab mode. If you have many related applets, displaying them under the main object in list mode could be a usability as well as performance issue. If you set the tab mode, all applets are displayed in a set of tabs right below the main object detail page and you can access applets of interest when you need to, avoiding scrolling and improving the application performance.
- A simple enhancement to hide/show the left navigation bar is pretty cool for operational users.
- On Demand also makes the application compatible with recent releases of standard browsers as well as extends support to new browsers such as Chrome.

On improved access to CRM data through new channels, Oracle released a new product, **CRM Desktop**, where your CRM On Demand data can be tightly integrated with your Outlook client. This makes it a lot easier for end users to synchronize and use information that cuts across their outlook and CRM On Demand. It is a great productivity enhancement tool for the end users. More features about the tool can be found at http://docs.oracle.com/cd/E35875_01/books/OnDemDesktopAdm.pdf.

Also the latest support for Safari browsers makes the CRM On Demand application iPad compatible, so it is now a convenient alternative to access CRM On Demand from iPads.

On functional enhancements, some noteworthy new features are listed as follows:

- It is a demand from customers of Oracle to support Opportunity hierarchy where business users can split a large opportunity to multiple smaller opportunities and link them in a hierarchical manner. This is similar to the account hierarchy feature in CRM On Demand. Now with recent releases of CRM On Demand, the opportunity hierarchy is supported.

- CRM On Demand now extends the availability of assessment features to the Activity object and also exposes the assessment scripts via web services making it easy to extend/build a custom application using an assessment scripts data model.

- Address object, which was a pure child object, is now made as a top-level object, making "Addresses" stored in the system reusable across the CRM On Demand system, avoiding duplication.

- Date effectivity in managing a user's access to records via books is a great new feature making it easier to manage books if the user switches jobs or moves from one department to another.

- Many of the relationship objects such as Account-Contact can now be customized by adding additional custom fields, facilitating easy capturing of more detailed relationship information.

On the automation and workflow side, CRM On Demand continuously facilitates flexible automation capabilities in the system by bringing in incremental enhancements such as support to more trigger events in workflows, enhanced web service capabilities, more cross object workflow validation features, usability enhancements in assessments scripts, and so on. Similarly on reports and dashboards, with every new releases of CRM On Demand you can find support for additional objects, new pre-built reports and dashboards such as reports to measure user adoption rate, and so on.

As it may not be possible to really list and detail every new feature in the recent releases of CRM On Demand, I recommend users view these webinars and additional reference/pointers listed in the webinars to get more info on new features added in Releases 19, 20, and 21 of CRM On Demand:

- R19 Features: `http://oukc.oracle.com/static09/opn/apps09/crmondemand/51848/WhatsNewInR19_2/index.html`

- R20 Features: `http://oukc.oracle.com/static12/opn/events12/99601/021312_99601_TOI_source/index.htm`

- R21 Features: `http://oukc.oracle.com/static12/opn/events12/103442/102612_103442/index.htm`

Summary

In this chapter we learned about various CRM On Demand support channels, how to access them, the procedure to register a service request, enhancement requests, upgrading your CRM On Demand instance to a newer release, and finally some really cool features made available in recent releases of CRM On Demand. Additional information about CRM On Demand support/help can be found at Oracle Community Forums, Blogs, and the Training and Support link in your CRM On Demand instance.

In the next chapter, we will discuss Oracle's partner offerings and how they can add value to your CRM On Demand implementation.

12
Oracle Partner Offerings

While being a strong, cloud-based application, Oracle CRM On Demand also provides a solid platform for extensibility. That is, the available solution can be extended to suit any customer needs. We have discussed this in detail, in *Chapter 8, Web Services Integration*.

If you take the analogy of a mobile phone, it acts as a wonderful device to call someone and speak to them. At the same time, its benefits become multifold when you start installing applications on it. Suddenly, it becomes an e-mail client, an e-book reader, even a movie player.

Along the same lines, there are many extensions available for Oracle CRM On Demand, which enhance its usability on many levels. This chapter discusses Oracle's partner ecosystem and the kinds of applications these partners have built for your use.

Oracle's partner ecosystem

Oracle as a corporation works closely with thousands of partners, many of them working on the CRM domain. These partners are involved in selling, implementing, and building value-added services, products, and applications on top of Oracle's offerings.

Partners of Oracle are part of a community called **Oracle Partner Network (OPN)**. All its members are split into various categories such as gold, silver, platinum, and so on.

In addition, these partners specialize in certain topics. For example, a partner may focus only on Oracle CRM On Demand, another partner may focus on Oracle database and J2EE, and so on. These specialization statuses are awarded to a customer after they go through a stringent process, satisfying various requirements such as:

- Successful, referenceable product implementations
- Certified consultants in various product areas such as sales, presales, support, and implementation
- Certified products (more on this later)

This rigid process ensures that a "Specialized Oracle Partner" is someone who is really an expert in the mentioned product. A customer can confidently engage them to implement or extend their existing Oracle solution.

Oracle CRM On Demand implementation partners

When it comes to implementing a SaaS solution such as Oracle CRM On Demand, customers face the following two important questions:

- Which solution meets my need very closely? (Or, in this case, whether Oracle CRM On Demand fits your needs or not.)
- How do I implement it as per my requirements?

On both these levels, OPN partners can help you to a large extent, making the best use of their Oracle CRM On Demand experience and expertise.

For example, when you are discussing whether Oracle CRM On Demand is the right fit for your current requirements, most likely a partner will be working with the Oracle sales team to provide you a consolidated proposal. This will have mappings between your business needs and features of Oracle CRM On Demand, identifying gaps, and the solutions to fill them.

Not all the requirements will fit with Oracle CRM On Demand fully. They can be split into the following five categories, depending on the action you need to perform on them:

- No gap: Feature available 100 percent out of the box
- Simple gap: Easily configurable in CRM On Demand
- Medium gap: Needs customization

- Large gap: May need integration
- No fit: Oracle CRM On Demand is not designed for this requirement

As your requirements are moved into one of these five buckets, you can clearly see whether Oracle CRM On Demand fits your current implementation needs or not. This is where a partner's product expertise comes in handy.

While this process is on, the partner may also be arranging for a customized demo of the Oracle CRM On Demand system. This will be different from the typical sales demos that you have seen earlier, because the partner will configure the CRM On Demand system as per your needs, and try to accommodate as many "no gap", "simple gap", and "medium gap" requirements as possible. Sometimes, if time permits, they may even build simple integration scenarios to show you what is doable for those large gaps.

Once this is completed, the OPN partner will show this customized demo to your team, so that you can make a better decision on how well Oracle CRM On Demand suits your needs.

This process is used by the partners to demonstrate the power of Oracle CRM On Demand, as well as their capability to implement it successfully. Based on this, the client can make an informed decision.

Coming to the second question, if a partner was involved during the earlier phase (or choosing Oracle CRM On Demand as the product), this decision (how to implement Oracle CRM On Demand) becomes quite easy. The client most likely goes with the same partner for implementation.

However, this is not an obvious choice. Till this stage, the client would have observed only the product (Oracle CRM On Demand) skills of the partner. Now, they need to look at the implementation skills. For example:

- CRM On Demand implementation process followed by the partner; is it in line with the Oracle recommendations?
- Their past experiences in this domain/size of an implementation
- Team structure, communication protocol, and so on
- Customer references

This is just a sample list; each client will have their own detailed process to freeze on a partner. Some of them may also decide to implement it on their own.

As you would have observed throughout this book, it is possible to implement Oracle CRM On Demand on your own. It provides very good tools to make sure this experience is pleasant, reliable, and not developer-dependent.

On the other hand, going with an experienced partner may also help your implementation, mainly because they have the product expertise and know what it takes to implement it quickly and successfully, following all best practices recommended by Oracle, or learned the hard way in one of their earlier implementations. This means the overall project implementation time will most likely be less than someone on a self-service mode.

To summarize, it is a classic "buy versus build" decision. There are tons of examples for Oracle CRM On Demand implementations done in-house, and a higher number of customers benefited by engaging an expert partner for this job.

Based on your needs and level of comfort, you can make a call. Oracle also supports its clients by recommending best partners in each region, domain, and so on.

In addition, Oracle also has its own team of implementation specialists, called **Oracle Consulting Services (OCS)**. OCS has taken the responsibility and delivered many Oracle CRM On Demand implementations across the globe. Sometimes, OCS may work with another partner for some specialized skills, making it a hybrid implementation.

Whoever performs the implementation, it typically takes care of the following tasks, depending on the agreement you have with them:

* Workshops: Conducting requirement gathering workshops
* Document: **Business Requirement Document (BRD)** sign off
* Design: High level and detailed
* Configurations: Objects, reports, workflows, and so on
* Integrations (if any)
* Testing: Unit testing, system testing, integration testing (as applicable)
* Deployment: Staging
* User acceptance testing: Training, support, and rework (as applicable)
* Deployment: Production
* Deployment support
* End user trainings: Content creation and delivery
* Documentations
* Overall project management
* Performance tuning services
* Change management or user adoption services
* Ongoing maintenance

Oracle CRM On Demand extensions

In addition to selling and implementing, a few of the OPN partners specializing in Oracle CRM On Demand have built a number of solutions on top of this platform. If you have a genuine business requirement, most likely there is already a solution available for it.

These solutions are typically called products, extensions, plugins, or applications. Irrespective of the name the partner uses, we have to understand that the solution exists on top of Oracle CRM On Demand. That is, you have to be an existing Oracle CRM On Demand customer to use these applications. They are not standalone entities you can buy.

When it comes to pricing, these solutions follow various patterns, as follows:

- SaaS: Similar to Oracle CRM On Demand; per user per month fee
- One-time fee
- Setup fee and SaaS
- Based on other metrics (for example, number of e-mails sent via the solution, number of quotes submitted, and so on)

Pricing of CRM On Demand extensions, typically depends on the way they are deployed. Typically following are the choices:

- SaaS: Implemented in the partner environment (it may be single tenant, or multi tenant)
- SaaS: Public cloud (for example, Amazon Web Services, Google App Engine, Oracle Cloud, and so on)
- SaaS: Private cloud; implemented in the customer cloud
- On premise
- Hybrid

Depending on the security requirements for this application, the client opts for one of these options and deployment is done. Pricing for the solution is determined based on this and various other factors.

In addition to the product cost, there may be a support cost involved. This will include answering end user queries and bug fixes. If there are any new feature requests, typically they are handled as additional change requests, which may involve additional costs.

How to make a purchase decision for a CRM On Demand extension

As the Oracle CRM On Demand extensibility platform is open, anybody can start building products for it easily. All you need are keen eyes to find out the gaps in features, client expectations, and creativity to visualize your solutions.

In a way this is good, as there are more and more products being released for Oracle CRM On Demand every day. That is, you have more options to choose from.

On the other hand, it also brings a high level of uncertainty in the client's mind, how to ensure the solution I am choosing is good enough for my requirements? Here are some useful tips/questions to ask that will help you during this stage.

Is the product certified?

Technically speaking, anybody can build and sell products on top of Oracle CRM On Demand. Those products may or may not satisfy the business requirements, or worst, they may be misusing your data, leading to serious privacy and business issues.

To make sure such issues are avoided and the CRM On Demand products are of the quality levels expected by its customers, Oracle has a dedicated program to test and certify such third-party products. This is a rigid process to ensure the product quality, security, user experience, and more.

This means that if there is a business requirement you have and two products seem to complement CRM On Demand by providing this feature you should go for the certified solution. This will most likely be better than the non-certified solution.

In addition to Oracle certifications, there are a number of other organizations which test and certify products on their usability, security, and other aspects. Examples include Human Factors International, Verizone Cybertru, and Checkmark. You may want to also use this information to decide on which applications are likely to perform better than other similar apps.

You can also have a look into the Oracle recommended partners list. These are the inner circle partners, whose products are tested and certified to work with CRM On Demand in a seamless and efficient manner.

This is a dynamic list, changing as Oracle adds new partners and products. You can access it via **My Setup**.

Here is an overview of a partners in this list, and the main products they provide:

No.	Partner/Product	Description
1	ActivePrime	A very popular data quality solution. CRM On Demand users can check for duplicates and clean information either during manual data entry, or in batches, or during migration from one server to another. Contains sophisticated business rules to decide how to identify and clean the data.
2	Antenna	Mobile CRM solution available across many platforms and networks. Allows CRM On Demand users to access and update their data on the go.
3	BigMachines	Helps in opportunity-to-quote-to-order process for CRM On Demand.
4	Cast Iron Systems	Configurable integrations to many industry standard SaaS solutions. Can be deployed in a matter of days, against the coded integrations which take a few weeks at least.
5	Click Tools	Marketing extension to Oracle CRM On Demand. Can be used to run campaigns, use calling scripts, build forms, run surveys, and so on.
6	EloQua	Multiple business tools for enhancing your Oracle CRM On Demand experience. For example, revenue building, marketing automation, and prospect profiler.
7	Hoovers	Gets more information and latest updates about your accounts and contacts, within CRM On Demand. It also provides rich insights to understand the customer and close deals faster.
8	InQuira (now part of Oracle, called Oracle Knowledge)	Intelligent search and knowledge base management solution, which can be used by your support staff to get more information about the current issue. Can also be deployed in the self-service mode.
9	Inside View	Identify and track sales opportunities across various channels, including the social media.
10	Experian QAS	Capture or validate accurate contact information in CRM On Demand, using a continuously updated knowledge base.

Can I try it?

This is an app economy, and companies are quite comfortable with "Freemium" models, where customers are provided a free version of the product with some limitations, which can later convert to a full version purchase.

For example, let us say you are thinking of going for a mobile CRM solution for your Oracle CRM On Demand. In addition to viewing the demo shown by the Oracle partner, you can also ask for a limited trial.

The word limited has many meanings here, explained as follows:

- Time restriction: For example, 30 days free trial
- Feature restriction: For example, only a single object enabled in a free trial
- Bandwidth restriction: For example, only 50 records can be used in a free trial
- Adware: The product has all the features, but will show nagging advertisements every now and then
- Base product is free, but the additional options are to be purchased

Our experience is that most of the Oracle CRM On Demand products have some or other trial version enabled in them. You can ask for it, and try it for few days before making a purchase decision.

What level of support is available?

Most of the innovation in the field of Oracle CRM On Demand extensions, is typically driven by small companies. This means, these products may not be as complete as you expect them to be. You need to do a careful analysis before making the actual purchase decision.

For example, a product may well cater to your requirements, but its documentation may be poor, or support channels inefficient, even non-existent. In such cases, it will be a huge issue if you face a problem at a later stage, or need a new feature to be developed.

This may sound like a usual risk we need to take with any product. But the fact is, you are more likely to hit this issue with SaaS application extensions and it is important to play safe.

To give a practical case study, a famous extension to CRM On Demand was using certain web services provided by Oracle. Many customers were using it to add more value to their sales processes in CRMOD.

When Oracle moved from Release 19 to Release 20, they discontinued one of those web services. As a result, the most important part of this extension stopped working.

Fortunately, the partner was well prepared for this scenario and they did a fresh development to fill this gap and released a patch immediately. All customers got this for free and the issue was sorted out.

Imagine what would have happened if the partner was not active. All the customers would've been forced to do fresh development, or go with some other partner to fill the gap. This won't be possible if the product documentation is not good, or the source code is not made available.

That brings us to the fourth question. We will discuss it a little later, after completing other aspects of support.

Oracle CRM On Demand extensions have varying levels of support. Most of them would provide web/e-mail support and a few may provide telephone support as well. There may be restrictions in terms of how many support tickets, or how many hours of support you may receive every month or for every quarter. For example, there are 50 hour packages, 100 hour packages, and so on. You may decide which package to go for, depending on your usage pattern and the number of users.

In addition to the mode of support and the quantity, it is important that you also consider what is covered as part of this support package. Mostly, it will only cover user queries and bug fixes. In some cases, it may also include small user interface changes such as logo, color, and fonts as well.

What about new feature requirements?

Typically, these are handled as change requests; that is there will be a small requirement-gathering session to freeze on the requirements, and a solution design prepared, approved by the customer, and then executed as a mini project. This will involve additional effort/cost, which may or may not be included in your support contract. In such cases, it is important for you to know what billing rate will be used for implementing those new requirements in future.

In addition to such paid support, companies also offer some freebies with these application purchases. For example, if there is a newer release of Oracle CRM On Demand, they will most likely offer a patch to take care of the backend changes. Similarly, there may be new features added to the product, which may be given away for free. Carefully note these points as well before signing a contract.

Is the source code available?

End User License Agreement (**EULA**) signed between the Oracle CRM On Demand customer, and the company that builds and sells Oracle CRM On Demand extensions has various items, one of them being source code access.

Typically, product price only includes the right to use the software. In some cases, the client may want to get access to the source code. It may be due to statutory requirements, or the company policy, or to make further extensions to the available features.

In any case, these two parties may have to sign another agreement between them to get access to the source code, along with applicable documentation, training, and so on. This agreement will include clauses such as price for the source code, fair usage terms, whether the customer can use this source code to build other products, who owns the intellectual property rights, and so on.

Is the solution built using an open or proprietary technology?

This is a very important aspect when it comes to future customizations. Even if you have the full source code, if the technology used to build it is proprietary, it is very difficult for the end customer to build further extensions to it.

Hence, it is preferred that companies opt for solutions built using open technologies, which would mean you can get talent in the general market who can extend the solution using the source code available.

Most popular extensions

There are hundreds of extension solutions available to Oracle CRM On Demand. While it is practically impossible to list all of them here, let us cover in brief, the most popular solutions that are built, implemented by Oracle partners across the globe, and being used heavily by end customers.

E-mail channel for CRM

In addition to CRM, sales, marketing, and support staff heavily use e-mails across the globe in almost every industry. They write rich text mails with attachments, to interact with prospects, customers, partners, and co-workers to share various product and service-related information. Customers also just write an e-mail whenever they need a product or a service.

Problem is, these e-mail interactions are missing the CRM system. An account record in CRM may remain empty, but hundreds of conversations would have happened via e-mail, which is not centralized. Later, if this account is transferred to someone else for any reason, the knowledge transfer on what has happened is already very difficult.

In addition, when e-mail becomes the de-facto communication channel, it is practically impossible to track the SLAs. Hence, all e-mail communications need to be centralized in a CRM system.

Some CRMs manage this by providing a button or toolbar in e-mail clients, where you can move a mail communication to CRM with a single click. But still, this is a manual process and end users need to remember to click this button. They hate working in two different systems all the time, and this leads to human errors. To summarize, their superiors and others don't get a complete picture.

These issues are better resolved by e-mail channel integrations to Oracle CRM On Demand. These software programs listen to a common mail ID, move all the communications to a corresponding account, contact, opportunity, service request, keep track of SLAs, and so on.

This means your staff need not switch between two systems and can use CRM as their only interface. They will use a familiar e-mail-like user interface, while the background system will take care of tracking every single communication, without any additional clicks/human errors.

Telephone channel for CRM

In addition to e-mails, telephone is another very popular mode of communication for CRM users and their end customers. This is especially true in the field of customer support, where call center staff handle tons of service requests, which are to be resolved by backend CRM users.

To tackle this problem, there are a number of Oracle CRM On Demand extensions that integrate with popular computer telephony systems such as Avaya, Cisco, Nortel, Alcatel, Genesys, Trixbox, and so on. To quote just a few examples, CRMIT provides a CTI toolkit integrating CRM On Demand with Avaya, and AMC Technology provides a built-in solution with Cisco CTI.

Basically, these systems provide an interface where the end user calls are directly shown in Oracle CRM On Demand. Even before the call center agent picks the call, the corresponding customer details are retrieved from CRM, so that they can be used to make the communication effective.

In addition, there are advanced features such as call wrap-up, call transfer, one click dialing, and so on, which make the integration between the CRM system and voice-based telephony system easy.

Mobile CRM

This is clearly the era of mobile phones. People interact with smart phones much more than any other device. From e-mails to travel bookings, everything is moving to mobile phones at a rapid pace.

CRM is no exception. Sales and support staff who are constantly on the move, prefer to get details about their leads, opportunities, service requests, and most importantly, activities and appointments via their handy phones. They want to access this data offline, request for more information, edit and create records offline, and later synchronize with their centralized system easily.

There are a number of Oracle CRM On Demand mobile solutions on the market, including a few from Oracle themselves. Examples include Oracle Mobile Sales Assistant, Oracle iSales, and CRMIT's mCRM. These solutions help you access your Oracle CRMOD data from mobile devices such as iPhones, iPads, Blackberry phones, Android phones, Android tablets, Windows Mobile phones, and more.

Almost all these solutions will provide basic access to CRM data, such as viewing, editing, deleting, creating, and so on. A few solutions have gone a level above and provide mobile-specific features such as one-click dialing, text messaging, maps, GPS integration, voice recognition, and so on. This helps in improving CRM usability, by making it much easier than any other platform.

Quote and order management

Oracle CRM On Demand focuses on the lead-to-order flow and takes care of this very effectively. Once the opportunity is won, it is transferred to a backend system for further processing and fulfillment.

In certain customer cases, the opportunity-to-order flow is not very straightforward; it involves quotes, price negotiations, approvals, and then it gets converted to an order. To add more complexity, there is a full-fledged pricing engine/rules to be implemented for calculation of the quote price.

There are number of Oracle CRM On Demand extensions such as BigMachines and Webcom, which take care of these requirements. They allow creation of quotes from opportunities, or as a standalone entity; pricing can be decided based on customer type, and then it can be overwritten on the quote level; the generated quotes can have tax calculation, shipping cost calculation, and then e-mailed to the client. This can start a series of negotiations during which the quote goes through a number of versions. Finally, (once approved) it gets converted to an order contract with specific terms and conditions.

Self-service portal

Among all the customer access channels, web self-service is the cheapest. If customers can come online, register themselves, search for the information they need, register complaints if required, and finally track them, all in a secure web portal, that will be a great CRM tool.

Thanks to Oracle CRM On Demand portal extensions by many partners, this is now possible. Your end customers, partners, dealers, even employees can interact with the CRM data over the web channel. Best part is, you have full control on what information they see, and what they don't.

Self-service portals are typically used for knowledge bases, FAQs, dealer network, and service request management purposes. They are strongly integrated with the company's corporate website and CRM, to bring best results.

Social collaboration tools

CRM is much more fun and easy to use, when it is combined with the power of social networks/collaborations. That's how social CRM systems are evolving.

Imagine your CRM system having an embedded social network. You can follow other colleagues (even customers, if you combine it with the self-service portal that was just discussed), form groups, write public, private messages, share files, URLs, follow CRM records such as opportunities, accounts, and so on, to know what's new. You will be sitting in a single CRM feed, responding to stuff, and indirectly you are adding more and more information to the underlying CRM to make it very updated.

This may sound like a user adoption tool, but in reality it is a very effective solution for improved CRM productivity. With more and more young staff being added to the corporate world, such solutions will soon become the norm.

There are a number of social collaboration tools available for Oracle CRM On Demand, with varying sets of features. But the users who started working on them conclude in an unanimous voice, this is the best way to interact with a CRM system.

CRMIT, an Oracle gold partner for CRM, offers most of these solutions as part of its CRM++ framework. This is one of the very few platforms providing extensions for multiple channels. Some of their popular products include Email Workbench, self-service portal, SocialCRM++, and mCRM.

Summary

Thus, in this chapter we learned about the Oracle Partner Network, various kinds of services and products that these partners offer, and how best to analyze and make a purchase decision on these solutions. In addition, we also discussed the various sample extensions that are most popular among CRM On Demand customers. For more information on the Oracle Partners who offer such solutions, and the actual product information, refer to http://partner.oracle.com/.

Index

A

Access Profile Wizard 97
actions
  about 125
  book, assigning 125, 126
  Create Task 127, 128
  email, sending 128, 129
  integration event, creating 126, 127
  ordering 125
  Update Field After Wait 130, 131
  values, updating 131
  Wait 132
Active Link Condition parameter 184
Add to CRM On Demand button 238
All File Usage list 202
Allotment Usage List page 201
Answers On Demand service
  about 205, 206
  business layer 206
  data layer 206
  interactivity 208, 209
  prebuilt dashboards 209, 210
  prebuilt reports 206, 207
  presentation layer 206
applets 109
application architecture 54, 55
Application Customization | Action Bar
      Layout 91
assessment scripts 172
Assignment Manager tool 65
assignment rules
  about 139
  applicable objects 140
  prerequisites 139
  rule group, defining 140

B

attachment files
  about 174
  Manage Attachments section 174

Batch 181
book access 103
book access profile 104
BPM 115
BRD 266
business layer 206
Business Process Management . See BPM
Business Requirement Document. See BRD

C

Cascading Picklists 78
collaboration 102
Company Administration data
  about 30
  Audit Trail section 42
  Company Profile 30-39
  company SignIn 40
  currency definition 43
  IP Address Restrictions 41
  languages, activating 41
  password control 40
  Sign In Audit section 42
company profile
  Company Administration data 30
  product catalog, creating 47
  sales forecasts, enabling 48, 49
  setting up 29
  user login IDs, creating 44-47
company-wide alerts
  creating 50

contact import
about 226
data file, choosing 227, 228
field, mapping 229
file validation 228
import utility, accessing 226
Contacts 22
content
about 165-167
assessment scripts type 171
attachment files type 174
product catalog type 168
reports/analytics Folders type 173
types 166
Create SR button 252
CRM 53
CRM data
about 19
marketing functions 19
sales functions 21
service functions 24
user role access levels 26-29
CRMOD. *See* **also CRM On Demand**
CRMOD
about 8
history 8
service 9
service infrastructure 10
CRMOD administration
about 13, 14
customizing 14, 15
CRMOD external content
accessing, On Demand Widgets
used 242-244
CRMOD service
about 9
pod 10
software 12
CRM On Demand
about 113
application architecture 54
data and integration tools, accessing 226
help 247
integration abilities 178
R19 Features 261
R20 Features 261
R21 Features 261

recent release features 258-260
Training and Support Centre 247
URL 51
usage manual 249, 250
web services, enabling 189-191
web services, listing 192
widgets 242
workflow configuration 116
**CRM On Demand Connected Mobile
Sales 241**
CRM On Demand extension
about 267
certification, testing 268, 269
new feature requirements 271
purchase decision, making 268
solution, building 272
source code availability 272
support level 270
trial 270
CRM On Demand usage manual
about 249
product enhancements 257
release notes 256
release upgrade activities 257
service request, creating 253, 254
service request, pre-creating steps 252, 253
support forums 255
support portal 251, 252
CRM organization 95
CRM system 19
CTE 11
Customer Relationship Management. *See*
CRM
Customer Test Environment. *See* **CTE**
customizability
about 55
data model 56
interface model 67
process model 57
customization 53
custom object 58
Custom Web Tabs 109

D

data accesses
about 100

book access 103-105
create access 100
team access 102, 103
View/Inherit Primary accesses 100
data and integration tools, CRM On Demand
accessing 226
data layer 206
data model
about 56
data management 57
files 56
transaction data 56
data model-level customization
about 72
fields, adding 73-75
fields, cascading 78-80
fields, deleting 73-75
fields, modifying 73-75
field validation rules, writing 76, 77
default access profile 97
default search method 109
DeletedItemQueryPage method 193
DeleteEvents method 194
Delete method 192
Design Analyses page 211
Detail page layouts
about 110
Action Bar layout 111
default sales process 110
Lead Conversion layout 111
UI default Theme 111
Display Name textbox 74
Display Options parameter 183
Download Custom WSDL button 191
dynamic layouts 86, 87

E

Echo argument 192
Edit Picklist window 77
End User License Agreement. *See* **EULA**
Error Instances
about 138
Batch Delete option 138

ETL 206
EULA 272
Execute method 192
Expression Builder tool 123
Extensible Mark-up Language. *See* **XML**
extensions
CRM e-mail channel 272
CRM telephone channel 273
Mobile CRM 274
order management 275
self-service portal 275
social collaboration tools 275, 276
Extraction-Transformation-Loading. *See* **ETL**

F

Field Validation lookup window 76
findNoneOf()function 76
forecast 24
Forecast Definition wizard 162
forecasting
methodology, selecting 159
forecasts
maintaining 162
updating 162
forecasts administering
about 158
duration, determining 159
frequency 160
roles, designating 160
setting up 159
type, determining 159
forecasts frequency
about 160
setting up 161, 162
Formula button 220

G

GetEvents method 194
GetMapping method 194
GetPicklistValues method 194
GetServerTime method 194
group 66
group assignment 99

H

Heads-up Display 32

I

Import UI Assistant tool 48
Insert method 192
integration abilities, CRM On Demand
    about 178, 179
    data, surfing from other system 181, 182
    data, transferring 180
    data, transferring at real time 180, 181
    decision chart 179
    integration events, configuring 186-189
    web applet, configuring 184, 185
    web link, configuring 182, 183
interface model
    about 67
    online interface 68
    special interfaces 68
    web services interface 68
isolation 104
ITS URL for SSO Authentications 39

L

language dependent codes. See LDC
language independent codes. See LIC
layout management
    about 80
    action bar layout 90, 91
    dynamic layout 86, 87
    homepage 90, 91
    list, managing 91, 92
    page layout 80-86
    search layout 87-89
LDC 193
Lead Conversion Administration
    about 144
    Lead Conversion Mapping 144
    lead, converting 144
    settings 144
lead conversion layout
    about 146, 147
    creating 147-149
Lead Conversion Mapping
    fields, mapping 145, 146

LIC 193
lists 109
LoginHistoryQueryPage method 194
LOVLanguageMode argument 193

M

Manage Analyses button 211
Manage Lists link 92
manager hierarchy 99
marketing functions, CRM data
    campaign 20
    lead 21
    recipient 20
MergeRecords method 194
Message Centre section
    using 50
MetadataChangeSummaryQueryPage
        method 194
Miscellaneous Application
        Customization 92, 93
Mobile CRM 274
My Profile page 111

N

Narrative reports 212

O

object model
    about 58, 60
    external objects 62, 63
    fields 60, 61
OCS 266
On Demand Widgets
    used, CRMOD external content
        accessing 242-244
online interface 68
OPN 263
opportunity 14
Oracle
    partner ecosystem 263
Oracle Consulting Services. See OCS
Oracle CRM On Demand
    extensions 267
    implementation partners 264-266
Oracle data loader 239

Oracle Migration Tool On Demand 240
Oracle Offline On Demand
  about 230, 231
  data, adding 233
  data, downloading 232
  data, updating 233
  uploading, to CRM on Demand 234
Oracle Partner Network. *See* OPN
Oracle PIM Sync On Demand. *See* PIM
organization 95
organizational chart 95
Outlook Email Integration On Demand
  about 237
  using 238, 239
owner access profile 97

P

page layout 80-86
Personal Information Manager. *See* PIM
PIM 38, 234-237
pod 10
portlet 39
prebuilt user roles
  Administrator 28
  Advanced User 27
  Executive 26
  Field Sales Rep 27
  Inside Sales Rep 27
  Regional Manager 27
  Sales and Marketing Manager 27
  Service Manager 27
  Service Rep 27
presentation layer 206
privileges
  about 112
  data channel accesses 112
  UI customization accesses 112
  user channel accesses 113
process model
  about 57
  business rules 64
  object model 58
  security model 65, 66

product catalog
  about 168
  examples 168
  product 170, 171
  product category 169
product enhancements 257
Prompt Properties section 222

Q

QueryPage method 192

R

Rate This Article option 249
Record Detail page 59
record type 58
Related Information link 98
release notes 256
report
  Answer, building 217
  building 216
reports/analytics folders 173, 174
report writing
  about 210
  columns, defining 217-220
  data presentation, defining 221
  filters, defining 217-220
  folders 211
  Manage Analyses button 211, 212
  Open Existing Analyses button 212
  prompts, defining 222
  subject areas 213, 215
Role Management Wizard 107
RowId column 217
rule
  about 141
  defining 141
  fields 142
rule criteria
  components 142
  defining 143
  fields 143
rule group
  about 140
  fields 141

S

SaaS 267
sales category
    about 157
    setting up 158
sales functions, CRM data
    account 21
    assets 24
    contact 22
    opportunities 22
    revenues 23, 24
    sales forecasts 24
    sales process 22, 24
sales methodology
    about 149
    process 149, 150
    sales category 157
    sales stages 151
    sales stage, setting up 151, 152
    stage 150
SalesProcessQueryPage method 194
sales stage
    automated tasks 155
    mandatory fields, adding 152, 153
    process coach 154
    setting up 151, 152
    useful resources 156
Sales Stage page 156
Search field 87
search layouts 87-89
security model 65
self-service portal 275
service functions, CRM data
    activity 25
    service requests 25
    solutions 25
service infrastructure, CRMOD 10, 11
Service Level Agreement. See SLA
SetPasswordAPI method 194
SetSessionTimeZone method 194
Show New HTML button 244
Siebel On Demand. See SOD
Simple Object Access Protocol. See SOAP
Single sign-on (SSO) 62
SLA 254
SOAP 177

social collaboration tools
    CRMIT 276
SOD 7
software as a service. See SaaS
special interfaces 68
standard object 58
Submit a Service Request link 251
support forums 255
support portal 251

T

tab 108
Tab layout 108
targeted search 109
team 65, 102
team access profile 102
Training and Support Centre
    homepage, options 248, 249

U

UpdateCascadingPicklists method 194
Update method 192
UpdatePicklist method 194
User Access Management 102
user group 99
user ID
    about 96-98
    issuing 51
    manager hierarchy 99
    owner 96
    user group 99
user identities. See user ID
user role
    about 105, 107
    default access profile 108
    definition items 106
    Detail page layouts 110
    Homepage layouts 109
    objects, accessing 107
    objects' homepage, accessing 108
    objects'tabs, accessing 108
    owner access profile 108
    privileges 112
    role name 107
    Search page layouts 109

user role access levels
  feature access 26
  prebuilt user roles 26
  record access 26
user roles 96
UserUsageQueryPage method 194

V

View and Inherit Primary accesses 101
ViewMode argument 193
visibility 100

W

Wait action 137
web contents
  Feed 185
  HTML 185
  URL 185
Web Link Target parameter 183
web service allotment usage
  file usage, monitoring 202
  history 201, 202
  record usage, monitoring 202
  service allotment, administering 200
  service allotment alerts, setting 200
  Web Services Utilization section 203
web services, CRM On Demand
  allotment 199
  benefits 199
  best practices 196, 198
  enabling 189-191
  limiters 199
  listing 192-195
  sessions, managing 195
Web Services Definition Language. *See*
  WSDL

Web Services Description Language. *See*
  WSDL
When modified record saved event 121
widgets, CRM On Demand
  Favorite Lists Widget 242
  Message Center Widget 242
  Reports Widget 243
  Simple List Widget 243
workflow
  about 117
  active 136, 137
  adding 117-119
  assignment rules 139
  deleting 136
  Error Instances 138
  event actions 133
  inactive 136, 137
  modifying 117, 118, 119
  ordering 133, 134, 135
  Pending Instances 138
  record types 120
  rule condition 122-124
  trigger events 121
  Workflow Monitor 137
workflow configuration
  about 116
  action component 117
  actions 125
  prerequisite steps 116, 117
  rule component 117
  trigger component 117
workflow rule condition
  steps 124, 125
WSDL 68, 177, 190

X

XML 177

Thank you for buying
Oracle CRM On Demand
Administration Essentials

About Packt Publishing

Packt, pronounced 'packed', published its first book "Mastering phpMyAdmin for Effective MySQL Management" in April 2004 and subsequently continued to specialize in publishing highly focused books on specific technologies and solutions.

Our books and publications share the experiences of your fellow IT professionals in adapting and customizing today's systems, applications, and frameworks. Our solution based books give you the knowledge and power to customize the software and technologies you're using to get the job done. Packt books are more specific and less general than the IT books you have seen in the past. Our unique business model allows us to bring you more focused information, giving you more of what you need to know, and less of what you don't.

Packt is a modern, yet unique publishing company, which focuses on producing quality, cutting-edge books for communities of developers, administrators, and newbies alike. For more information, please visit our website: www.packtpub.com.

About Packt Enterprise

In 2010, Packt launched two new brands, Packt Enterprise and Packt Open Source, in order to continue its focus on specialization. This book is part of the Packt Enterprise brand, home to books published on enterprise software – software created by major vendors, including (but not limited to) IBM, Microsoft and Oracle, often for use in other corporations. Its titles will offer information relevant to a range of users of this software, including administrators, developers, architects, and end users.

Writing for Packt

We welcome all inquiries from people who are interested in authoring. Book proposals should be sent to author@packtpub.com. If your book idea is still at an early stage and you would like to discuss it first before writing a formal book proposal, contact us; one of our commissioning editors will get in touch with you.

We're not just looking for published authors; if you have strong technical skills but no writing experience, our experienced editors can help you develop a writing career, or simply get some additional reward for your expertise.

Oracle Siebel CRM 8 Developer's Handbook

ISBN: 978-1-84968-186-5   Paperback: 576 pages

A practical guide to configuring, automating, and extending Siebel CRM applications

1. Use Siebel Tools to configure and automate Siebel CRM applications

2. Understand the Siebel Repository and its object types

3. Configure the Siebel CRM user interface – applets, views, and screens

4. Configure the Siebel business layer – business components and business objects

Oracle JD Edwards EnterpriseOne 9.0: Supply Chain Management Cookbook

ISBN: 978-1-84968-196-4   Paperback: 370 pages

Over 130 simple but incredibly effective recipes for configuring supporting, and enhancing EnterpriseOne SCM

1. Master all that the EnterpriseOne SCM modules have to offer with this book and e-book full of step by step instructions

2. Go deeper into SCM functionality with special orders and approvals

3. This recipe-based guide packed with images, and concluding with a real-world Supply Chain blueprint, helps you fully absorb each step by step task

Please check **www.PacktPub.com** for information on our titles

Oracle Essbase 11
Development Cookbook

Jose R. Ruiz

[PACKT] enterprise

Oracle Essbase 11 Development Cookbook

ISBN: 978-1-84968-326-5   Paperback: 400 pages

Over 90 advanced development recipes to build and take your Oracle Essbase Applications further

1. This book and e-book will provide you with the tools needed to successfully build and deploy your Essbase application

2. Includes the major components that need to be considered when designing an Essbase application

3. This book can be used to build calculations, design process automation, add security, integrate data, and report off an Essbase cube

Oracle Fusion Middleware Patterns
Real-world composite applications using SOA, BPM, Enterprise 2.0, Business Intelligence, Identity Management and Application Infrastructure

Harish Gaur   Markus Zirn   [PACKT] enterprise

Oracle Fusion Middleware Patterns

ISBN: 978-1-84719-832-7   Paperback: 224 pages

10 unique architecture patterns enabled by Oracle Fusion Middleware

1. First-hand technical solutions utilizing the complete and integrated Oracle Fusion Middleware Suite in hardcopy and ebook formats

2. From-the-trenches experience of leading IT Professionals

3. Learn about application integration and how to combine the integrated tools of the Oracle Fusion Middleware Suite - and do away with thousands of lines of code

Please check **www.PacktPub.com** for information on our titles

CPSIA information can be obtained at www.ICGtesting.com
Printed in the USA
BVOW062138301212

309415BV00005B/134/P

9 781849 685009